Opinions of an
Old Contrarian

Opinions of an Old Contrarian

By Guy Friddell

The Pilot PRESS

edited by Joe Coccaro

Published by The Pilot Press

Distributed by:
Insiders' Publishing Inc.
105 Budleigh St.
PO Box 2057
Manteo, NC 27954
(919) 473-6100

First Edition
1st printing

ISBN 1-57380-055-4

TABLE OF CONTENTS

Dedication: *To Gin and her grandchildren.*

Acknowledgments

In pulling together columns from more than 40 years, the author is indebted to the willingness of The Virginian-Pilot and the Times-Dispatch to permit their use here. He also thanks Dietz Press for supplying four columns it published in "Jackstraws."

For helping locate the columns, he thanks The Virginian-Pilot's library director, Ann Johnson, and her ever-supportive staff as well as Kathy Albers and The Times-Dispatch's library staff for assistance through the years.

Janet Shaughnessy, a Virginian-Pilot designer, lent elegance with the book jacket and humor through her caricatures. Computer systems chief Randy Jessee kept the author's word processor and the author in good repair, as usual.

Joseph Coccaro, the book's patient editor, had a creative shaping hand in every aspect of it. To work with him is a pleasure.

For designing and bringing about the format, the author is indebted to Steve Jernigan and to all the other talented staffers of Insiders' Guide.

Always there is Gin, the author's wife. She infuses the book as she did his life and continues to do so after her death and will always. That holds true for every person of any age and condition whom she touched. This book is more her work than his.

Chapter One

The Magic Of Christmas

World in a Manger

"You should have been at the Christmas pageant at Meadowbrook," Gin said.

"It went well?"

"There was one problem," she said. "We had to substitute for Joseph. Everything had been going so smoothly. Glynnis had pulled it all together, including a Hanukkah scene. The auditorium was packed with parents enjoying every minute. But halfway through, just before Mary and Joseph and the three kings and three shepherds were to go on stage, a little girl playing Mary said to me in a faint voice, 'Where's Joseph?' "

"That must have startled you," I said.

"It did. We had 125 children in the library just behind the stage, with another 225 stationed in classrooms nearby, all of them drawing and playing dominos until their turns came to go on stage, and suddenly no Joseph. I'd noticed his costume lying across the table, but it hadn't hit me that Joseph wasn't in it until that minute."

"So what did you do?" I asked.

"I grabbed up a little boy and said to him, "You can be Joseph, can't you?"

"The most beatific smile you ever saw came upon his face, and I realized that this was the first time in his life he had ever played a major part. I wrapped his Afro haircut in an Arab head-dress, and another black child, wearing a gold turban as a king and looking every inch of one, said, 'One of the three kings was black, so maybe Joseph was black,'

" 'All you have to do,' I told Joseph, 'is follow Mary all through the pageant.' Mary, a shy little girl with big brown eyes, was dressed in a light blue gown with brocade. She never makes a mistake, anyway, and she knew all the cues. 'Just whisper to Joseph what to do,' I told her.

"About that time somebody told Mr. Chapel, the principal, who was keeping order in the halls and backstage, that Joseph was missing, and for just a second his face had a wild expression as if he thought the whole pageant was going to fold; but he recovered as quickly when he heard we had a substitute. On stage Joseph followed Mary's every step and that big smile never left his face. The pageant went perfectly.

"Next morning, I put my arm around the original Joseph, and said, 'What happened to you, old fellow?' He's very conscientious, and I knew he'd have a valid excuse, so he regained his confidence. So everything turned out all right.

"One teacher, I remember, said, 'That's typical of the father, not to show up for the birth.'

"In the final scene, with all 350 on stage, glowing in the lights in their finery with all the parents standing and applauding madly, it suddenly came to me that every race — red, black, white, brown, yellow — and several nationalities were up there. It looked like the whole world was in the manger."

"Including," I said to the teacher, "a black Joseph."

"Smiling," she said.

The Town That Could

This is the 43rd anniversary of the Christmas that Gin baked her first turkey. That summer we had moved into a former Army barracks at Camp Shanks converted into three-room apartments as Shanks Village for ex-GIs attending school 20 miles down river at Columbia University in New York. A modest deposit gave us a table, four chairs, and two cots that we shoved together to take a mattress. Each had an old-fashioned icebox and tiny stove. It seemed a palace.

She taught fourth-graders over the mountain in a small town by a big river while I went to journalism school and worked for the town's newspaper. The editor paid me 30 cents an inch for stories about Shanks. His ruler was generous. Assigning me to cover the county as well, he put me on the regular payroll. I filled the car's tank at the gas pump out back. I think of him often, with gratitude.

Dwight Eisenhower, Columbia's new president, toured Shanks and told us he was glad to see that we had learned that happiness was more than "a lot of goldurned overstuffed furniture."

Just before Christmas, entering the newsroom, I confronted a mountain of dressed turkeys in the middle of the floor. "Help yourself," said the editor. "That's your bonus. Go home!" I pulled one from the pile like a Pilgrim shouldering a turkey he had shot in the woods.

It weighed 20 pounds. We started to cut off the plump drumsticks and cook them separately, but a friend contrived a rig that would fit the turkey in the oven. Gin pored over "The Joy of Cooking," a wedding gift. Never have I seen such fierce concentration. She also decided to bake an angel food cake — with peppermint icing — and invited three couples who could not go home for Christmas. It looked to me like the thing had got out of hand.

We loved the town and its people. It was a good town. The

first-rate school system was integrated long before the U.S. Supreme Court ordered the nation's schools desegregated. That decree was still seven years off even when we arrived. The School Board interviewed each new teacher. One member, noticing Gin's accent, asked whether she, a Southerner, would have difficulty teaching black pupils.

"Children are children," she said. She might have added that she loved them all, especially those who merited extra attention, which is the way with most teachers. Each child is gifted in some way, they hold.

The principal, a perky, progressive, elderly lady, gave Gin forms that the boys signed for swimming lessons after school at the YMCA. The girls' turn would come in May. The next day, Gin learned that her black students had been turned away. She went to the Y to ask why.

It just hadn't been done with the blacks, it seemed, although, as she observed, black and white alike should learn to swim with the big river lying out there blue and alluring. "Is there a law against their learning to swim here?" she asked, in innocence, the kind that confounds officialdom every time.

Our barracks had two law students who couldn't find a statute that barred black children from lessons. The school became interested, and Y officials decided that all children, if they wished, could attend. It was a grand town, getting along the very best it could. The member who had been concerned with how Gin would do with an integrated class remarked that she was the last one he'd expected to raise the question.

She watched from afar and waited until every boy had entered the gym for his first lesson.

Each fourth-grade class presented a Christmas show. Gin's retold "Snow White." At the close, a black child who had been held back two grades (handicapped, it turned out, by poor vision), sang "Some Day My Prince Will Come." It was the child's first triumph and it drew a standing ovation.

Gin's first Christmas turkey, everybody said, was the best ever, although one friend did note that the cake's peppermint icing had cleared his sinuses for the next two years. Remembering it all, I can say but one thing to her, even now.

Shanks for the memories.

Best Tree Ever

Put up the tree Sunday. The hardest part, as always, was picking it out.

From a distance, every tree on the lot looks as if it could be on a Christmas card. You can't see the trees for the forest. A little closer, and flaws begin to appear, and, suddenly, as you walk the green aisles, none in the ranks steps forward to say, "Here am I. Look at me!" If Hamlet found it hard to decide whether to be or not to be, he should have gone looking for a Christmas tree. That is the question that would have brought the Dane down to earth.

The most appealing foliage Sunday was that sheathing the white pines with long, glossy, green needles shining in the sun as if they were lustrous hides of healthy animals. The texture of the wide-spreading fronds of five-inch needles, when you brushed your hand against them, was as soft as plumage. It stirred me, too, because, through childhood, most families, hard-up in the Depression, went out into the fields and cut a pine. Dragging the tree to the car seemed to take twice as long as the trip to find it.

The drawback with white pines is that vast cavities are often just under thinned-out patches on the surface. I'd about settled for a Douglas fir when right in my path, as if it had manifested itself, stood a tall white pine. Two feet up its trunk it billowed into a towering, bosomy triangle of thickset branches. A walk around it did not disclose a blemish in its sumptuous self. It was, at last, like seeing someone across a dance floor and knowing the two of you were well met.

A salesman, Bill Doughtie, offered to clip a few dead branches around its base and give the bottom of the trunk a clean, level cut, the better to put the tree on a stand. The way I'd done, nigh on 44 years, was lie on my back as the three boys lifted the tree above me and then lowered it through my guiding hands into the center of the stand. It took a good many sightings and adjustments to bring the tree into a straight stance.

Doughtie simply laid the tree on its side, sawed six inches off the bottom of the trunk, put the stand up against the end, and, centering a chunk of wood on the outside of the stand, gave it a smart whack with a heavy mallet, driving the prongs into the base of the tree — and the job was done.

How, over four decades, had I managed not to stumble on such an easy, forthright way to join tree to stand? He righted the tree, and it stood straight, a lovely shape on a two-foot stem of a base. Viewing it from a seat on a bale of hay, I studied the tallest, shapeliest tree we'd ever found.

"You know what this tree looks like," I said to salesman Tim Lane. "It looks like a very pretty girl in a very short dress."

He laughed.

"It looks like a ballerina ready to pirouette," I said, "but it is a half a foot higher than our ceiling."

Doughtie sawed another six inches off the trunk and righted it.

6

I could almost see the tree smoothing down its abundant, flossy branches.

"Now what?" said Lane.

"This tree," I said, "is girlish."

At home a son and his son, 3, helped escort the tree inside and we set about disentangling three strands of bulbs, a suspenseful venture, until, plugged into the wall socket, they all flashed into a ganglia of red, green, and blue lights. We arrayed the tree in finery. The mother of the three-year-old noticed that the soft green fronds reflected the lights, cloaked them in a halo, and, she said, made them seem even larger.

"It's as if," said the three-year-old's father, "they're shining through a deep forest."

"It's the best tree we ever had," Gin said.

But then we always say that.

A New Routine

The most suspenseful Christmas in our house was in 1971. It was agonizing. Reaching home about 2 a.m. from Christmas Eve shopping, I flung myself on the sofa, intending to rest a minute and then bring the gifts from the car trunk and wake Gin to do the wrapping. Four hours later the three boys were shaking me. "Christmas gifts! Where are the presents?" shouted one.

"Guybo's already up and dressed!" marveled the second.

The third teenager went and waked his mother.

"All right, everybody," I said, "we're starting a new routine. We're going to all troop out to the car and open the trunk for one grand and glorious surprise!"

We over-ruled her desire to send everybody back to bed while she wrapped gifts, but it didn't make any difference anyway because when we all trooped out to the car and I reached in my coat jacket, the keys to the trunk were gone.

So we trooped back inside and searched the sofa and, gradually, the entire room, and then fanned out through the house.

"No telling where he might have wandered," said the youngest.

The oldest just couldn't believe what had happened. Only the week before he had tied the car keys by a shoe string to a piece of plywood about the size of a folded handkerchief. "So you won't lose them," he had said, handing me the ensemble.

By noon friends began dropping by, the boys' as well as ours, and nothing would have it but that each new party have a go at looking around the house for the keys. The day was a melee, a cross between an Easter Egg hunt and the opening of a model home in a new subdivision. Finally, near 5 p.m., and near exhausted, I flung myself again on the sofa and felt, pressing inside my right-hand back pocket, a squarish object.

"Hey, everybody," I called. "I found the keys."

Well, How's She Look?

I thought our household had discussed every possible point about a Christmas tree — tall or short, fat or slim, fir or pine, real or artificial, early or late, icicles or not, bought or found — but there was one more.

We got the tree on its feet last night and after an hour the youngest boy found the box of decorations and we untangled and tested the strands of colored lights to see how many had made it through the year undimmed.

In childhood you wondered whether Santa would show; now the suspense is all in whether the strings of lights will go on. They are very special lights, much larger than you see nowadays, not the little winkey-blinkey kind but big fellows that flash off and on independently in bursts of red, green, blue, orange, yellow, so that when the tree is plugged in, it jumps with color.

The three boys and I were on our knees, trying the lights, when Gin, looking down at us, her hands behind her back, said she had a wonderful surprise, and held out four boxes of white lights. "For 25 years, I've always wanted a tree with white lights," she said quickly.

"I'D SOONER HANG THIS TREE WITH CHITTER-LINGS!" I shouted.

And for once there was male solidarity as one after the other offered argument; but she was as set as I had ever seen her. When the oldest boy tried to end the debate by plugging in the colored lights, she grabbed the other end of the string, and he, joined by his brothers, pulled back; and there was a tug of war in the living room, all lit by dancing colors.

To watch it was exhausting. I lay on the sofa to get my second wind and dozed off amid all the clashing voices and flashing lights. When I awoke the boys were gone — had she decked them all with boughs of holly? — and she was moving, humming, about the tree, which was, indeed, a dazzling sight.

In the first place, I saw, the lights were not white but golden. As she lifted a lighted string into place, she seemed to be handling a string of fireflies. And as she worked, I thought of stars, a new constellation, and a hive of golden bees, swarming, or a burning bush. I followed the line of one drooping strand that took as precipitous a dip as the roller coaster at Ocean View. She went right on happily, arraying the tree as if it were a bride, even placing white ornaments, winged cherubs, and what not. She must have been planning for this tree a long time, I thought.

Turning, seeing that I was watching, she stood back a little to look, and asked: "What do you think of it?"

"It beats chitterlings," I told her.

We Miss You, Ebenezer

You've wondered, perhaps, what happened to Ebenezer Scrooge after that memorable Christmas morning when he threw open his upstairs bedroom window and shouted to a boy loitering in the street below, "What's today?" Did his rebirth take after the visits of the three Ghosts of Christmas? Or did he backslide, as most of us do? It took.

Not only did Scrooge become a person who "knew how to keep Christmas well," as Mr. Dickens reported; he kept Christmas every day. Even his figure altered. His spare, rigid frame unbent and filled out. Flintlike features softened. Smiles wreathed the face that for years had been downturned into a frown.

From a creature focused on getting of money to beget money, Scrooge became dedicated to giving the stuff away to whomever he found in need. Let a man, unsteady on his feet, stop him on a London street and ask, with fragrant breath, for a shilling to go see his old mother in Liverpool and Scrooge not only pressed a coin in the man's hand, but, gripping his elbow, would put him protesting on the train to Liverpool and stand, waving, as the train pulled away with the stranger glowering at the window.

As Scrooge dealt with people in need — he was always trying to place a score or more in jobs or with suitable agencies — he became aware of the kingdom's charitable institutions and drew on his financial reserves to bolster their good works. He shared his wealth with the same zeal and shrewdness with which he had hugged it.

In giving a copious amount to the London Alms House, he provided that three inmates sample the gruel periodically. If they found it wanting, the funds would revert to the Ebenezer Scrooge Counting House. A grant to the Haven for the Aged was coupled with a mandate that the oldest party test the cots to see that linens were clean and mattresses firm.

Scrooge was hailed through the realm for his cheerful — and careful — giving. Other wealthy people, wishing to do good without the bother, entrusted large sums to Scrooge's Year-Round Christmas Stocking. The Cosmos Club proclaimed him London's First Citizen. The Lord Mayor gave him a key to the city. "You already have unlocked our hearts," the Lord Mayor said.

Scrooge was presented at Court, where the Queen, in a low voice, tete a tete, asked him three questions. (How do you spell Ebenezer? Did you really see Ghosts? Do you like the white or the dark meat of the turkey?)

In the House of Commons, a member of Labor demanded that Scrooge be appointed to head the government's welfare agencies, a motion that failed to carry only because the Conservatives felt that his talents might be lost in the bureaucracy. Let the private sector do the job, they cried.

Scrooge became a member of 58 charitable boards and 23 civic groups. The Jaycees made him head of their get-out-the-vote drive. Did money need to be raised for unfortunates anywhere? Send for Ebenezer Scrooge, was the cry. So busy was Scrooge at doing good that he turned the management of the Counting House to his rollicking nephew, who became president, and Bob Cratchit, treasurer. Nephew Fred extended the business into all the kingdom's major cities and across the Channel in Boulogne. "It had such a grand sound," he said. "Boulogne!"

In fact, the business overexpanded, and one fatal day the cash flow dried to a trickle and then to naught. Three weeks before Christmas, Scrooge wound up in the alms house he had endowed. It wasn't so bad, he found. What it lacked in frills it made up in the company, a good deal more interesting than that of the Lord Mayor. He did miss his family, though. And, then, Christmas Eve, they appeared, Nephew Fred and his dimpled wife and all the Cratchits, down to Tiny Tim, quite cured, waving his crutch.

"You've come to see me!" cried Scrooge, overjoyed.

"We've come to stay," said his nephew. "We're bankrupt, busted, broke."

"Stoney broke," Bob Cratchit added.

"Sit down and have some gruel," invited the delighted Scrooge as they gathered around him.

"I say, Uncle," Fred called from the other end of the table, "This gruel is not half bad. Quite good, in fact."

"It better be," Scrooge said.

As they ate and chattered and smiled and nodded his way, Scrooge thought it quite the best Christmas yet. He felt closer to them than ever before. It is one thing to give of your substance to the poor. It is another to be among the poor. He tapped on his mug.

"I have never been happier," he told them. "This is the essence of Christmas, simply to be with loved ones, your family or the larger human family."

"A bit of goose would help," his nephew called.

"Pshaw!" Scrooge replied, "who'll know tomorrow whether we had goose today. You always over-ate anyway."

Did Scrooge but know it, Tiny Tim was already organizing a rock group, the Lame, the Halt, and the Blind, that would soon become the first to invade America and make a wad of money with which he would bail the family out of the alms house, somewhat to Scrooge's regret. He had needed a respite from board meetings.

But leave them there for now, eating the gruel, looking in one another's loving eyes, and Tiny Tim crying, again, "God bless us, every one!"

Ms. Santa

Christmas stories are drifting in, including one from a young couple whose 2-year-old son discovered that Santa Claus was not of the sort portrayed universally.

The three were shopping for a Christmas tree, the father said, when a white-bearded Santa-like figure appeared, strolling about the lot. "There's Santa now," said the mother, and their son bolted toward the red-clad figure for his first encounter with the magical elf.

A few yards away the father recognized that this Santa was, unmistakably, a woman, with a light feminine voice and a thin face at odds with the white beard and mustache. He hoped that she might wave away the boy's inquiries by not speaking, or by saying she was in a costume. But no, she bent to consult him on his wishes.

There was no robust ho-ho-ho with her, no expansive gesturing, larger than life, no resonant voice capable of commanding reindeer in the clouds, no sense of evanescence in being able to disappear down a chimney. The tone and tenor of her remarks were the sort any woman might use in chatting with a child.

As the three drove home, the boy was silent. "You could tell he was pondering what had happened," his father noted. After a while, he said in a soft voice, "Santa is a lady."

"Don't you think that it might have been Santa's helper or Mrs. Claus?" asked the father.

"No," he said, "it was Santa."

"Then I knew I was in trouble," his father said. Before reaching home, they saw two male Santas of the standard sort, whose images, the parents hoped, would override that of the feminine Santa.

Of course, no one objects to a woman's depicting Santa Claus, if she can carry it off. Many an actress can play a male role superbly. Mary Martin comes to mind as Peter Pan. There will never be another actor, man or woman, to match Martin's crow of delight as she flew through the air with the verve of a tomboy, if not a boy. Some men can convey the guise of women. Alec Guinness did it persuasively. Many men don't have the panache, much less the figure and face, to summon Santa for a child. There is many a lackadaisical male Santa.

Those employing the season's merry symbol ought to understand you can't throw in just anybody in whiskers and a red suit. Playing a myth is a challenge when every aspect can be examined by a skeptical or adoring child. The audience, most of the time, is on his knee, memorizing his features, looking into his eyes. His impression, if done well, may carry through life.

Too often what the employer and the actor fail to do is take Santa Claus seriously. They don't believe in the rogue who slips around doing kindnesses as if they were crimes.

The effect on the 2-year-old, his mother said, was not traumatic. It was simply confusing. There was one reassuring development. At home Christmas Eve, the child was more concerned about whether milk and cookies had been left for Santa Claus than in the gifts he might bring. And next morning, the 2-year-old ignored the presents as he raced to the hearth to see if the cookies were gone, the glass emptied.

His face radiant, he said, "He was here!"

A Wise Example

With Christmas here, sober-sided citizens begin worrying that we will forget "The True Meaning of Christmas." The implication is that the message is lost in our focus on material things.

In the name of Donder and Blitzen, do they think we have been running around buying all these objects - electric toasters and trains—for ourselves? We have been trying to express through limited means our illimitable love for others. Sometimes, if the means are ample, we go overboard. But how wise were the Three Wise Men presenting gold, frankincense and myrrh to a baby?

Not a one of them brought a rattle. Or a puppy. But they had come a long way, following a star, without being sure of what lay at the end.

Some people are blessed at being able to find what are called thoughtful presents as if the gifts themselves could think. Often they are small, inexpensive items which say a lot. My way is to buy at one swoop a single universal gift that will fit everybody.

May as well tell you that this year's gift for the men is a pair of Robo Grip pliers guaranteed to open the rustiest pipe. Women can use it to tear open heavy, waxed plastic in which cereals are wrapped.

But this time, while the men have pliers, the women's gifts are varied, as are the grandchildren's, thanks to an elegant young woman who discovered me standing, a pensive hippo, in a museum gift shop. Taking pity, she pointed out presents. Everything she touched shone as if she were a fairy god mother. The apt gifts will shock—and enthrall—the nieces and daughters-and sisters-in-law.

Our youngest son was explaining to a friend the other day that when he and his two brothers reached 12, I left the shopping to Gin. "Christmas day, Guybo would wrap whatever came to hand—an old dog's collar or plaques or paperweights civic clubs had given him in lieu of cash for speaking.

"One Christmas he bought 36 toy slates. For the women he chalked two or three words of praise on each slate and for the men forthright epithets. 'Horse hockey' is one that comes to mind. You can't imagine the glee those slates aroused in my grandfather, Coach Pitt. Then well into his 80s, he went from slate to slate, laughing, and, when he finished examining them, having forgotten the first ones, he made the rounds again.

"Listen," the youngest son said, "when you receive for Christmas a casually wrapped brick out of the front yard, you begin to understand how immaterial material things are. I'll never forget the delight that those slates aroused in Coach."

Ring It Up

The youngest brother called Monday to report he had found for his son a game, called Nok-Hockey, that he and his two brothers had played as children.

I remembered. That game nearly got me arrested in 1958. Their mother discovered late Christmas Eve there was no eye-popper under the tree, no game that would make the three forget all else.

So near midnight, I was at the locked doors of a newfangled discount store, begging through the glass to get in, folding my hands as in prayer.

The guard shook his head, and I, feigning dejection, walked off; but when he looked away, I began running all-out along the face of the building. And, turning the north corner, saw, appalled, that the side stretched 150 yards to the rear west corner.

Never mind, dig in, RUN, you fool, and reach that back door before it closes. Midway, I sprawled on wet soil. Get up, mutt. MOVE!

I rounded the west corner and saw, dismayed, that some misguided architect had placed the rear door at the far south end, 400 yards away. I had practically run around the entire confounded building!

Don't maunder, clown. GO! GO!

Racing along the rear, I reached the open door, plunged through plastic strips and shot past two guards on metal folding chairs. One, tilting back, fell to the floor as a wild-eyed, muddy-faced madman, bolting by them, opened the double doors, vanished.

"HEY!" a guard yelled as the doors were closing. "YOU CAN'T GO IN THERE!"

Inside, housewares were to the left. Clothes to the right. Where were toys?

Try the east aisles. Use your wits. Slink, a coyote, below the shelves. But hurry, in a fast crouch, knucks grazing the floor for balance, Akut the Ape.

Behind me, a cry: "YONDER HE GOES!" A yell: "BLOCK THE AISLES!"

Aha, THE TOYS, at last! Dolls? Nothing doing! Parcheesi? Forget it! And in the corner, long boxes of heavy cardboard. NOK-HOCKEY. I grabbed one. And turned to see my pursuers gathering around. "You'll have to wrest it from me," I said. They paused. "Somebody call the manager," somebody said.

Somebody did. He took in the scene.

"What the hell, it's Christmas," he said. "Ring it up!"

At home, wrapping gifts, Gin raised her eyes, shining in the tree's reflected lights, and saw the box.

"Was it hard to find?"

"Nothing to speak of."

 She thought of her three sons, thwacking wood sticks. She smiled. A thumping good Christmas!

On the phone Monday, the youngest said the 3-foot new version was plastic.

The old wood one had extended 6 feet.

"You found it," I told him. Nothing's the same. Nothing.

And thought: Keep running. Just keep running.

Chapter Two

Young 'uns

Airborne

Josh and I said hello as we sat side by side on the big plane.
A fifth-grader, he was going to visit his gran'ma in Chattanooga.
I was headed for Houston to the GOP Convention.

"Are you nervous?" he asked — and looked me in the eye.

"No need to be."

"Do these planes crash a lot?"

"Very seldom. This one won't."

He worked the window shade.

"Will there be lines around the states, like on the maps?"
he asked.

"No, but there will be other ways — rivers, lakes, mountains — to tell them apart."

As he talked he was busy as a chipmunk checking a rock pile.

The plane came to life. It moved.

"I trust the pilots," he said.

"So do I."

"Will there be a lot of noise?"

"Just at first."

"Do you mind if I pull the window shade?" he asked.

"Pull away."

The plane reached a shrill whine. He pulled down the shade,
then raised it a bit.

"Bye bye," he said softly.

But he kept peeping out and, finally, murmuring something
about not being chicken, he raised the shade for good.

"Boy!" he said gazing at the ground going by.

He braced against the seat back, extended his arms stiffly in
front of him, fists clenched as if on the controls, and imitated the

sound of the roaring engines. As the plane's nose rose, he pulled his clenched fists back slowly. We were airborne.

"Good going," I said.

"Great pilots," he said.

"This is really my second flight," he said. "On the first I was a baby."

"How old?"

"Two."

"What do you remember about it?"

He narrowed his eyes.

"My mother holding me up to push the buttons."

We discussed the plane's speed, its altitude, shining white clouds that looked like the South Pole.

"What is your occupation?" he asked, stumbling a bit on the big word.

"A reporter with The Virginian-Pilot," I said.

His eyes widened.

"I work there too!"

"Where 'bouts?"

"I'm a carrier. I'll ask my boss if he knows you!"

We marveled at the coincidence of coworkers winding up on the same plane in the sky. Soon we were descending to Charlotte to change planes and go our separate ways.

"It was more funner taking off," he observed.

He watched the landscape, thick with trees coming up at us. "I saw a deer!" he said.

We landed, said see you, and I stood to pull my bag from the overhead compartment. It wasn't there.

"Look in the one across the aisle," he said — and pointed.

Nothing like a seasoned traveler to help a fellow.

More Than a Doll

Beside me on a flight Wednesday to Atlanta was Elizabeth, 3, chipmunk-quick, ever active, asking questions, not whining, just curious, bent on exhausting a subject, closing a series of rapid-fire inquiries on seatbelts by asking: "Does the captain wear one?"

And then, suddenly, she was scrambling to reach the aisle to go see if the pilot had one on, and, if not, why. Her mother caught her just before she charged the cockpit.

Not once, when flight attendants reminded me to buckle the belt, had it occurred to me to ask, "Let's go see if the pilot's wearing one."

Her mother brought out two dolls, Barbie and Ken, who, Elizabeth told me, was "Ken Barbie," giving Barbie a little extra status, it seemed.

The child's fingers flew in fastening Barbie's clothes, as if she were capable of caring for an infant or, as I watched her, dressing a wound or addressing a computer. Her young mother bent to help, and, both heads bowed over the tiny doll, they seemed peers, sisters even, immersed in their play-task.

When Elizabeth and her parents visited Chicago, their cabbie veered in and out of traffic. Leaning toward him when he stopped, Elizabeth said, "I want you to know one thing. That's the worst damn ride I ever had!"

Some psychologists say that girls and boys are conditioned from birth toward interests in dolls or trucks. Was Elizabeth's attentiveness to the doll innate or acquired?

"It was there from the start," her mother said. Next day, I asked Gin, who has watched boys and girls, in school and out, most of her life.

It's natural with them, she said. "That's the part that's mystifying. Girls don't see the doll or figure as a little object as they would some other toy."

The thing becomes a person to them.

"A girl holds it close, carefully. Watch a boy the same age." She laughed, remembering how two boys, going on 3, handle a Pinocchio their size. "They have a kind of careless way of toting him. They're apt to pick him by his arm or foot. The other day Bo picked him up by his nose! Now, a little girl doesn't ever do that. She's conscious of that being a baby of some kind."

Watching Elizabeth learning her way around the plane, I remarked to her mother, "You all, from the first, have the edge on us."

She laughed, which is what women generally do when it's pointed out that they are smarter, quicker than men. Mention that to an audience of women and some nod in agreement, and most of them smile. Offer it to a men's gathering, and, except for a few, you might as well have endorsed communism. Some frown or flush at the notion. Others look stunned at the thought, as if they've been pole-axed, like a steer about to crumple to its knees.

In "What Every Woman Knows," playwright James Barrie suggests that a woman is smarter than her spouse — and smart enough not to let him know it, helping along the unsuspecting dolt from backstage. Now, becoming leaders in public and private enterprise, women are coming onto the stage, where they belong. No sense in continuing to waste time and energy exerting guidance from behind the scenes. Things are in crises that need their talents to be applied directly at the front, unfiltered. Think how recent presidents have erred.

Many women are finding ways for dual roles, putting their careers on hold or working part-time while they rear children, enjoying motherhood. But it is demanding, tough. And, of course, women, as well as the children, require the fathers' active investment of self at home. It is as enriching to them as to their families. And let a father hear that his daughter can't do anything as well or better than a man, and you have a first-rate feminist in the making.

One day Elizabeth will be in the cockpit.

Wearing a seatbelt.

Knock! Knock!

In the car in the rain at night, the 5-year-old and I were waiting for his brother, 7, to be released from some activity, and, to lighten the vigil, he proposed a riddle.

"What is yellow, weighs 1,000 lbs., and sings?"

"Beats me."

"Two 500 lb. canaries," he said, laughing. "How do you stop a skunk from smelling?"

"How?"

"You hold its nose," he said.

"I can't top yours," I said.

"Yes you can. Try," he urged.

"All right, what has four wheels, stinks, and flies?"

"I give up," he said.

"A garbage truck."

"A garbage truck can't fly!"

"But it draws flies."

"What's worse than finding a worm in an apple?" I asked.

"A half a worm!" he said. "Why did the letter Y cross the road?"

"Why?"

"To join the MCA."

"I like that," I said.

"What do you do if you see a lion?" he asked.

'Tell me."

"You hope he doesn't see you!" he said, in glee at my obtusity.

"How long have you known me?" he asked.

"Are we still doing riddles?"

"Just answer," he said.

"I've known you five years."

"Knock! Knock!" he said.

"Who's there?" I asked.

"I thought you said you knew me!" he said. "But you didn't."

"How old are you?" he asked.

"Is that a knock-knock question?"

"No, for real."

"All right, 75."

"That's old-d-d! When will you be 85?"

"Tonight, the way things are going."

"Why didn't the skeleton cross the road?" he asked.

"I can't imagine."

"He didn't have the guts to try it!" The boy was gleeful.

"Your turn," he said.

"What's black and white and red all over?" I asked, reaching back.

"I give up."

"A newspaper."

"It's not red," he said.

"But it's read all over town."

At that moment his brother's face loomed at the rain-wet window. He got in the car.

"Ask him that last one," urged the 5-year-old.

So I asked the older boy what was black, white and red all over.

"A zebra with a diaper rash!"

"Who told you that?"

"My teacher, two years ago."

Don't tell me schooling is for naught!

In the rain, I drove slowly. "Why aren't we going faster?" the older brother asked.

"Ain't no cause to hurry."

"A RIDDLE!" cried the younger boy. "Guybo made a riddle!"

Life's a riddle, I told him.

Awesome!

The sight of a tent, a teepee, in the window of a Lillian Vernon discount store caught my eye and lured me inside.

Several months ago, a grandchild, now 6, had told his seven cousins he had seen an Indian in a teepee in the wilderness of our back yard. When exploration failed to turn up the Indian or teepee, an aunt, bending down, asked him where he thought the Indian had gone.

He looked her in the eye.

"Probably he went out West," he said. Well done! I thought, at least one of eight has a bit of me in him.

So, seeing in the store window the teepee's eight poles bunched atop its widespread siding, the stout canvas just about the off-white you see in Frederick Remington's paintings of the plains, I bought the teepee, the last of the lot.

Next morning, the child's father came over early and raised the teepee out back under the giant, three-spired deodar cedar tree, tallest for miles around. Its trunk is huge. Two large off-shoots are thicker than the trunks of any other nearby tree. It rears upward, a great three-masted schooner or Jack's beanstalk, depending on your view.

Upon arriving at the house, children, without saying hello, rush to the back yard to climb the always-evergreen deodar tree. It is festooned with a rigging of vines thick as a man's wrists on which sailors or Tarzans and Janes can swing or slide to earth.

Now it shaded a white teepee.

"Don't any of you brothers tell your wives about the tent," I said. "If the mothers find out, overwhelming love will compel them to heighten anticipation by hinting something exciting is out back. Hustle the children into the house until they all arrive, then loose them at once to find the teepee on their own, without warning.

"How the teepee got there must be a mystery. Let it subside in their minds until, years later, one asks another, 'Do you have any recollection, a long time ago, of seeing a teepee, or even an Indian, under the deodar tree?' "

The children, arriving, became involved in caroms until, the game waning, someone said, "Let's climb the tree!" They were gone as a swoop of swallows. If the mothers knew, and they must have, they had kept the secret.

I slid open the big glass door to peer into the impenetrable green wall of brush and trees out back. Amid a sudden outburst of voices, going on and on, the only words to be discerned, over and over, were shouts of "See! ... See! ... See!"

A father, joining them, found his 7-year-old staring at the white tent under the dark-green tree.

"Awesome!" the boy said.

Much later, in the house, an aunt asked the 6-year-old if he wished to put the tent in his own yard. "No," he said, "the Indian might come back."

Don't Look Down!

She returned from a day at the State Fair with grandchildren as if she had been to Mars and back, outside the spacecraft. "We went on the Ferris wheel," she said. And I understood. The most frightening ride of my life, scarier than the Loch Ness Monster, was on a Ferris wheel long ago at the State Fair. With me were our three boys and two of their cousins — the five ranging in age from 3 to 7 years.

The darn thing reared eight stories, scraping high-piled clouds in the picture-puzzle sky. "Let's ride the merry-go-round for teensie tots," I suggested.

No, no, nothing would do but the confounded Ferris wheel. We all piled in the last of the long, swinging seats stuttering upward as they were loaded one by one. "This seat don't have a bar across the front to hold onto!" the oldest boy discovered.

"This seat doesn't have a bar — HEY!" I shouted, "IT RE-ALLY DON'T HAVE NO BAR TO HOLD ONTO!"

And I said to the operator at the lever, ' "I say, old chap, may I point out this seat don't have — "

S-W-O-O-O-S-S-H-H!

The wheel took off in a rush, with the eight of us seated backwards, sky and earth changing place. "DON'T LOOK DOWN!" I shouted, and, looking down, felt my stomach turn two Immelmanns. Bracing a foot at one end, I threw myself lengthways and backwards across the front of the seat and, gripping the other end with my hand, made an impromptu bar for the little troop. "EVERYBODY HANG ON TO GUYBO!" I shouted. "SUTT, ARE YOU CLINGING TO MY FOOT?"

There is a point, as you reach the peak of the turn, suddenly facing forward, it seems as if the seat will fly off into the sky and come to rest in the next county. As we swooped to the top and started down, I felt, distinctly, the six of us, clumped like a mass of seaweed, rise slightly in the air and then fall back into the seat, ker-plunk. Sing, you fool, sing, to lighten things, I thought — and bawled, "DID YOUR MO-THER COME FROM IRE-LAND? DID SHE WEAR A BONNY SMILE?"

As we swept by the operator, motionless at the lever, I yelled, "GET US OFF THIS THING!"

He didn't even turn his head. By George, I thought, when we do get off this infernal ride, IF we get off, I am going to wrench a bar from one of the other seats and pound that rock-eared operator into the ground and sue everybody in sight. It became apparent that he, bent on drawing spectators, using us as an exercise in fright, was not going to stop the wheel and let us off until he had a crowd to refill the seats.

And, sure enough, spectators doubled up in mirth at the sight of me, an outstretched human bar as the wheel whirled around. We may be on this wheel like doomed mythological characters forever, I thought.

But at last it slowed, the earth settled into place, and, one at a time, the seats emptied. Kind people helped me out. The children piled off and, hopping about, shouted things like: "I wasn't scared a bit!" and "Why did Guybo act so funny?"

Except for the three-year-old who stood in silence to one side.

Poor tyke, I thought, he hadn't uttered a word the whole time. Just clung vise-like to my neck. I cleared my throat. Fine! I could still talk.

"Wink," I said to him, "are you all right?"

He was gazing up at the towering Ferris wheel.

"Let's go again," he said.

God Made Dirt, So Dirt Can't Hurt

Eraser clappers of the world, relax. Your jobs are safe.

For a while it appeared that the U.S. Department of Labor might forbid Virginia Beach teachers to assign pupils to routine chores in cleaning lunchrooms and classes. No one would want children to do heavy work, but teachers have used little deeds — dusting erasers, carrying notes to the office, feeding fish in the aquarium — as a way of nurturing a sense of responsibility.

In the fourth grade if someone had asked for volunteers to sweep the chimney, I'd have been the first to spring forward, broom in hand. And it was a big chimney, filled with swifts in summer. It was not that our teachers weren't kind and caring. I can summon their names and dear faces. They were gifted, self-sacrificing. If they married, they had to give up teaching. I loved them. But I didn't like school, not a bit. Didn't like forsaking my dog Tony (named for Tom Mix's horse); didn't like wearing shoes all spring; didn't like leaving the woods stretching for miles; didn't like closing a "Miss Minerva" book at home to go to class and do sums; didn't want to stop playing Cowboys and Indians or Kick the Can or Follow the Leader. Today most children love to go to school. And, of course, I wouldn't do anything to lessen their zeal.

I ask, casually, if they like school, and when they nod and smile, I'm awed. And grateful. They should like school. It's fun to learn. But I'd do anything to get out of it. The chore we liked most was dusting erasers. Cleaning the blackboards with a damp rag wasn't a bad job either. It was like unpainting a painting. One time when I'd finished cleaning the boards in Miss Eubanks' room, I slipped next door and announced to Miss Shepherd I'd come over to do the blackboards for her.

"Nobody can do boards like me, Miz Shepherd," I said.

"As I do," she said.

"Miz Shepherd, you shouldn't be doing blackboards. Lemme," I said.

But dusting the erasers was where I shone. When the teacher asked, "Now boys and girls, who would like to dust the — "

WHAM! ZOOM! I was out of my seat, hurdling desks, and standing in front of her, hand raised, when she said " — erasers?"

Best thing about it was you had to dust them outside. Couldn't have white chalk dust clouding the room, setting everybody to coughing. I took the erasers to the fartherest reach of the school yard, so as to take more time in getting back. Perched on a rock, I clapped erasers together, white puffs exploding at every blow. After all were done, I did 'em again, trying to drag out the duty 'til Little Recess. One morning, clapping erasers, I heard a droning in the distance and saw a dot on the horizon, getting bigger and bigger until it became a full-size silver airship, three blocks long, the dirigible Los Angeles thundering overhead, darkening the sky as if a roll-top desk were being slid across it.

The school's windows were filled with spectators watching that zeppelin sail above us. Exulting, I reached up in the air and made a great sweeping motion as if to erase that ol' airship right out of the sky.

I'm glad some parents are interested enough to ask about policy — and that teachers are wise enough not to overdo the duty. Time ever comes they ban pupils dusting erasers, I'll go down and do 'em.

Anything to get outside.

How 'bout a Break

Amid all the hullabaloo over what schools should and shouldn't do, nobody thought to tell us that many schools no longer have recess. That may help explain why so many difficulties beset education. Recess every day is all that kept me in school. Otherwise it would have been unendurable. I wouldn't have been a dropout — I simply couldn't have gone in the first place. A stay-out.

I'd have hid in the woods.

Why, Atlanta schools had two: Little Recess, a half hour mid-morning, and Big Recess, an hour at noon with lunch followed by a release out doors. Some of us bolted our lunch to bolt outdoors. Furthermore, in the fifth grade at 11:30, Miss Minter read us Mark Twain's "Huckleberry Finn," America's greatest novel. To hear of Huck was a kind of recess from the time and place where we were. Miss Minter did it without asking anybody. That was why nobody could tell Miss Minter not to do it. Anyway, parents didn't meddle then in what they knew little about: namely, how to teach school.

At recess we did what we pleased: marbles, jump rope, kick the can, dodge ball, hopscotch, kites, tag, tops, hoops, mumblety-peg, or just sat on a log and not think. Let the subconscious take over. We learned by playing as biologists tell us young animals do. Some adults want children at a task all day, something most grown people don't pretend to do. Nearly all wangle breaks of some sort.

I learned of Norfolk's policy of recesslessness on Career Day. A bright youth was assigned to watch me at what is laughingly called work. We were discussing favorite subjects, and, hearing that mine had been recess, a teacher escorting the youth remarked that recess was no longer in use in Norfolk. To me, it was like finding the sun didn't come out. She missed it, too, she said, but students have so much to do there's no time for a break.

A check among friends disclosed that recess is not universal around Virginia. In North Carolina a school district requires pupils to earn recess through merits awarded for good conduct. As punishment, a malefactor has to stand on a wall and watch his fellows at recess.

One Richmond mother remarked that teachers would seem to need a turn outdoors as much or more than the pupils.

If you care to know what recess can do, take a look at the oldest generation. But not at me. There's such a thing as excess recess. I'm still on recess.

Chapter Three

The Better Half

Snow in August

On an August morning, leaving the front door ajar, we started walking down the driveway to give the Labrador retriever a run in the field across the way. Looking at the bare drive, Gin asked, "When, if ever, are you going to put down gravel?"

"Soon."

"Soon," she sighed, "never comes."

"I never promised you a rose garden," I said, "but I did say we'd buy gravel, and we will. Dear girl, whatever you do, never lose faith. After 46 years of your keeping hope alive, I just couldn't stand it if you lost heart at this late stage."

The phone rang and she dashed to answer it and chat with Martha or Charlotte or Bunny or Jackie or Jean or Mary or Wanda or Caroline or Elizabeth or Frances or Mary Lee or any one of her three daughters-in-law.

Mind in neutral, I was drowsing in the sun when suddenly there pulled up before me at the drive a huge dump truck. Filled with gravel.

A hillock of gravel, blinding white in the light. As I gawked, a smiling youth leaned out the cab window — I thought he was going to ask directions — and he began saying something about not wanting to take the load back to the plant and offering it, at a remarkable price, to me.

"I can spread it in 15 minutes," he said.

"Do it!"

He backed the truck in the drive, and he went to work. Deft, swift, he put down that gravel as if he were icing a cake. He even extended it up into the area around the brick path and spread a double layer at the entrance to the drive. What a pleasure to watch him work.

And then, the job done and paid for, the genie was gone. I went inside the house and sat with a cup of coffee, black, at the kitchen table. And waited.

"Well, I'll let you go," I heard her saying to Mary or whoever was on the phone down the hall. There was the click of the receiver as she hung it up.

"I'm going to the grocery store," she called. "Be right back."

"Ta-ta!" I said.

There was the sound of the front door opening. Then a silence, deep as a well, broken by her shouting, "COME HERE QUICKLY!"

I ran to her side and looked out. And gazed upon what seemed to be fresh-fallen snow that filled the drive and reached up the walkway to the door and even spread out to hide a bare spot beyond what was the buried brick border.

Her face, turned to me, was a mixture of shock, mystification and dawning laughter at the sudden Antarctic at our door.

"How did this happen?" she asked.

"Some things in this old world we just accept without inquiry," I said.

"What does that mean?" she insisted.

"Why, you kept the faith," I replied.

Elizabeth Taylor

The World War II veteran looked up from the Hampton hospital bed into the visitor's thick-lashed, violet eyes. "I never expected to see Cleopatra in person," said the grizzled patient to the woman bending over him.

Elizabeth Taylor Warner smiled. "I left my barge outside," she said. In her most protracted role, the 46-year-old actress is campaigning around Virginia for her husband, former Navy Secretary John W. Warner Jr., candidate for the U.S. Senate. Women, if anything, seem more intrigued with her than do men.

"It's her eyes," explained one young woman, waiting for the actress' arrival at a morning coffee in suburban Hampton. "I want to see if they're really violet."

Some, nostalgic, seek in the matron's face traces of the pig-tailed girl in "National Velvet." Others come for the sheer spectacle of a raven-haired Hollywood celebrity stepping out of a car like an ordinary hausfrau onto a quiet street between close-clipped lawns.

"Because she's a survivor," said another young woman. "She's gone through ordeals — marriages, illnesses, career crises — any one of which would destroy the average woman."

Whatever the reason, 60 women greeted her at the day's first stop in the ranch-house home of the wife of the Hampton GOP chairman. Mrs. Warner was wearing a tan headband, a bronze-colored blouse, a beige gabardine skirt, open-toe pumps, and, around her neck, a gold chain strung with Byzantine coins. She carried a brown-leather pocketbook with, said one woman, the Gucci look.

She moved among the guests, chatting quietly, and they were too awed to recall a minute later what she had said. "Who can quote exact words when you're so excited?" said one. After mingling half an hour, the women crowded into the living room, and Mrs. Warner spoke three minutes.

"I won't speak on the issues," she said, so softly that the audience strained to pick up every syllable. "I just want to say that each and every one of you is important to our campaign. We need your help so badly." Then she referred to the death of the Republican Senate nominee, Richard D. Obenshain, whom her husband replaced as the candidate in August.

"As you know, because of the tragic circumstances, we're starting pretty late. I know some of you are still hurting because of Dick's death, but I just have to ask you to help us as Republican women. You women are the real kind of power behind the Republican Party, and, without your help, we won't make it.

"And John is such a fine man. He has such integrity and honesty. I really believe that he is the man who should be the U.S. senator. So I'm asking for your help and I thank you."

When she had finished, just before the women broke into applause, a little "ah-h-h-h-h!" escaped them, as if the veteran of 50 films was a gifted child called upon to perform for elders.

After another coffee, Mrs. Warner, accompanied by secretary and driver, toured wards of the Veterans Administration hospital on the shore of Hampton Roads. In the foyer of a ward she moved among a double row of wheelchairs bearing patients with spinal injuries.

"I saw you let the snake out of the box," said one, referring to "Cleopatra."

"It's easy to remember a pretty lady," said a doctor standing nearby.

"He remembers the snake!" she said, laughing.

In the rear of the room, largely unnoticed, a youth craned in his wheelchair to take in the scene, a delighted grin on his face. She, finishing the review between the rows, went around them and walked toward him. He, smiling, drew back his shriveled hands and raised his right elbow quickly in greeting, and she touched it.

As the entourage was leaving, a young doctor, sidling up to a colleague hosting the tour, muttered, "You lucky devil!"

Not by the least quiver of his moustache did the dignified guide indicate that he had heard. Patients, nurses, orderlies and doctors poured into a large day room, and she moved through the eddying crowd while flashbulbs popped.

A doctor, posing with her for a picture, broke away from the knot of spectators, his knees wobbling as if he were on roller skates. "My wife's gunna kill me!" he cried. In a moment, however, he was back, explaining his duties, while she, enormous violet eyes fixed upon him, murmured questions. Then, his discourse finished, he drew away, nodding twice, quickly to himself, as if to say: That's well done.

Someone produced a pencil and a pad of paper, then the room became a waving forest of pencils, as she inscribed, bold as skywriting: Elizabeth Taylor Warner. "My son had your picture on his desk years ago," quavered an elderly nurse.

"Years ago it was on his desk! — Where is it now?" she countered, laughing. Amid the escalating hubbub, a gray-haired patient approached a reporter. "I've been playing the piano 35 years by ear," he said. "Do you think it would be all right for me to play now?"

Assured that would be splendid, the patient went to an old upright in the corner. Presently "Red Sails in the Sunset" broke over the pandemonium and continued throughout the levee.

Leaving, she cried, full-throated, "Byee-e-e-e, guy-y-y-ys!"

In an elevator, crowded into a corner by a phalanx of medics, she sighed, "A wallflower!" In the next ward, the accompanying doctor marveled at her deft banter with patients. "After all," she said, "I've been doing this since I was 12."

As each doctor dropped off the tour, he abandoned his professional decorum, and consented, on the urging of nurses, to pose for a picture—shoulders back, stomach in, chin up — beside her.

At the day's last coffee, she moved around a huge semicircle of black women seated in lawn chairs in a pine-shaded backyard, then, walking to the center, made her soft appeal. "I would like to tell you just one small thing about my husband," she said. "He's a man that cares. He's a man that listens. He will take time out for every personal phone call. He cares about people in general — we both do — and we want to make this world just a little bit better for all of us, and for your children and grandchildren. And he has the honesty, integrity and energy to do that, and with your help and God's will, we will make it."

In the day's final stop on the way to the airport, she talked with the mentally retarded clients and the staff of the Sarah Bonwell Hudgins Regional Center, marveling at the handiwork, comparing it favorably to what she had seen at facilities in other states. Asked at the close how she had stood the lengthy day, she replied, "My feet are okay." Then she added, "It's only when I take my shoes off that they collapse!"

But then the day had been short compared to one on the set. "When you get up at 6 o'clock, work all day under trying conditions, go home at 8, grab a bite to eat, and memorize lines — there's nothing cushy about it."

"Naturally now I meet more people on a one-to-one basis, and it's not fantasy or fiction — it's real life. You don't have anybody else's words or thoughts to express. You're on your own, and you talk about real people and issues. They're all very warm, which is the reason they want to get near you and be photographed, and you can only respond in return. Their friendliness is contagious."

She had been in the public eye since she was a child, she continued, and her family in England had been oriented to politics. Both her godparents were in Parliament. "And when I was

5 years old, my pony threw Anthony Eden," she said. "In Hollywood, I was much more sheltered — that's the way the studios used to put it — they wouldn't let you get out and meet people as much as this.

"And I really enjoy it because I like people," said Elizabeth Taylor Warner. "I've been a volunteer all my life — which is nothing the studio can stop!"

Imogene Coca

Imogene's in town appearing with her husband, King Donovan, in "Plaza Suite" by Neil Simon. Imogene Coca, that is, who, with Sid Caesar, has been to television what Chaplin was to films. And who, when she was 11, was told by her mother to take dancing lessons, and, being an obedient child, did. Her mother had been in the chorus on Broadway. Her father, a musical conductor in Philadelphia's theaters, took the child with him to rehearsals.

"I kind of fell in love with what I saw, most particularly the dramatic shows," Imogene Coca said. "I never dug the comics. I thought comedy was silly, but when people acted or wore lovely clothes I became entranced, and here I am a comedienne, or so they tell me."

Just such a phrase — "or so they tell me" — expresses what was most likely an early, now habitual, self-effacement in conversation. It discloses a shyness which may seem at odds with the wild, creative antics that take hold when she is on stage.

Just starting dancing lessons, she appeared in a recital, and not having learned much about dancing at that point, she sang a song, "Oh by Gee, by Gosh, by Gum."

"I had never been before an audience and I was scared. Comedy, I think, can come out of desperation, and I found myself doing really crazy things. I went quite berserk on the stage and stopped the show, and my father said, 'My goodness.' That summer I was booked into vaudeville. My father was such a good musician, they didn't dare turn me down. Nepotism, pure nepotism!"

The next three summers, she studied dancing in Atlantic City, where her father had seasonal engagements.

"My teacher, Miss Viola — I never knew her last name, nobody called her anything but Miss Viola — taught me pantomime, though I didn't realize then it was that. We would sit on the floor and be flowers, back from the time they were seeds until they grew and became full blossoms and then lost their petals in the wind and disintegrated. And we were fountains and all sorts of things. She was a wonderful teacher. After I finished the eighth grade, I went to work as a dancer in New York, and I've been in the theater ever since."

In one show, rehearsing in a cold hall, she slipped on an actor's coat between numbers — "He was quite tall, and it was a polo coat that came to my ankles" — and while waiting for her number, looked over in the corner of the stage where one of the boys was doing a funny, little step.

"I thought, 'Gee, that looks like fun.' I went over and looked at his feet and started doing the same step. Some others joined us, and suddenly the producer of the show said, 'What are you all doing?' We said, 'Nothing. Nothing.'

"But he needed a bit number while he was changing scenery in the first and second act, and he said, 'I want you to do exactly what you're doing — and think of more. Wear what you've got on!"

"On opening night it was a big hit and they said I was a comedienne, which came as a big shock to me."

Her outsized features call to mind cartoonish penny valentines of the 1930s. She activates the huge rolling eyes, the wide lavish mouth, the generous snub nose to convey swift-changing shades of emotion. And with it all, petite Coca is utterly feminine, quite pretty with a beauty heightened by intelligence. Her mind — quick-moving, shimmering — is as fun to follow as a dragonfly.

She danced next at Tamiment, a summer camp for adults in the Poconos, with a company headed by Max Leibman. When Leibman began putting together "Your Show of Shows," he remembered the shy girl with the huge smile, and brought her into the cast, and put her with Sid Caesar.

"Sid and I — it's terribly dull, but we've never had an argument — respect each other and we have different sets of friends and never socialize much, but when we work together it's almost like ESP.

"There was never any pulling because we had the same reactions. I'd think, 'Oh dear, this isn't going to be very good' — and inevitably Sid would question the sketch, so I never had to say anything.

"I think of Sid primarily as a brilliant actor who does comedy. Even when he does a monologue, he's going into a character. He's being someone else, not himself."

They had brilliant writers, she said, but often the two of them improvised dialogue. "Once, on a Thursday, we were rehearsing a sketch for a Saturday show and Sid said to me, 'Do you think this is any good?' And I said, 'No-o-o-o-o-o!' and Max said it was terrible.

'Let's suppose,' said Max, 'that Coca has wrecked the car and doesn't want you to know it.' So we got up and improvised, and Max had a couple of secretaries catch the lines and then he called in the writers and told them not to say a word, but just to watch. And the writers were wonderful. They started to laugh and began saying, 'Maybe, instead of saying this ...'

"And there was a fine feeling, and it was all because of Max, who held our temperaments in. He gave you freedom and yet you realized someone was sitting there, who, if things got out of hand, would say whoa. And things never got out of hand. Max is also a writer, so we weren't strapped for material. It was nothing for Max to come up after a run-through on Saturday and replace material. Once he replaced 20 minutes an hour before we went on the air.

"We'd get terribly nervous when we heard the show's theme, like going on to a ledge 100 stories up, but then suddenly there was no time to get tense and there were no cue cards, no teleprompters. I never knew where the camera was — we had five of them — and we had an audience of almost a thousand so you were playing to it and your fellow actors and it never occurred to me that all those people were watching on screens at home.

"I realize television exposure is great, but you know when you're creating something and it really turns you on, that becomes all-important and the audience is exciting wherever it is."

They don't make shows any more like "Your Show of Shows," but one day, Sid and Imogene believe, they'll make them again, and meanwhile, he is in a dinner theater in Atlanta and she is in one in Norfolk, and, as Coca said the other day, the audience, wherever, is exciting. And so is she.

Jacqueline Kennedy Onassis

Her wispy soft voice trailed off at the end of sentences without her enunciating crisply the final word, her mouth slightly ajar as if breathless, keeping that last word as well as the hearer dangling, while her big eyes looked into the distance, a shy little girl. That vaporous image sheathed the steel Jacqueline Kennedy Onassis needed to survive. She bore adversities without whimpering, regal head high.

Her childhood was broken by divorce. Then there were her husband's infidelities. She suffered a stillbirth and the death of an infant. She strove to preserve her identity amid the close-knit, clamorous Kennedys, whose women smacked of a pride of lionesses.

Then Dallas and a sniper's shots. Pink suit blood-spattered, she hugged his shattered head. With fortitude unmatched by women in Sparta, she presided over a funeral worthy of him, their children, and us. To gain independence, she risked the nation's scorn in a marriage to a Greek shipping tycoon, then returned, after his death, to take up toil in a New York publishing house. She dwelled on her children. When writer Doris Kearns Goodwin said she wished that her own children could be as caring of one another as were John and Caroline, Jacqueline replied, "That's the best thing I've done, bar none."

Still, the children were part of the clan. So she went to the 1964 Democratic convention in Atlantic City where Robert Kennedy was dueling with President Johnson for the party's heart. Dressed in white sleeveless brocade, she held a reception in a Boardwalk hotel. To each person who came by and suddenly could say little, she said, in a deep voice, "Thank you."

Three times that day, she went to the stage and thanked those present for many kindnesses, "but most of all for helping him in 1960." Outside, teenagers chanted her name. When the last well-dressed guest cleared the receiving line, Robert Kennedy asked the committee, "Couldn't we let some of the — uh — younger people come in?"

It was not to be. Outside, she waved to the youthful, screaming crowd while police locked arms to hold it back. Inside, actress Florence Eldridge was reading a poem in his memory:

I have a rendezvous with Death

At some disputed barricade,

When Spring comes back with rustling shade

And apple blossoms fill the air —

I have a rendezvous with Death

When Spring brings back blue days and fair.

"Why that poem?" I asked the actress.

"He asked her to memorize it. He must have had a premonition."

"When did he ask her to memorize it?"

"On their honeymoon," she said.

Girded by loved ones, she died with the grace and dignity with which she had lived. "She did it on her own way and in her own terms," said her son, his tones and features echoing and mirroring Jacqueline.

Queen Elizabeth

An acerb fashion critic — whom we shall not dignify with a name — included Queen Elizabeth II on a list of the world's worst-dressed women. "God save the moths," the churl had the cheek to say.

My loyalty to Elizabeth II is such that if she declared war with or without the consent of Parliament against anybody, I would take up arms again. We met in 1957 when she and Prince Philip visited Williamsburg. Assigned to cover the royal couple, I expected to be bored — and was bowled over.

Her majesty was wearing a blue outfit — scarab blue, a woman told me — with touches of fur at the wrists, neck, and maybe on the hat. Her complexion was as delicate as fine china, and her eyes, big as carriage lamps, rivaled the sky in color. When she walked across the field at Patrick Henry Airport, a blue-jowled photographer murmured: "Look at her jabbering away! Ain't she cute?" My thoughts, exactly.

In Williamsburg, as she moved at the head of an entourage between a constant, narrow corridor of spectators, her sapphire eyes — large and luminous — turned from side to side, and she smiled as if delighted to be stabbed by 15,000 rapt gazes. Occasionally a woman would try to curtsy, as if pulling a pan of biscuits from the oven — you don't get much chance to curtsy these days around here — and the queen would beam upon her.

Her walk was at a processional pace, except that she had a way of picking up her feet smartly, like a chicken walking on a hot hearth, and then advancing them almost in slow motion to the next hot brick.

Once, through some eddy among the escorts, she was left unattended but poised. She looked around, smiling, like a child in a wonderland. It was all I could do to keep from springing to her side, drawing an imaginary sword and shouting to the crowd: "En garde!"

She glided as a white swan, silently; and close behind sauntered Philip. Slim, tall, bent slightly at the waist, hands clasped behind his back so that his arms resembled closed wings, he was a great blue heron stalking through a pond. The breeze wafted his thinning hair in a crest. His big, beaked profile scanned what lay before him, alert for frog or crawfish. Mesmerized by the brilliant passage of the swan, a spectator would look up and find the keen-eyed heron regarding him. Every now and then he would spear a question from the waters.

"And what, sir, do you do?" he asked a stout, goggle-eyed fellow, still dazzled by the shining apparition of the queen.

"Why Ah'm a member of the General Assembly of Virginiyuh!" goggle eyes replied.

"Oh?" quipped Philip. "Is that all?" And, nodding, strolled on.

In my haste to reach Williamsburg that morning, I had donned a suit jacket of navy blue felt, it seemed, an antique-looking garb, so that the British assumed I was a member of the American party with deplorable taste in attire, an eccentric member of the CIA perhaps, and the Secret Service must have thought I was just another mad Englishman. So my vantage point was favorable.

Elizabeth II, I decided, was quite shy beneath her impeccable, unbreakable facade of poise, and Philip was somewhat saturnine, caustic. That night I waited in the lobby of the Williamsburg Inn with a pride of rouged lionesses, women reporters from New York and Washington. They were lounging about, sarcastic about the queen, wary of Philip.

Suddenly into our midst the queen sailed, radiant in white, sparkling with diamonds like a snow-covered pine in the sun. Glancing at us shyly, she smiled briefly on her way to the formal dinner in the Inn. None of us could muster a question. Then, open notebook and pencil in hand, gawking as she passed, I felt a presence at my right shoulder and looked up into piercing eyes. "Quick, write something!" the heron said.

Three Violets

The postage stamp bore purple flowers, and as I bent to look, I was reminded of dozens of African violets filling a sunlit room. It was the 1950s, and that room was the lair of the state movie censors, three widowed grandmothers who met me one afternoon as a long-lost nephew come home, not a reporter come to expose them. "Go see what they do down there," my curious city editor had said.

The trio — Lollie Whitehead, Margaret Gregory, Russell Wagers — worked in Richmond in a niche of the now-gone state office building, a yellowed 10-story corner cupboard. Their two-room suite sparkled. White curtains stirred at open windows above the James River. Victorian decor embraced a bowl of gold-fish. It looked much as their own rooms in the Jefferson Hotel, a few blocks away.

The viewing room had platform rockers before a huge screen. The projectionist, a disembodied voice, did their bidding as they previewed the afternoon's lot of movies. The dark room, flick-ering screen, humming projector made us prone to doze, never all at once. We paused now and then for tea.

They chatted as if on a porch. Peck, one noted, had a touch of gray at the temples; Elizabeth, a hint of a double chin. They snipped a few seconds from a kiss between Clark and Ava; did a cosmetic job on Taylor's chin after asking my advice as a viewer. "By all means," I said.

Every so often the city editor inquired how the censor story was going. "Splendidly," I said. The knowledgeable trio had good taste. Always civil, they rotated among them the post of chair as if it were an heirloom. Their husbands had been active in the Democratic Organization. Often, between films, we talked politics. During the Depression, Lollie, an aide for the Works Progress Administration, hired starving artists to do paintings for state buildings. Theater owners, who were levied to pay their wages, cherished the three graces and hid behind their skirts from purveyors of risque films, the sort frowned upon by conservative Virginians, that day's tastemakers.

Many salesmen, hearing of the trio's rigorous reputation, just bypassed Virginia in their rounds. Other states, impelled by reformers yammering about the First Amendment, gradually expelled their censors. Ultimately the wave reached Virginia. An officer from the attorney general's office told the three, morosely, their day was done.

And they, I'm sure, consoled him with a cup of tea. And I bade adieu, fondly, in person and in print, to the gentle, lovely censors amid a riot of purple and lavender African violets.

"I can see now," said the city editor, "why you took so long to write what was a fairly simple story."

Pat Nixon

Some people are describing Patricia Nixon as fragile, even brittle. Perhaps, but she had a citadel of inner strength. Her husband called her "the greatest campaigner in the world." She won the palm at the close of the 1972 Republican Convention.

The Nixons came down from the podium to greet all comers at the base of the mock Roman forum. A line ascended six steps to shake hands with the couple under the glare of TV lights. As the delegates descended the steps on the other side, returning from fantasy to reality, their glowing faces went blank.

Dressed in silk of flaming pink, a high ruff at the neck with loose sleeves gathered into long cuffs over her thin wrists, Mrs. Nixon betrayed no feeling that the last demand was anything but a pure delight.

An old pro, straw hat pushed back, leaned to whisper a word to the president, who beamed as if he had been slipped the key to victory.

A bluff, rotund person shook Mrs. Nixon's hand, and, so doing, her entire arm as if it were a dangling doll's. A grinning jack-o-lantern held her hand high, dosey-do. A third clung to it and, departing, was so long releasing it that he was only a second short of pulling her back down the steps with him.

Each of three chunky men in aloha shirts shook her hand in a double clasp until her body trembled. Another, asking for an autograph, held the program belt-high so that stately Mrs. Nixon, stooping to write, seemed about to topple. A woman delegate embarked on a story, a recipe on how to stew prunes, perhaps. No impatience showed in the face with the high cheek bones, the pursed, rosebud lips, and the slant hazel eyes. Hands clasped before her, Mrs. Nixon bent to catch and treasure each tedious word. As young girls came by, the First Lady, murmuring, touched a necklace or leaned forward to brush back a curl displaced on a smooth forehead.

On a three-story screen behind the podium, an image of the president in profile — lips pursed, black brows knit, a deep shadow along the ski-slope assertive nose, the eyes deeply reflective — regarded the smiling, laughing, hand-shaking man and his wife at the foot of the forum.

Now the president was saying they had a light schedule next day — only five speeches in four cities — so they had to depart. The crowd groaned, and he said they would stay 10 more minutes. Mrs. Nixon did three little dance steps and put her hand lightly to her back. The younger ones, last in line, began taking liberties, especially 13-year-old girls, shaking in baby fat, pushing forward to kiss the First Lady or hug her, placing their heads a moment on her shoulder. Well, three days of cheering had earned them that moment, she may have figured. Then came a stringbean teenage boy all a-jangle with buttons on his shirt. Shaking her hand, he suddenly, like a kid butting its nanny, lurched forward and kissed her on the cheek. She, laughing, raised her hand to the spot.

He bounded down the steps, shot through the crowd around the podium, and, still running, knees pumping high, bolted headlong through the hall, looking for his peers to tell about the favor, running as hard as he could out into the tear-gassed night and away from the 1972 Republican National Convention.

I wonder, 20 years later, does he remember?

Rosalynn Carter

If Rosalynn Carter was, as Jimmy Carter used to say during the 1976 campaign, his "other self," and "secret weapon," she is even more so today. Only she could get away with delivering some of the lines that she musters in his defense. Chatting with

200 Democrats at a buffet last week in the Virginia Beach Pavilion, she said, "He's a much wiser man than he was four years ago." The line drew an enthusiastic response and no sooner had the applause died than she added: "When we first came to Washington, we were outsiders and we were full of confidence that we could conquer Washington overnight. Well, let me tell you that it doesn't work that way!"

This is a thrust at Republican Ronald Reagan's candidacy, but it takes cool footwork on her part since the dominant theme in 1976 was that Carter, an outsider, was much better equipped to change things in Washington than was President Gerald Ford.

Another of Mrs. Carter's stops was with members of the Democratic Women's Clubs. When the First Lady had swept them off their feet and departed, a resolute young woman from Southwest Virginia confided that when a friend at home was leaning toward voting for Reagan, she straightened her out quickly. "We've already had one governor," she told her. "Do we want another governor in the White House?"

That Reagan would be charged with Carter's four-year learning process could scarcely have been foreseen by the GOP strategists. Mrs. Carter's remarks are accepted in part because, as one country-music song says, she is expected to "stand by her man." But it goes deeper than that. Another reason is that she delivers a devastating punch in a gush of chatter as a hostess describing her troubles in cooking the Christmas goose. The audience has hardly grasped the import of one line before Mrs. Carter has moved along in her frilly recital and is launching another stinger. The Georgia-accented words fall soft as peach petals, disguising the bee.

Then there is her beguiling foxlike face with wide-spaced eyes over high cheekbones, broad snub nose, wide-smiling mouth, and long chin. She has the durability of plaited tensile steel, but she looks frail as a flower so that women find themselves sympathizing with a sister and the men begin pulling for her subconsciously. As she pattered along, Lt. Gov. Charles S. Robb began nodding solemnly and State Democratic Chairman Richard Davis, red-faced, beaming, his head tilted back, seemed to have caught a beatific vision through the Pavilion ceiling. A fatuous smile hovered on the face of a balding middle-aged reporter, pencil poised witlessly over his notebook.

Her speech concluded, Mrs. Carter moved slowly, shaking hands and talking, with the people pressing around her. As she advanced, flanked by Secret Service agents, down an aisle formed by a rope, she paused and became engaged in intent conversation with Robert Richards about the progress of a mental-health bill. From the attentive way, hands folded before her, she peered in his face, the two could have been tete-a-tete on the White House balcony instead of standing in a milling throng. It had been a long day — five stops, including a press conference, in four hours through two cities — and at least one turnout must have been disheartening in size, but the constant expenditure of charm never flickered. Up close, the face is beginning to pucker a trifle with age, as if pulverized under the terrible public scrutiny of stares and cameras, but the laugh is lilting. Wearing a soft brown dress flecked with minute gray dots, she appeared, russet-haired, a herald for autumn.

Near the end of the line at the exit, the crowd had melted away, and, looking up and finding no one to greet, she seemed uncertain momentarily; but then photographers, scenting a last chance, swung into position and focused their cameras. For a second she looked as lost a doe caught in a car's headlights; but just before the cameras clicked, she squared her shoulders and started forward, looking and smiling directly into the lenses as if sighting and old, dear friend.

Nancy Reagan

Nancy Reagan, chestnut hair piled high on her high-held head, sat through a luncheon of the National Federation of Republican Women and listened to speaker after speaker, including Mrs. Betty Ford, without speaking herself. Curious, this reporter asked afterwards why she hadn't spoken. Mrs. Reagan trained her large hazel eyes on him. "I wasn't asked," she said. "I'd have been happy to speak."

Her daughter Maureen, less self-contained, declared, "I think it was awful tacky."

But unshakable poise seems to be part of Mrs. Reagan's armor. The composure never cracks. It was another tiny instance of obstacles to be overcome in her husband's run against an incumbent president.

On a bus rolling down a freeway to a home for the aged outside Kansas City, the reporter paused by Mrs. Reagan and asked what one thing she would like to say about him as they neared the zero hour for the roll call on the Republican presidential nomination. She reflected a second.

"He's done an incredible job all by himself with only a handful of people from Sacramento, a staff of about 10 people who have been with us 10 years, against all the power on the other side," she said. "For him to have done what he's done is absolutely wonderful, and I'm very, very proud of him."

And suppose after all that work, he loses the nomination tonight, would he accept the vice presidential nomination?

"Absolutely not, unequivocally not! I'll make you a bet of $100, and I'm not a betting woman. He wouldn't take it under any circumstances. He turned it down in 1968. He's not interested in being vice president. He feels he can do more to further his beliefs, his philosophies, his policies, by being independent and resuming doing what he was doing before — which was his radio, his column, and his speaking. He just feels he can do more that way."

The same flat refusal extended, she said, to any bid to run on a third-party ticket.

She is a petite, pretty woman, a former actress who played opposite her husband in "Hellcats of the Navy." They met when he was president of the Screen Actors Guild, and she went to him with a complaint about receiving propaganda through the mails.

There are four children in the Reagan family — two from his previous marriage to actress Jane Wyman and two from their own marriage of 24 years.

How did she respond to people who tried to disparage her husband by saying he was only an actor? She listened to the question, her smile never wavering, and remarked briefly: "They had a lapse of eight years in there while he was governor of California."

As the bus rolled along, all of the political action and the large audiences were back in bustling hotels in Kansas City. Less than a dozen reporters accompanied Mrs. Reagan. And some stayed aboard the bus while she insisted on meeting and talking to every one of the residents of the home for the aged.

"It is a natural thing for me to do, a natural interest," she told one of them. "My father was a doctor."

She began visiting hospitals when her husband was governor of California. On one such visit in 1969 she learned of the newly developing Foster Grandparents Program and became a sort of godmother to it. "I never just give my name to something," she said, "I take on a program only when I can become actively involved."

The program, which encourages elderly people to become volunteer parents to physically and mentally handicapped children, has spread to other states.

"It is one of the few programs where there are benefits for both sides," she said. "The children need more love than any hospital can possibly give them, and the senior citizens, who are too neglected in our society, have so much love to give."

She is a thin woman, and her generous features — the abundant chestnut hair, large eyes, pointed chin and wide mouth — make the head seem unusually large on the petite figure, almost, the reporter thought, like the spinster on the Old Maid card in the game of that name. With Nancy Reagan as the Old Maid, however, the object of the game would be to get, not jettison, that card.

Reports had it that she is reserved, and so she appeared on the rostrum as she listened to Betty Ford addressing 200 Republican "women of achievement."

But not on the bus rolling through the Kansas countryside.

Barbara Bush

In a seven-minute speech, Barbara Bush did more Wednesday to help her husband's campaign for re-election than did all the rest of the speakers that day combined. Oh, but it was shrewd, throughout.

She had waited with interest, she said, to see how George would reply to a reporter's question as to what accomplishment he was most proud of. Building suspense, she listed a half-dozen — things like the collapse of communism — each fit to be carved in marble.

But, as she suspected, it was the same answer he always gives: "that our children still come home." Before this family values theme plays out, every father in America will be guilt-ridden, especially newspapermen.

Barbara's speech, of course, was a covert reproach to Bill and Hillary Clinton's marital difficulties. In truth, those troubles are more likely the norm these days than is the perpetual honeymoon of the Bushes. If all the spouses who have had domestic infelicities voted for the Arkansas governor, he would win, hands down.

When 22 members of the Bush family, including a horde of adorable children, flooded the stage on family night, I could only think what W.C. Fields would say of the scene. An irony is that in the 1988 convention, when Bush was asked how his campaign might be improved, he said he and Barbara were impressed by the devotion conveyed by the Dukakis family.

In Barbara Bush's grandmotherly visage, the viewers caught sight of a disciplinarian accustomed to raising a brood of sons. They saw it as she sliced the air with both hands flat to shush the audience's applause. She is to be obeyed.

Mad as Hell

"Mad as Hell," by Jack Germond and Jules Witcover, argues that the Bush-Clinton-Perot debate at the University of Richmond was the most influential of the three in the 1992 presidential race. Some Bush people deplored the town-meeting format and the anchoring by ABC's Carole Simpson. She has received "a lot of very hateful mail," Simpson told me by phone. "That's distressing. I was trying to bend over backwards to be as fair and impartial as possible."

Before the debate, she warmed up the 209 citizens. In red, moving, laughing, she won their trust. She asked for sample questions: "The simpler the better, and you show everybody how smart you are," she advised. "Please don't make speeches. I'll cut you off." A woman said, "I don't want to put the president on the spot." Simpson replied, "Why not? This is the spot." A youth handed her a note. "This is on the hairy edge," she said. A shy blonde raised a hand: "I don't really want to ask a question. I just wanted to practice raising my hand." Simpson smiled. "And you did well!" To another she said, "That's too long. That's small print and lots of lines... "Who's got a dynamite first?" Of one, she said. "This is good, but I want a grabber."

Don't applaud or laugh, she said. "You're supposed to observe silently. Can you do that?" They promised. "Could we limit the candidates' responses to get more questions?" a man asked. She promised. She told the crew, "If they start to do what Quayle and Gore did, I may have to step in." The 209 applauded. "Are you going to wear those shoes?" a man asked. She slipped away and reappeared in a black patent-leather pair. They roared. Just before 9, they went rigid. "Are you loose?" she asked. "You don't look loose. What's happened to you? You all have tensed up on me. You were fine before you went to the bathroom. This is historic," she said. "It's only going to work if you cooperate." Near 9, they began chatting. "You're too noisy," she cried. "I need you!" They fell silent, bonded.

The three candidates, as if shaken from a jokester's sleeve, came in.

"Good eve-ning..." she said, every syllable crisp. She remonstrated with a president, chided a billionaire, goaded a governor.

Her warmup, she told me, "was my attempt to make them comfortable with the format and me. It's what I do as a reporter with many interviews." Some critics assert she stacked the audience. "I didn't have any control of even who I called on. That was directed by the control room," she said. "I had no control at all over who composed or posed the questions." She traveled to 27 countries with Bush and happens "to like him very much as an individual. I wouldn't do anything to embarrass him."

In the control room, the authors note, the producer told her by phone whom to call on and where to go so he could direct the TV cameras. It made for a stirring evening — and book.

Chapter Four

No One Said It'd Be Easy

Never Mind!

Had to make a speech at a church in Richmond not so long ago. Turned out there's another church just up the road, which led to utter confusion.

Running a half hour late, abiding by speed limits but taking short cuts to avoid stop lights, my mind a blur, I overshot the first church and wound up in the parking lot of the second.

Purely understandable error; happen to anybody. There ought to be a constitutional amendment preventing two churches from being only three blocks apart.

Dashed inside the wrong church, panting like the Hound of the Baskervilles, ran up and down and around the halls on two floors and the church basement looking for the office — you ever notice how well-hidden church offices are? — found it, burst inside, leaned on the counter, wheezing, near exhaustion, proclaiming to a secretary my intention to make a speech, late though it be.

"Better late than never," I said.

"No speeches here tonight," she said, looking in a well-thumbed brown spiral notebook.

"Got to be!"

"Can't be," she said.

"Keep looking!"

She closed the book.

"There's a group around the corner," she said. "But..."

"Lead me to it!"

She did and flung open the door of the meeting room.

"Here's somebody to make a speech," she called.

What a lovely intro!

A woman, giving a report, looked up, rattled at the intrusion, and sat down. My guide left. Leaving me looking at the most startled bunch of people I'd ever faced, as if they'd just heard the trump of doom, as my great aunt used to say.

Tell these affrighted people two or three stories, I thought, to put them — and me — at ease, get our bearings. All will be well, never fear.

The first two stories drew scant response, a nervous giggle or two, and, midway through the third one, I glanced around and was taken aback to see that the man who had pleaded for me to speak wasn't even in the audience. Dashed odd attitude, that!

Looked closer into their baffled faces. A strange lot, God wot! By George, not one in the room was familiar to me! What gives here?

Then it hit me. "Let me bring up something you may have overlooked," I said to those bewildered people.

"You all are in the wrong church!"

Then I fled, but, through the closing door, one old gent called, "Aren't you going to finish that story?"

Bowled Over by a Box

The other evening I had to use a can opener to open a box of cereal.

The cereal — cornflakes — is a basic single-grain brand without fruits, nuts and bolts. It rests lightly on the stomach. And the box used to be easy as pie to open. Long ago, the outside was waxed to keep the cornflakes fresh. You just opened the box and there they were. Then someone packed the cornflakes in a pouch of wax-like paper, which was OK. It tore easily. But the third innovation of molding everything within slick plastic undid us. There scarcely is a product that's easy to open.

The toughest, I found, is the cereal box. I set the box on the kitchen counter, placed a bowl beside it, opened the top of the box — everything going smoothly so far, as Napoleon said just before Waterloo — and started to tear apart the plastic wrap containing the cornflakes. I defy anybody to open that vacuum-packed plastic wrap with his bare hands, or bared teeth, which is what, at one stage, I tried to do, gnawing like a maddened beaver, to no avail. Had they handed Hercules a 13th labor, a box of vacuum packed cereal, and said, "Herk, open this, old sport," it would have brought him to his knees.

I looked around for a sharp knife; they were all in the dishwasher. The plastic withstood a fork. Next, rummaging around, I came up with an ice pick and punched a series of holes which didn't weaken the plastic enough to tear. In a respite, to calm myself, I fetched a dish of peaches from the ice box, dumped them in the bowl, and poured on milk and sugar.

You fool, I said to myself, now look what you have done. You have put the milk and peaches into a bowl first which means that, if you ever get through that confounded plastic wrapper, you are going to have to pour the cornflakes on top of milk and peaches, whereas anybody, even the merest child, understands that the peaches and milk ought to be put on top of the cornflakes. In other words, you ignoramus, the cereal should go in the bowl first. Get a hold of yourself.

So I got out another cereal bowl, dumped the peaches and milk into it, and placed that second bowl alongside the now empty former peach-and-milk bowl which would receive the cornflakes upon which I would then dump the milk and peaches from the second bowl. So, in order on the counter, were a cereal box, a bowl of peaches and milk, and an empty bowl that formerly held the peaches and milk. Somewhere in there was a wasted motion, I realized.

Possibly, it had not been necessary to dump the peaches and milk into the second bowl, but, no matter, get back to the original objective, which is to open that infernal plastic wrapping. Calling into play an old-fashioned, hand-held can opener which I found under the sink, I ripped a half inch slit in the plastic pouch, but it still held. So I skipped a half inch or so and gouged another slit in the plastic and yet another and another until the wrapping was serrated with slits.

Then, so as to get a good two-handed grip on the plastic pouch, I pulled it half way out of the box, and, holding one end of the pouch with my left hand, I yanked with the right hand with all my might, whereupon the pouch came loose from the box, and as it gave way, my right hand swept both bowls, peaches, and milk crashing to the floor.

There was silence. Then, from the living room came a voice: "What are you doing in the kitchen?"

"Opening a box of cereal," I said.

Him am I

On arriving that first day in Houston for the Republican convention, I was trudging with my luggage across the hotel lobby, head bent, my mind a blank.

I was in a vacant or a pensive mood, the same stage at which the poet Wordsworth encountered daffodils nodding and dancing in the breeze. No such scene greeted me. I entered the elevator, eyes down, without noticing that it was paneled in mirrors until lifting my head I saw myself facing me, an abject sight but one with which I have come to feel fairly much at home.

Taking him all in all, I have not found him to be as bad a guy as one might think at first, or even second or hundredth, glance. What happened next occurred in a flash, but that was long enough for a multitude of impressions to arise.

I was standing sideways to the elevator door, facing the mirrored right wall, and even before I realized that the elevator was a four-sided booth of mirrors, I noticed a reflection positioned to the right of my image in the mirror with its back to me.

So my frontal image faced me, but to its right was another woeful one offering a rear view, and my first thought was that the fellow, whoever he was standing with his back turned, was a homely cuss. Whoever he is with his back to me, I thought, he ought to turn around and put his best face forward or spend the daylight hours inside. As I gazed at the rear of this intruder, sharing my elevator, I felt it was the most unimposing back I had ever laid eyes on.

A great bald furrow, about the size of the ozone hole, began near the front of his graying head and widened steadily as it moved to the rear, sweeping all before it. This churl, I thought, should wear a hat or paper sack. Either that or back-pedal away from people or circle ever frontward around them, never extending his back to the public gaze. The public can stand but so much. He should go sideways down the street, his back to walls.

Absorbed with studying the droll figure, I realized that he was wearing a white linen coat, exactly like mine. What gall for this miscreant to go around attired in the habiliments of an ordinary citizen!

The lining of his coat had become loosened and dipped a bit below the right hem, just as mine had done as a result of snagging itself as I tussled with the suitcase upon disembarking from the plane.

Startled at the revelation, I realized: WHY, HE IS ME! Or, rather, HIM AM I! My grammar was as scrambled as my senses, but any way you put it, we two were one. One learns, being homely, to adjust to the inevitable. My thoughts turned to Robert Burns and his plaint: O wad some Pow'r the giftie gie us. To see ourselves as others see us!

By George, I thought, the giver has given me the opportunity to see me from the back as others do. Just as a dog can take a humiliating dusting and arise, wagging his tail, and go on as before, so I became entranced with the images of the back-turned me, eight of them receding, ever smaller, into the distance.

I tried backing away from the mirror before me and found, doing so, that the distance seemed to shorten between me and the first of the eight images of my back. I fell into a kind shuffling jig, back and forth, trying to find the optimum point at which to get the clearest view of the rear of my noggin.

Suddenly the elevator door opened and a family of three stood framed watching a balding gaffer doing a soft shoe shuffle with his image in the mirror. He stopped, turned, took a little bow, as if receiving plaudits, and then backed smack against the mirrored wall behind him.

The Great Overhang

Got a haircut the other day.

Which had, always, a peculiar effect upon those who saw it fresh.

"You had a haircut," they say. And reel back.

That's all right. I've seen grown men break into a run at the sight. Their identification of the haircut is not quite a flat statement. A hint of surprise creeps in their voices at the sudden apparition. Usually, after a beat or two, they recover in time to mask alarm. That little space of time is the sort that took place among ancient Greeks upon confronting face to face the terrible Gorgon, just before they turned to stone.

But the other day, having notified me I'd had a haircut, a young colleague said, "It makes your ears look big."

"Like Ross Perot?"

"Not that bad," she said.

How gratifying to hear such a note of consolation. Still, shaving the other morning, regarding the face in the mirror, one had to admit the ears were close enough to Rose Perot's to flag a train.

Another young colleague — they are all young, all of a sudden — skidded to a halt in the hall, crying, eyes wide, "Guy-y-y-y, you had a haircut!" Regaining composure, she said, "I just wasn't aware you had enough hair to have a haircut."

Yet another, who had proclaimed the haircut, said the next day, "Your haircut looks better today."

All this comes from my having what barbers call "a problem head." They seat me in the far chair with the raw recruit from barber college. "You have," an old-timer told me, "three-quarters back on your head a sink-hole."

It is unnerving, he said, to come upon that declivity. The barber fights his way out of the sump and tops an enormous bulge on the last quarter of the head.

It is known, among barbers, as "the great overhang." They are on top, clipping away merrily, relieved at having cleared the sink-hole, when venturing along the backside they are in deep trouble.

One barber, a fellow Georgian from Atlanta, likened it to going astray on top of Stone Mountain, that huge outcropping of granite rising 30 stories high, a sheer gray wall against the sky. Atop its rock plateau, a foolhardy sightseer, growing bold, slips under a hip-high steel hawser to go near the edge of the gently sloping crest.

The slope steepens. Starting back, he begins slipping on slick lichen. He falls to his knees, then lies flat, spread-eagled, to keep from going into a slide down the precipitous side. He waits, petrified, for a rope to pull him to safety. The rookie barber, gamboling atop the bulge, goes a step too far, over the edge, fighting for a toehold, scissors quickening. Too late, an older barber calls, "WATCH THAT OVERHANG, CLIF!"

Any way you look at it, it is an ordeal, especially for the barber.

A Mad Dash

A friend asked if any stressful circumstances beset me in New York at the Democratic National Convention. Yes, I said, and one of them demanded some agility.

I was riding the steepest escalator in the hemisphere and realized, three quarters down, that I had left my wallet on the turnstile.

Wheeling, I bounded up the oncoming stairs. Why not let the escalator reach the bottom and then come up the other way, you ask.

Like a noble salmon climbing rushing rapids, one obeys nature's dictates and swims up, up, up toward the wallet.

A lot of picky people, the same ones who honk at you and yell when you have become entrapped on a one-way street, grasped at my elbow as I leaped by them — three steps up, and two back —to say that I was going the wrong way.

"ANY FOOL CAN SEE THAT!" I shot back as I went by one and, my legs still churning, came back to him.

"One doesn't," he said.

But I kept going, even as I thought, what the deuce, Jack's beanstalk wasn't growing down at him as he climbed.

Other passengers' faces soon began stiffening at the sight of this manic acrobat jumping up the downgoing stairs like Uncle Wiggley, the storybook rabbit.

Half-way along was a large impediment in the person of a florid fellow who spread his arms wide — Horatius at the bridge to repel the Etruscans. But I ducked under them, jostling him a bit as I drove toward the broad sunny uplands, as Winston Churchill would have it.

"YOU NUT," Horatius yelled, "WHAT THE DEVIL DO YOU THINK YOU ARE DOING, HEADING UP THE DOWN WAY?"

"JOGGING!" I screamed. "I DO THIS TWICE A DAY!"

Enraged, he started in hot pursuit of me, bounding up three and gliding back two himself.

"YOU SEE, IT AIN'T EASY," I taunted.

Two friends seized him. "HE'S A NUT, HARRY, LET HIM GO," one yelled.

Aha, I thought, it's Harry, not Horatius.

"YOU'RE AN IMPOSTOR!" I yelled.

"UNHAND ME!" he cried, as all four of us fell in a heap, seaweed borne toward the vortex.

Slipping through the massed humanity, gaining the top in one last leap, I saw the wallet on the turnstile.

I retrieved it and peered warily down the escalator. Mad Harry was being led away, an angry Minotaur, by his friends.

I got aboard the repentant escalator. Even in the midst of the frenzied assault on Everest, there shot through my mind a thought, as happens on occasion, that my plight was like those that snared Charlie Chaplin's Little Tramp.

He could have slipped my contretemps into his movie, "Modern Times," except that at the top of the escalator, a mob of outraged citizens would overtake and pile on him. From that mass, as it dissipated, he would arise, bereft of his wallet.

But from his torn attire he would begin to produce wallet after wallet that he had picked from their pockets while they whaled away at him.

And then he would walk with jaunty step and twirling cane past the inexorable escalator, as I did, undeterred, but still somewhat wary of Harry.

To No Avail

How is it some people can command attention without even trying?

I bet you at their birth, amid a passel of infants, nurses went to them first. They just have savoir-faire, as loaded with it as a shag dog with ticks. Others — such as I, or if you prefer the colloquial, such as me — couldn't catch a fly's eye with a swatter.

Once, in a restaurant of fine cuisine, a young lady in our party of six asked me to signal the waiter. She wanted a glass of water. "Have mine," I suggested, ever the diplomat, knowing we were in for trouble if we waited on me to snare a waiter. "It is only half drunk."

But no, she wanted her own glass of water. That is the "me generation" for you. No satisfying them without going all out. But, noblesse oblige, she would have her water, by cob! So as the next waiter was passing dim-lit in the night, I raised my hand high like a frantic fifth-grader asking to be excused.

The waiter looked through me as if I were, well, a fifth-grader, and bore on. When he hove into view on the next flyby, I was ready, braced with one hand to arise with a rush like a covey of quail, gripping with the other hand a napkin to flag him down, and was struggling upward from an awkward half crouch when I tipped the chair over and, trying to reach back to steady it, lost my balance and went down backward with it.

If a clown could perfect that act, he would be a sensation in the center ring with Ringling Bros. I actually fell into a sitting position on my back in the chair, my feet above my head. My feet, flying upward, caught the table edge and brought my water glass tumbling to the floor, most of it on me. That caught the Flying Dutchman's attention. Also that of the owner and the manager rushing from out back. And I, clambering to my feet with as much dignity as could be mustered amid shambles, the first man learning to get off all fours, bowed to them and said, with a slight wave toward her, "I say, this young lady would like some water, if it won't be too much trouble.

"And," I said, "If it is, don't bother. I can go back there in the kitchen to fetch it myself."

How inspiring it was to see them leaping about to bring her that glass of water.

Another trial is to quiet a room by tapping a water glass. At a recent banquet, the host asked me, at his right elbow, to sound the water glass. The whack I gave it with a spoon would have cracked the Liberty Bell. Nobody bothered to look up.

"That's crystal," he said. "Let me try." He flipped an index finger against the rim and drew a light ping. The company fell silent.

The most trying, humiliating feat of all is snagging a taxi. During the GOP National Convention in Dallas, three of us — Margaret Edds, Warren Fiske and I — watched from the sidewalk as the cabs raced by.

Warren and I, determined to be gallant, while tactful Margaret waited, waved a tentative hand now and then, and the cabs, if anything, picked up speed. So at last we two thrust into the avenue, waving arms, shouting all out. We cavorted about like maddened mummers in a street parade.

To no avail. Until Margaret, sedate, stepped forward slightly on the pavement. Three cabs screeched to a halt.

I think she raised her right eyebrow.

Chapter Five

Un-Conventional

Battle at Bay

When John Stewart Battle decided to lead Virginia's delegation in refusing to sign a loyalty pledge, he had feared that political careers of young Virginia Democrats would suffer. His own, he said, would end anyway with the close of his four-year term as governor.

But he made two stirring speeches last night and before dawn today that turned the Democratic National Convention in its tracks and impelled forces that:

(1) Seated the Virginia delegation which had filed a declaration of independence instead of signing the loyalty pledge.

(2) Seated Virginia's two Southern allies, South Carolina and Louisiana, which also had refused to sign the "strait-jacket" pledge.

(3) Boomed the candidacy of Adlai Stevenson, whose backers threw their support to the trio.

Virginians took their seats expecting to be expelled as nonpledgers. Battle got up from his place by the Virginia standard.

"Where's he going?" asked a delegate, watching Battle's broad back moving away. "John's going right up and get on the rostrum," said U.S. Sen. Harry Byrd. "He's going to present our case."

Battle came forward, his big jaw set as he looked at the turbulent floor. "I am not here to argue this case," he began in deep, measured tones. "I simply wish my fellow Democrats who are here today to know plainly and simply the reasons for our position."

The delegates quieted. First, Battle said, there was no effort to keep the nominees of the convention off the Virginia ballot. A state law provided that they be put on the ballot.

"What we object to is doing something which may be construed as binding this delegation and the Democrats of Virginia to any future actions of this convention. We are unwilling to enter into a pledge which would have that effect, and we therefore have not signed. We took that position in the beginning, and we do not recede from it now." Battle paused, then said: "We believe in the freedom of thought and action which is taught by Thomas Jefferson, in whose county I happen to live, and we believe that the patron saint of this party, if he were here tonight, would approve our action."

And now his voice rang out in stern determination, "And we're not going to jeopardize that freedom for you or for us."

Amid thrumming waves of applause, Battle walked to his seat. Byrd gripped his shoulder. "John," he said, "after that speech, we don't have to worry about going back to the people of Virginia."

Battle's face was weary but relaxed. "Where's my hat?" he asked. "I had one here somewhere."

In a scramble, U.S. Sen. Harry Byrd found he had placed it inside his own natty Panama. "Well, let's go," said Battle. But a Maryland delegate moved that the convention view Battle's statement with favor.

Battle took off his hat.

Chairman Rayburn called for a voice vote. Ayes and noes both sounded like Niagara Falls. He agreed to a roll call of the States.

When it began, Judge Leander Perez of New Orleans came to see Byrd and Battle. His broad, tan face, with heavily carved features like an English walnut, was beaming, but it had a touch of anxiety.

"Suppose they seat Virginia and not us?" he asked.

"What do you suggest?" Byrd said.

"Move for an amendment seating all three — or none," said Perez.

"Bear down on the great State of South Carolina and its distinguished statesman, Jimmy Byrnes," Perez advised. "You can't stretch us too far. We're just country boys."

Out of the throng flailing his arms like a spent swimmer came big Senator Maybank, of South Carolina. He pulled Byrd and Battle close to him and said hoarsely, his eyes pleading, craggy face wet with sweat: "Don't give us up, don't give us up."

Battle clapped him on the shoulder. "We're together to the end." And as Maybank flailed away, Byrd said, "I'd hate for them to seat us, and not seat the other two."

About that time Illinois voted 45 no and 15 votes aye.

"Those big delegations are going to vote against us," predicted Byrd.

"We're gone now," said Byrd, "but we're making a whale of a showing."

Texas came back with 52 votes aye. As the roll call continued, all Virginia delegates were standing, most on chairs, a clustered, jumbled skyline in a plain of faces.

Battle raised on tiptoe for a last good look around the hall.

The breakthrough came when Illinois announced a switch of 52 to 8 in favor of Virginia. Through that gap the bandwagon rolled. The final count was 648-512 for Virginia.

There came Boss Jim Farley among a line of party dignitaries congratulating Senator Byrd. "I'm glad you're back in the party, Harry," called Farley. "I'm not concerned about technicalities."

"I know you're not, brother," returned Byrd. "I know you of old."

The band played "Stout Hearted Men." When Battle approached the rostrum pandemonium cut loose. Battle waited five minutes, smiling, slightly, and then Rayburn told him, "You better go ahead."

But Illinois Senator Paul Douglas was determined to adjourn the convention and try to rally Kefauver forces. He seesawed below shouting a hoarse chant for recognition. When some order was restored, Battle stepped forward, and this time his face hardened to a fist. Douglas bent his head a moment beneath Battle's glare.

"I sat in the same seat of the Virginia House of Delegates occupied by Thomas Jefferson," roared Battle. "I now occupy the same office he once held. When I am at home the sun's rays glisten over the eastern hills on Monticello, shrine of our patron saint.

"I think I have a right to be heard before the Democratic National Convention. I shall never betray your confidence."

He paused and went on in deeper tones, "There is one State in the Union that since the founding of the Democratic party has never voted Republican. That's the state of South Carolina. I am pleased at what you voted this afternoon, but my heart is saddened when I see the great state of South Carolina denied a seat.

"It would be fair, reasonable and equitable to reunite this party of ours. I have the honor to move that the people of South Carolina be permitted to take their seats in this convention."

He made a similar motion for Louisiana and it, too, carried.

The long day's work was done. Battle had won.

1956: When Harry Walks

He doesn't just walk. Harry Truman marches as if to the beat of a big brass band, shoulders back, cane swinging, stepping to cadence, straight on, reporters falling over each other at his heels. During the Democratic convention he has kept the nation guessing whom he'll back for president. Thirty reporters scrambled in his wake this morning as he swung down Michigan Boulevard, swung along, shoulders squared, his step smacking through puddles on the broad sidewalk while they fished for an answer.

"Nobody knows but me," he crowed. "Nobody knows but me!"

They jostled one another for position, trying to take notes while dodging each other and his swinging cane, stumbling into the gutter.

"I guess," he called, "you wish we'd hit a red light."

Finally he did, and they were waiting on the curb for the light to change, like seabirds on a sandbar, when a taxi came careening around the corner. As it was hurtling hell-bent into Michigan Boulevard, the cabbie caught sight of that fighting profile with the fish-hook grin and scarecrow-sharp nose standing out of the flat face, light of battle glinting off his glasses. Leaning from the cab window, nearly running up the steps of the Art Institute of Chicago, the cabbie screamed, "Give 'em hell, Harry!"

Didn't he always?

1956: A Demonstation For John Battle

John S. Battle, once the first moments passed, took the duty of being Virginia's favorite son presidential candidate with low-keyed ease. In the International Amphitheater, he draped his arm over the seat beside him with the air of a man relaxing on a midway ride at the State Fair. He knew he was going to come out right where he started — lawyer John S. Battle, ex-Governor — but if there were any amusement in the ride, he'd find it.

South Carolina's Gov. Timmerman came up and bent down to Battle's ear. "John, my people are doing the same thing to me. But I've got a question of political ethics. Should I stay on the floor or leave when they're placing my name in nomination?"

"Aw, just stay there," said Battle. "That's what the big boys are doing."

Word of Battle's candidacy spread among newspapermen and they dropped by to shake his hand, a little wistfully, as if they were toasting what should be but couldn't. A Mississippi belle rushed up and said in an accent you could spread on bread: "Guv'nor, we Mississippians ah insulted you didn't let us know you were running."

"My candidacy sprang up overnight, but it's a rather nice compliment," Battle drawled. Nominating speeches ran on, bobbins in a cotton-mill. "All of 'em are 'great' men," Battle observed of the candidates.

Lewis MacMurran of Newport News called to Sidney Kellam of Virginia Beach: "Us favorite sons ought to stick together. One walk for the other."

"Better not," advised Kellam, "or you'll be walking all afternoon."

Passing in popeyed excitement, a Texan yelled to Kellam. "Come on down deep in the heart of Texas, and I'll let you carry me back to ol' Virginny!"

"We got some in the peerade," said Kellam, agreeably.

There was a running debate on whether they would demonstrate and if they should find a band. "What in the world are you all up to?" growled Battle. "Don't y'all be doing all that. Relax."

"Dignity, that's better," said C. K. Hutchens. A broadcaster asked Battle what his chances were. "I haven't written my acceptance speech," drawled Battle. His shoulders shook with laughter. Governor Stanley was on stage, starting to speak. Battle stuck out his jaw at the praises being heaped on him.

"Our governor looks better than any of them," said Kellam. "He's making the best speech of his life."

Time came for the "demonstration." The organ began playing "Carry Me Back to Ole Virginny." Naturally, the Virginians stood up and began singing as they always do. The song from the tiny cluster of 60 or so people standing in the center of the vast arena around the gray-haired Battle was in dramatic contrast to snake-winding, howling demonstrations.

The arena stilled and Massachusetts, the neighboring delegation, took up the refrain, a black delegate leading. Other delegations joined in all across the arena. Battle smiled, his mouth closed tight, and gave those applauding him a jerky salute. Tears rolled down his cheeks. The three nominating speakers — Stanley, J. Vaughan Gary and Harry Byrd Jr. — got congratulations. "Yours was the best speech of the afternoon," Cynthia Boatwright of Wise told Stanley.

"I had the best candidate," Stanley said.

JFK And LBJ

Virginians met John F. Kennedy during the 1956 Democratic National Convention when he dropped by the seated delegation seeking their votes for the party's vice presidential nomination. They looked up and there he was, the golden boy of politics, smiling and looking both urbane and as young as an Eagle Scout. Mesmerized, they gave him their support. He lost.

In 1960, the Kennedys launched an all-out campaign for the presidential nomination which boiled down to a contest between Senator Kennedy and Senate Majority Leader Lyndon Johnson of Texas.

William C. Battle, Governor Battle's son, became Kennedy's Virginia campaign manager. Young Battle and his wife Barry spent the Fourth of July with the Kennedys at Hyannisport. Even then, Kennedy was mulling over possible choices for a running mate should he win the presidential nomination.

On the golf course, he asked Battle whom he should pick. "Lyndon Johnson", Battle told him. Kennedy needed him to carry Texas and Johnson also had the support of the Virginia delegates.

"In the middle of a back swing, I remember," Battle said, "he asked me why Johnson would want to be vice president."

"Because," I told him, "Johnson as the minority leader had power, but if the Democrats won, the power would shift to the White House."

Meanwhile, in Virginia, the state Democratic convention bound the delegates to support Johnson for president. Their hands having been hog-tied, U.S. Sen. Harry F. Byrd, the Democratic boss, skipped the national convention and went with Virginia House Speaker E. Blackburn Moore to climb mountains in Switzerland.

The Virginia delegation remained bound under the unit rule but that did not deter Governor Lindsay Almond from making a stirring tribute to Kennedy during a morning caucus of the Virginia delegates. In his piston-stroke oratory, Almond declared: "I looked in the clear blue eyes of that young man and I was inspired. He towers like a mighty oak over the other pigmy candidates." The morning after Kennedy won the nomination he called Battle to his suite for advice. Of those attending the conference Battle and Senator Abe Ribicoff of Connecticut were the only two who recommended Johnson. When Johnson won the vice presidential nomination, Governor Almond made one of the seconding speeches.

Two images persist. John Kennedy pointing that imperious index finger at the delegates like the Uncle Sam on a recruitment poster and Lyndon Johnson towering on the platform, his arms upraised in a great rectangle as he wheeled slowly from one side of the hall to the other, a prowling radar screen attuned to seeking power.

1964: Uncle Sams And Daddy Ike

The champ came to Chicago. Just looking at Ike you forget what many regard as his failures. He stood in the convertible, turning to the right and the left as if he felt it his duty to look personally into the eyes of everyone, raising his arms to the sky, looking up at the people in windows, giving a little extra wiggle from his wrists, as if he were trying to reach them for a mutual hug. A snowstorm of confetti almost hid him. The dots of paper slid off his bald pate and caught in the fringe of hair, crowning him with a rakish halo beneath which Ike beamed.

When he and Mamie, holding hands, appeared on stage that night, waves of applause tossed great surfs of sound around the red-faced, laughing president. Demonstrators came down the aisles but they were submerged in the roar and color from the convention floor. The delegates themselves were putting on their own unrehearsed, unbought, undirected, unequaled demonstration.

Ike brought Mamie forward, and she waved, some of her girlishness returning in the excitement of the cheers. At last it quieted, and in a second Ike had taken them all the way back to the first whistle-stops of 1952 when he said, "From our hearts, Mamie and I thank you...."

The Republicans and some independents will call Richard Nixon's acceptance speech the greatest since his defense of his campaign funds. "I am the man to carry this burden," he said. "That decision is yours."

Repeatedly he brought the audience to its feet roaring approval as when he answered Khrushchev's prophesy of burying us by declaring "His grandchildren will live under freedom."

A closing scene was after midnight in the vast parking lot redolent of the musty red odor of the stockyards. I was idling along when suddenly, behind a barricade of yellow sawhorses as if marking the end of the road, were 47 Uncle Sams standing in loose array, thick as Wordsworth's daffodils. Fat Uncle Sams, thin ones, tall and short, weathered looking Uncle Sams, young ones with only a peach fuzz on their cheeks, Uncle Sams everywhere. A poet could not but be gay in such a jocund company.

Each Uncle Sam wore red-and-white striped trousers, a blue

swallow-tail coat, and a soft gray top-hat that was narrow at the brim and flared out at the crown like an old-time locomotive smokestack. They said nothing, just stood, tiredly, far out in the lot in the flare and shadows thrown by the klieg lights far away at the back entrance of the amphitheater. One of their number, a gray-haired gent, looking remarkably like the real Uncle Sam, came out of the darkness and said: "Fellows, the bus won't be here for another 24 hours. Shall we wait or get back to town the best way we can?"

They shuffled a moment, and, like cows leaving a pasture, started forward in the darkness. I fell in with them. Next to me was a black Uncle Sam, a stout, round-shouldered man, carrying his coat over one arm, his hat pushed back on his head, his left shirt-tail out. All of them walked flat-footed in weariness and silence.

"What is it?" I asked him. "This," he said, "is the Uncle Sam Republican Club Marching Unit of Buffalo, N.Y. We came here on a bus to march in the demonstration. Now we are going home.

"I hope we don't have to march all the way," he added.

"Who's eligible to join?"

"Any good Republican" he said.

"What's a good Republican?"

"Anybody who voted Republican in the last election or anybody who is going to vote Republican in the next election or anybody who likes to march and has the money to buy a uniform. We have been marching since 1896 and we have been coming to the convention since 1920."

They reached the street and scattered, getting into taxis, disappearing into the El, climbing aboard city buses, heading into restaurants, Uncle Sams going in every direction and in a moment they were gone.

1964: Tears for Kennedy, Cheers for LBJ

To step into a convention demonstration is to plunge into a warm, humid sea in which strange fish swim or to walk through a looking glass into a childhood fantasy in which adults behave with Wonderland logic.

Amid the pandemonium surrounding Lyndon Johnson, I came upon a Pennsylvania grandmother, 69, wearing atop her head two long sausage-shaped balloons bent double, tied together, and fastened by a scarf looped under her chin. Beneath her propeller of pink and blue balloons, she might have just touched down from Mars or Mother Goose.

"Why?" I yelled, as we clung together while the sea of demonstration pitched about us. "I just got tired of holding them," she said. A wave of running youths parted us and, borne away, she shrieked, "I bet I'm the only one out here wearing one of these things."

Over us poured a deluge of red, white and blue sticky stars, the kind you got for finishing a book in the third grade. A tanned, brazen-faced woman had pasted a handful in a pattern on her broad forehead, a bold, swirling comet of tiny stars, a constellation such as is traced in the dotted lines of a human figure in astronomy books, Diana the huntress dropped to earth, striding the floor of the convention.

Then came, floating drunkenly on the surface, a brown canvas sombrero big as a beach umbrella, and beneath it, struggling with the braces on his shoulders, a young man, a prince reduced to thumb size and doomed to bear a large toadstool.

Un-Conventional

Next night was another, unscheduled demonstration. Reporters, typing in the basement pressrooms, stopped typing and looked up at a special rising urgency in the applause over television. On screen was Robert Kennedy.

As the applause drummed on and on behind the sad face, a European correspondent said he saw tears in his eyes and observed, "He can't hold them back." A minute later, the European reporter added, "I can't hold them back, either."

Two minutes later I watched from the press corral at the front of the hall. The wide bands of giant spotlights in the roof had been cut off. Shafts of brilliance from TV klieg lamps lit the floor in an orange gloom as at the mouth of a cavern in early dawn or late afternoon. Standards of the 50 states stood like proud stalagmites.

The whole hall was a-flutter with fragile white pennants in the delegates' hands, whitecaps on the roaring surf louder than the waves breaking on the beach outside. The white pennants hailed LBJ in red and blue lettering, but they were not waving for him, nor the brother on the podium, nor even the Party. That truly genuine demonstration was for a man who was not even there.

Until that moment the docile delegates had gone along with stage directions, but at the edge of their consciousness was the muted memory of a tall, urbane, yet boyish young man and now they stood and voiced their wordless anguish at what had happened last November and their human frustration at not being able to set it right.

There was no music, no marching, nothing except crashing applause, steady as a summer downpour, and at any gesture to stop it, the tempo raised even higher and heavier, as does the rain when it seems that now surely it could not beat harder, but it did, on and on, as if it would never stop.

87

When it did, finally, Robert Kennedy read from Shakespeare the verse about cutting the departed Romeo into tiny stars to spangle the heavens and, amid all the gadgetry of the media, the delegates applauded the old, ever fresh words, glowing in contrast to the synthetic stars showered upon them the night before.

1964: The Hump

President Johnson's disclosure of his choice of a running mate was like the lighting of a 10-inch firecracker on the Fourth of July. You know it's going off, you know how it's going to sound, but the bang always catches you by surprise.

First, there was Johnson approaching the firecracker, the platform, in such a tumult that you caught only abstract glimpses of him, a sort of jigsaw Johnson, a big Pinnochio nose here, a large ear there, a forehead wrinkled in pleasure, the silver gray hair like the lines on worn beach wood, the prim scarecrow-stitched mouth suddenly opening to yawning elephant dimensions.

Cautiously, he put a can over the firecracker, announcing the dozens, the hundreds rather, of persons he had consulted, and then he was building suspense as fire ran down the fuse. Hubert Humphrey stood back in the wings, unsmiling, under a blue drape that gave a pale cast to his tense features.

The President kept adding one qualifying phrase after another, until finally, groaning in mirth, the crowd settled back to a seemingly endless string of them as the President put in one more, "my trusted colleague," and then, triumphantly and right then

— Bang! — Johnson leaned forward and shouted triumphantly "SENATTAHR HUBERT HUMPHREY!"— elated at having caught everyone off guard.

Humphrey, smiling, turned from pale blue to happy pink as he came out into the din. While the Humprheys took the acclaim of the convention, Johnson strode around the rear of the stand, the father who knows best. And near midnight the father decided there had been enough speeches and postponed Senattahr Humphrey's speech a day. But starting to leave, Johnson could not resist an unexpected excursion back and forth across the front of the hall to press the flesh with a thousand surprised stragglers.

Intent on grabbing every hand in sight, reaching to the right for delegates and up to his left for reporters looking down from the press section. As the President moved along, harvesting hands extended to him from out front and against the wall, Senator Humphrey tagged along, laughing and shaking hands with the delegates out front to his right. Back by the wall, Richmonder Ted Maeder called to the Vice Presidential nominee, "Senator Humphrey, don't forget us on the left."

Humphrey turned, smiled, and waved — and kept on shaking hands with the people on the right.

1964: The Hammer of Dissonance

"We want in, we want in, we want in..." the chant of would-be Scranton demonstrators shut out in the convention hall lobby, summed up William Scranton's position precisely. Of course, four years ago, Goldwater's demonstrators were put in a similar plight when a Nixon doorman took up their cards at one door and directed them through another that dumped them outside.

The Pennsylvania Governor was aware of the parallels as he praised the system that permits a candidate to arise from the debris of defeat and capture his party's nomination in four years, and no one is likely again to underestimate the power of working at the grassroots. "Let us pledge not to desert our party, but to strengthen it," said Scranton. "I say come, let us work within our party, not from outside it."

Newspapermen lined the back side of their corral on the convention floor to look down at Governor and Mrs. Scranton leaving the platform after his acknowledgment of defeat. Standing next to me was an assistant sergeant at arms, a teenager, and just as the couple was passing below us and turning to leave, he called to them, quietly but clearly, "Thank you."

She heard, and turned, and gave him a swift, absolutely dazzling smile. I guess she will treasure that last word in the Cow Palace.

"Where are you from?" I asked him.

"Louisiana."

"You're for Scranton?"

"Of course not."

"Why'd you thank him?"

"I respect him."

Richard M. Nixon's speech of peace-making had the glowing quality of the last chapter in a novel by Charles Dickens in which all the characters receive a measure of happiness. He made peace with his rival peers, with the delegates, with the press, and even —as one felt watching him go joyously about the work he knew best — with himself. In the pitch of the present, he dismissed the might-have-beens.

His performance was virtuoso. He is a Toscanini in playing upon a political convention, drawing forth great roaring sounds, and swiftly turning the sheets before him on the podium as if they formed a musical score. Fans of his or not, many felt a satisfaction at seeing such skills employed again as he put together the pieces of the political party and his own image, the picture of the politician to whom hope is never lost.

He built steadily to a crescendo to bring his hearers to the moment that would signal Barry Goldwater's entrance. At the rear of the runway to the podium, flash cameras made a fitful flickering, as of an approaching storm, suited to Beethoven. The flickering went on an unseasonable time, as if the storm, a summer number, might change its mind and go away. (Suppose, one imagined, he suddenly sent up word he didn't want the darn thing after all.) But then, Barry Goldwater appeared, and it thundered.

But nothing, not even a Nixon buildup, was going to change Mr. Goldwater's pace. He stood there, left hand shoved in his pocket, and he talked to 50,000 casually as if chatting in a precinct meeting. He threw away dramatic lines his writers had whetted for hours; he leveled what could have been oratorical peaks into humdrum plateaus. There was something endearing about the way he massacred that speech.

In his brisk way with a news conference, the Arizona Senator can be quite effective. Speaking off the cuff at a rally, he is impressive; but in delivering a set speech from a text, he gives it all the oomph of reading an eye chart. In his organization's awesome exhibition of power, one was inclined to forget Goldwater's distaste for emoting and orating.

And then, in this fashion, his voice as flat and matter-of-fact as a hoarse saw pulling back and forth through a board, he suddenly flung in one sentence on extremism the Thor-like hammer that brought down in crashing dissonance all the soothing themes orchestrated by Nixon the harmonizer.

"You're Going To Get Gassed, Baby"

The 1968 Democratic Convention began for me in an airport limousine, riding into Chicago, as I talked to a Harvard sophomore, 18, a political science buff.

"You're going to watch the convention, then?" I asked.

"No," he said, "I'm going to take part in the demonstration outside."

"You think there'll be one?"

"I know there will. People will be coming from everywhere."

He had never seen a demonstration. He spoke as if it were a part of growing up, like joining the Scouts.

About 2 a.m. Thursday after the convention had adjourned, the park across Michigan Avenue from the Hotel Conrad Hilton was dense with a shouting throng.

Facing that upheaval was an impassive line of police in helmets of baby-rattle blue. Across the street they lined the front of the cliff-like Hilton.

Youths huddled in blankets around fires. Others curled, gorilla-like, in trees. The air was aromatic with marijuana. Searchlights fell on a wide patch where they sat, sang, and yelled "Pig!" at police.

Their leader called with a bullhorn to the hotel windows: "Blink your lights if you're for us!"

A dozen lights flashed across the massive surface and he urged the occupants to come down and speak.

The delegate would declare his name, state and sympathy to cheers. But one said he had been with Eugene McCarthy, their hero, in New Hampshire where 3,000 youths had showed what could be done with reasonable election laws.

"Go back to your homes and change your laws," he pleaded.

A girl, cursing, shrieked: "This is it! NOW!" Others took it up and hooted him down. National guardsmen arrived to relieve the police.

"You're going to be gassed, baby," a stringy-haired middle-aged woman advised me. The youths tied handkerchiefs over their mouths. "Sit!" their leaders said. They began barking "Sieg! Sieg! Sieg!" To soldiers they sang: "Join us! Join us!"

The police, once moving, ran amok and clubbed anything in their path as heartily as children knocking over dandelion puff balls.

I joined those running headlong to put distance between us and them. The police riot spread as they moved "to sweep the streets."

A well-dressed crowd, issuing from a movie, faced a wall of police advancing at a trot, nightsticks held out belt-high, charging rhinos. The theater-goers broke and ran.

A reporter for Ridder Publications, wearing a vinyl jacket, had joined the demonstrators for three days. An aggressive fraction of the police was at fault, he said, but among the demonstrators, a motley lot directed by the National Mobilization Committee to End the War in Vietnam (MOB) were provocateurs skilled in rock throwing, name calling and hoisting the Viet Cong flag.

The police were focusing on newsmen taking names of victims. Just then one pointed to the Ridder reporter and shouted to two others, "There's the one!"

He ran and got away because he was young, nimble and hurdled two automobiles.

The Hilton's lobby was a make-shift hospital as Eugene McCarthy and his physician brother moved among the fallen. Years later, McCarthy told me that he stayed till he was sure the youths were safe.

Soviet tanks had invaded Czechoslovakia that week. As McCarthy's party was taking off in his plane, the pilot intoned on the intercom: "We're now leaving Prague!"

In the convention hall at the stockyards, where Hubert Humphrey struggled to save his crumbling party, the action had been as tense as the theater on the streets. Afterward, as delegates stumbled from early morning dark into the uncut glare of TV klieg lights, youths packing the Hilton's twin staircases chanted, "You-killed-the-party! You-killed-the-party!"

At a news conference, saying he was "captain of the team," Humphrey pledged to end the Vietnam War; but Coach Lyndon Johnson reined him in until near the end, too late, and Republicans used riot scenes to defeat him narrowly.

As the convention hall emptied, I spied a knot of two dozen people high in the farthest reach of the balconies. I climbed to them. They were young men and women, working on regulations to run the party on one man, one vote, admitting minorities and reducing the bosses' powers. Employing those rules four years later, the Democrats nominated George McGovern. He lost in a landslide that carried away a host of Democrats, including William B. Spong Jr. of Portsmouth, one of the finest ever to serve in the U.S. Senate.

I wonder what happened to that Harvard sophomore.

1972: An Impartial Presider

When the McGovern forces dropped Larry O'Brien as Chairman of the Democratic National Committee, some Democrats mourned the loss of an impartial presider and others the passing of an able campaign manager. They might have added that he was as satisfying a figure-head as has ever graced any political party's national convention.

Deep portentous tones issued from a huge, curly head, which with small eyes, ample nose, and pursed mouth gave him the look of an immense chicken strutting about its run, the platform. He looked like the man-sized dominecker with which Charlie Chaplin struggled furiously through a two-reeler, or like the outraged hen-head that pops up in Picasso's panorama of war, screaming silently.

At one point in the proceedings, he intoned to the 3,000 delegates, "I've been told that this podium should be congratulated on the way it has conducted these sessions..." — and then, as the always dutiful audience set up a spatter of clapping at this self-congratulatory observation, the Chairman shook his head benignly, and banged the keg sized gavel with yard-long handle, and said, no, it was rather the delegates themselves who deserved praise — so that everybody would be pleased.

"Then we will remember the convention, this convention in this place," he said, heavily, like a chicken pecking scattered corn, "as the place where the Democratic party came back, came back to life."

How he would have delighted the heart of Charles Dickens!

O'Brien's greatest moment arrived when a subordinate read to the vast hall a resolution acclaiming him for his masterful conduct of the proceedings. The delegates arose and gave him an ovation. As waves of applause rolled to the platform, Mr. O'Brien roamed about, a slight, blissful smile on his big lips, looking indulgently at the agitated sea of faces, tossing the gavel from hand to hand, playfully, as though it were a tennis racket, approaching the block on the podium now and then and pretending to pound on it, but stopping that huge mallet-head skillfully just a feather's distance short of impact, and finally, when the applause was dying beyond all coaxing, suddenly bringing down the gavel sharply, which had the effect of summoning another spate of handclapping. The performance should be fixed somehow in Roberts Rules of Order.

1972: Miami Heat

For a moment Collins Avenue in Miami Beach seemed about to become as riot-torn as Michigan Boulevard in Chicago in 1968.

But in Sunday night's brief confrontation between police and activists order was restored because (1) the demonstrators are a shade less zealous than were those in 1968 and (2) the Miami area police are a good deal more astute than were those in Chicago four years ago. Indeed, police officers here, calculating, moved their troops as men on a chess board.

The protesters in blue denim began parading along the street and sidewalk in front of the GOP's swank hotel headquarters just as Republican couples in evening dress were arriving to attend a Gala celebrating President Nixon's impending nomination. The demonstrators locked arms across the entrance drive and forced party-goers to stumble through shrubbery or turn back.

On the green slope in front of the portico brown-uniformed state troopers, holding yard-long night sticks waist high, formed a second line. At first they looked on impassively at the harassment of guests trying to enter the hotel.

Protesters were chanting "Rome-was-sacked-in-a-day — Rome-was-sacked-in-a-day" and "Keep-out-the-rich — Keep-out-the-rich." A young couple, looking no older than the demonstrators, started to push through the line, but he fell, and the crowd began to boil around them.

From the lawn half-a-dozen persons rushed to their aid, and a middle-aged man, Ralph Andrews of California, pulled them to safety. Bald as Daddy Warbucks, wearing round horn-rims, he had a lapel button announcing that he was chairman of Baldheaded Republicans. He turned to shout at the youths: "What's the matter with you?"

"The chant — Keep-out-the-Rich — is a joke," said the young man. "I'm living on a college campus making the salary of a college president. I borrowed this tuxedo from one of my students." He identified himself as Dr. William Benowsky, California delegate and president of Pepperdine College.

"Those students out there," he said nodding at the protesters, "are behind the times. Our college is the central district of Los Angeles, with a student body that is 25 percent black, and our kids believe in working a change in constructive ways. I don't know what's behind them out there."

A protester thrust his face forward, and shouted, "Then why do you support the Vietnam War and the mad bomber."

"I've been against the war all along," said Dr. Benowsky, "and I'm supporting the man who's doing something to end it."

He and his wife made their way into the Fontainbleu lobby, where Art Linkletter, the Gala's emcee, stood penguin-like at the entrance to the grand ballroom, and declared of the demonstration: "It's idiotic, stupid, jerky, it's exactly opposite to anything that has to do with democracy."

John Wayne, wearing a russet toupee, shrugged off questions and shouldered his way through the throng at the ballroom door as easily as he had walked through the pickets. He left a broad wake in the crowd. William Buckley bowed to admirers, and asked: "Hahr yew? We came around the back way. Was it rough out there?"

Out there, at 7:52, the state troopers began to move, marching down the curving drive, meeting reserve squads coming north, and, turning toward the protesters and holding their night sticks with both hands straight before them to ward off blows, formed a steadily advancing brown broom. The activists fell back in disarray. Flash bulbs flickered like heat lightning between the two slowly moving forces. The troopers halted, so did the demonstrators and a girl, Miss Molly Backup, a Harvard-Radcliffe student, called through a bullhorn: "We did real good. We kept out the rich."

Word came that Dade County police were coming up from the opposite end of Collins Avenue.

"We should move at a quick pace back to Flamingo Park," she called, "or we will be caught between several lines of cops."

The Dade County police appeared, marching on the right side of the avenue.

"If we do not move relatively quickly to the left side of the street, we will be trapped. Keep chanting and march arms linked," she called.

The activists scattered down the left side, and a lieutenant observed, "They took the opening we left for them."

Throughout there was nearly absolute quiet in the brown ranks. A reporter asking questions was referred by an enlisted man to a noncom who pointed out his commanding officer, who had nothing to say. But, at one point, as the brown broom was sweeping forward slowly and surely, a corporal muttered to a sergeant, "I'm just waiting for one to swing at me, and I'll bust his ass."

1976: Dimpled Chin and Darkly Glowing

None of Cary Grant's 80 pictures won an Oscar, but he deserved one for his appearance on the final night of the Republican Convention that nominated President Ford.

Other actors yearn for an Academy Award as certification they exist. He needs none. Cary Grant is, well, Cary Grant. The only disappointment for his fans has been that they are denied the satisfaction of seeing him sleek as a seal in his tux, a gliding panther in his movements, accept an award with a light, deprecating remark. Oscar has been the loser there.

Nor are the women of America bothered by the several failed marriages of that shade somewhere in Hollywood; they are focused on the real Cary Grant, the one darkly glowing up on the screen, not a hair displaced. Aside from his astounding good looks, including a dimpled chin, he is always in his roles a man whom women can trust. They'd feel intrigued — and secure — in his company. His easy manners, his athletic grace elicit men's approval. They can't feel envy; they are too busy imagining themselves in his mold.

The convention, over which there was usually a hum like that of bees fanning a hive in hot weather, went silent when Cary Grant appeared, snow-thatched, wearing dark-rimmed glasses, still the handsomest man in the place, any place. The old smoothie's assignment seemed to be to nominate Betty Ford. For what, wasn't plain. First lady, maybe. It was enough that he was up there, in the flesh, on the rostrum.

The women were enchanted by his debonair air. The men were bemused that anybody that old could look that young. Of all the speakers this convention week, he had the most attentive audience. Oh, the delegates cheered the others. And ate hot dogs and read newspapers while they orated. For Grant, they listened. And, incredibly, he seemed to be making light of women's rights.

"I'm here to introduce a remarkable woman," he said with his air of casual elegance. "Oh, I know you have many remarkable women in your party. After all, what's any party without remarkable women?" He noted Betty Ford's aim "to further the cause of women's rights," observing, "Women have always been one of my favorite causes. Ah, well, time goes on."

It's quite understandable that women everywhere "wish to be treated as intelligent equals," Grant confided, adding magnanimously, "as indeed they should be." Then he trailed into patter, which wasn't altogether clear in meaning — thereby on a par with the general level of conventions — about the wisdom of wives and husbands exchanging confidences at the end of the day, "pillow talk," he said.

That Grant, bantering, was gently teasing the ERA seemed inconceivable, but when I checked this impression with several feminists in the Virginia delegation after his departure, they nodded calmly, serene-eyed. Apparently, Cary Grant, as long as he came before them in person, could say anything he pleased.

1976: Democratic Family Reunion

When Democratic Chairman Robert Strauss announced the showing of a 15-minute film Thursday night, boos and shouts of "Oh-h-h-h-h No!" arose among the 20,000 at the Democratic National Convention.

They were ready for Jimmy Carter, even those not of his camp. It had been a skillful buildup. First Hubert Humphrey came to pass the liberal torch to his protege, Walter Mondale. Various speakers had quoted founding fathers. Humphrey outdid them all by quoting from his own speech of two nights before about the need of a new breed of leaders.

Then Mondale brought them to their feet with a direct shot at President Ford's pardon of Richard Nixon. So they settled back, grumbling, to watch the film — and saw as skillful a political commercial as could be devised.

Slick, rapid, it depicted the lone candidate bent on meeting every voter in America and, in a daring ploy, repeated newspaper cartoons satirizing his grin — thereby minimizing any such future cartoons. There was little indication of the cold logistics of the Carter campaign, nor much of his brilliant young operatives, including Gerald Rafshoon, who designed the film.

Time now for the candidate, and in a summer lightning of flashbulbs Carter appeared, not on the platform, but at an entrance to the floor itself. While Eddy Duchin's band played the slam-bang theme — "Why Not the Best?" — from the film, Carter made his way slowly, handshaking, past delegations in New Jersey, Illinois, Virginia, Kansas, Utah, and Wyoming — a visual demonstration of his campaign.

Through much of the dramatic progress, Carter was lost to view. "Jimmy always was the smallest boy in the class," his mother had told an interviewer. He climbed to the rostrum and stood a moment, bathed in the klieg lights and the adoration of his followers to the continuous thunder of applause.

And when it quieted, he said: "My name is Jimmy Carter, and I'm running for president of the United States."

That drew a roar of laughter.

"It's been a long time since I've said those words the first time," he added, "and now I've come here to accept your nomination to be president of this great country."

If the film had been skillful, the speech topped it. Various hands, including Patrick Anderson's and former writers' for the Kennedys, had contributed to it, but really it as Carter's, the master speech, a compilation in one place from 3,000 speeches in 30 primaries.

And there had been a sharpening. In Norfolk last summer he noted the ironic injustice that the poor always seemed to go to prison while the well-to-do, able to hire the best lawyers, went free. In the Garden the line emerged as a slant lance at the Watergaters and Nixon: "I see no reason why big-shot crooks should go free while the poor ones go to jail."

"It is now a time for healing," he said, and then, leading the listeners up the stairs:

"We want to have faith again!

"We want to be proud again!

"We want the truth again!"

The forces of the desperate anguish in third line hit the harder for following two more general ones. He spoke of love, and, as often, his voice dropped on the word as if love were a lump in his throat:

"I have spoken many times about love, but love must be aggressively translated into simple justice."

It also translates into one of the most effective, hardest-hitting speeches ever delivered by one political party against another. The summary of his attitudes also disclosed populist overtones as he categorized sharply how the poor suffered and the rich went unscathed in trying times. The speech done, his family joined him on the rostrum — Rosalynn, in flaming ruby red, and the chidlren.

Earlier, in a litany, he had invoked the political figures in the Democratic family, even bringing back, to generous applause, Lyndon Johnson, who alive and exiled at the ranch in 1968 dared not show his face at that convention.

Now Strauss bawled out the names of living Democrats, scemingly down to the doormen, and they filed onto the rostrum until it looked like a crowded lifeboat.

Then the Rev. Martin Luther King Sr. came to the rostrum to pronounce the benediction, after a few words.

If Jimmy Carter speaks of love in gentle tones the old man thunders the Old Testament. For a moment he turned Madison Square Garden into a fundamentalist revival tent. What a delight to picture the likes of Patrick Moynihan and John Kenneth Glabraith under the rich blessing that needed no public address system.

All walking and all talking would have to cease, except the work of the Lord, who surely is in this place, commanded Daddy King.

"Yes. He is," came back a shout from someone in the gallery.

"Surely the Lord sent Jimmy Carter to come on out and bring America back where she belongs," King thundered.

"Yes. He did," answered the voice.

Then Daddy King pronounced the benediction, and the 1976 Democratic National Convention was over.

And brothers and sisters, it was something!

1980: "We Want Ted"

Jimmy Carter won the nomination, but Ted Kennedy stole the show at the Democratic National Convention — and then muffed it.

Having made a splendid speech Wednesday, all Kennedy had to do, once on the platform before the cheering delegates Thursday night, was raise Carter's hand and smile. That grace note would have consolidated his newfound hold on the hearts of many viewers.

But, his face set, except for an infrequent slight smile, he moved slowly around the platform as if in a trance, seeming to try to avoid the rival he had come to congratulate. An especially excruciating scene occurred when he stood within a few feet of Rosalynn Carter, and, instead of stepping forward to talk with her, hung back, as though dazed. Mrs. Carter, her slight figure drawn bow-tight, her tremulous, large eyes fixed on his face, waited, and when he made no sign of cordiality, she simply stood her ground.

Whatever the explanation of Kennedy's actions, he managed, moving slowly like a robot, to enter a bower at one corner of the platform and clinch a raised fist toward the vast plain of faces across the floor, a salute to which his followers responded with a roar. Perhaps the Bostonian's pride was injured by the Georgian's piteous, well-nigh demeaning plea — "The party needs you, I need you" — for his support. Perhaps he felt used.

Contrast Kennedy's mournful passage around the thronged platform, a reproachful Banquo's ghost, to his happy spontaneity when visiting the Hispanic-American caucus two days before. He arrived in their hall as Cesar Chavez was concluding a call to the delegates to boycott carrots. Reaching the lectern, Kennedy grabbed the cellophane package of carrots, waved them over his head, and shouted in a mock-stern tone, "If I am elected, those carrots will not be served at the White House!"

"A la victoria!" cried the ecstatic delegates, raising their pointed index fingers like a bull's horns.

Carter's performance Thursday night was below par, probably because he began the day by jogging in Central Park. At his age, under the world's heaviest burden, he ought to eschew such pointless exertion. He dropped phrases, words, and sentences from his text and tried to patch them in place. When, for emphasis, he raised his voice to a shout, what often emerged was a meaningless roar.

It was an able enough defense of his administration and, from a viewpoint of the realities of the country's temper, it made more sense than much of Kennedy's ringing oration, which, like Ronald Reagan's persuasive pitch to Republicans, often was heavily nostalgic. But seldom has a speech been delivered in as miserable a fashion as was Carter's.

And seldom has an evening been as filled with tensions. About midway one began to wish simply that the president would hurry and finish without incurring embarrassment or hurt.

Sporadically the senator's supporters, waving blue and white placards, shouted "We want Ted!," whereupon Carter's backers, shaking green and white signs, drowned them out with shouts of "We Want Jimmy" — a blue sea contesting a green forest. Throughout Kennedy had been the dominant force, and the last day many delegates were more interested in seeing Kennedy, their darling, than in hearing Carter.

Stalling for time until Kennedy arrived, Bob Strauss took the mike at the lectern and began, a man possessed, to reel off names of dignitaries to come to the podium. As he continued, it appeared that he was bent on cramming everybody in Madison Square Garden, packed as densely as canned asparagus, on the platform. Kennedy's arrival on the platform forestalled that experiment, and presented the spectacle of the delegates' idol wandering around the landscape like one of the walking wounded.

The Carters' restraint during the ordeal may well work to their advantage in time, but not in nearly as great a degree as would have been true had Kennedy been able to summon one last beau geste — a balm to the newly nominated candidates, to the convention, and to himself.

1984: Ready and Able

SAN FRANCISCO — If Walter F. Mondale's putting Geraldine A. Ferraro on his ticket made history, one would wish to remember where one heard the news.

Hurrying along a corridor in the Chicago airport, I came upon a dozen people huddled around a tiny portable TV set. On the screen was Mondale flanked by Ferraro.

"This is an exciting choice," Mondale intoned in his plodding cadence, as if plowing rocks.

At that, his audience took matters in its own hands and broke into applause.

Mondale looked surprised, then brightened and said: "Let me say that again. THIS is an EXCITING choice."

He said it that time with considerably more animation. In

choosing Ferraro, Mondale scored a breakthrough. He broke the tedium of the sober earnestness of his delivery. His friends say that humor runs through his private conversations and it flashed in St. Paul, Minn. for a second, although it is hard to believe, now that Mary Tyler Moore has left, that anybody there has a sense of humor. It is too cold.

The head of the National Women's Political Caucus said Mondale "electrified the electorate." That raised an image of all of us, our hair standing on end, electrified, getting the news. Certainly he electrified himself as much as if he had stuck his finger in a socket.

In those clustered around the portable TV, one well-dressed young fellow leaned forward to catch Ferraro's every word. Obviously, he favored her. Two attractive young women were so absorbed, eyes shining, that their faces seemed drawn to a point. Mondalers, I decided.

Not only did they favor him, I found later, they were his staffers on their way to San Francisco. On the plane, two bright young aides to House Majority Leader Jim Wright of Texas said they had rushed into a bar to catch the news.

What was the reaction in the bar? One fellow looked up, they reported, and said, "Caved in, huh?"

That was all he had to say.

Another had remarked somberly: "Just what we need."

My two young friends judged that the second man was kidding. So my poll had one for Ferraro, one against, a 50-50 split in the electrified electorate. It made just as much sense as those surveys taken by newspapers or TV networks that do not have a much larger sampling.

On this issue in particular there's no way of divining how people will vote because you're dealing with the most unpredictable element in society: its women. You can gauge, often, by a man's special interest how he will vote. But women are independent thinkers. Some, suspicious, may vote against Mondale simply because he chose a woman to get their votes.

Their independence knows no bounds. Long ago my wife began voting against my candidate simply to neutralize my ballot. How are pollsters going to judge the spousal nullification factor? I began talking against my candidate simply to sway her to his side and when she saw through that, did a double reverse by talking for him. It became so complicated that at the polls, I didn't know how the devil to vote. She did.

In the end, my guess is that many people will not decide about Ferraro because she is a woman so much as what she is as a person. Impressive in her early career is the fact that she worked her way through Fordham University Law School at night by teaching second grade. Either one of those efforts demands is as much as being vice president.

A big influence on Mondale was the persuasive power of House Speaker Thomas P. "Tip" O'Neill Jr. He wanted, he said, pizazz on the ticket. He got it in St. Paul.

1984: Master Communicator

Master communicator Ronald Reagan was at his deftest last night in accepting the Republican presidential nomination.

His skillfully wrought speech was replete with imagery — "maybe we could get the Lord back in our school rooms"; one-liners — to say that Democarats spend like drunken sailors "would be unfair to drunken sailors. The sailors are spending their own money"; and a new way of measuring the political spectrum — not "left" or "right" but "up" and "down," the Republicans being on the upbeat.

Reviewing foreign policy, he dwelled on a success, Grenada, where "19 of our fine young men lost their lives." But he skipped Lebanon, where questions of policy and tactics hover over the death in ambush of nearly 250 Marines. For that matter, the Democrats are chary of criticisms on that score.

Once again Reagan sounded the roll call of charismatic Democratic presidents; the better to woo dissatisfied Democrats into Republican green pastures. He explained his own conversion to Republicanism by observing that the Democratic Party strayed from its cost-cutting policies of early 1932.

"Did I leave the Democratic Party or did the leadership of that party leave not just me but millions of patriotic Democrats?".

Not only does Reagan have the audacity to kidnap the Democratic leaders, he set out to divide the party into two parts — the Democrats who met in San Francisco and the "Democrats of the main stream ... who share our Republican vision of America" — and made it clear that he has designs on taking the latter half into the Republican camp.

The Republicans four times played "Happy Days Are Here Again," the jaunty tune that Democrats regard as "our song."

Before he had finished, Reagan managed to make the Olympic games seem a Republican production and he even embraced the Statue of Liberty.

Even reading the speech, one could hear Reagan's husky baritone and see him, eyes twinkling, cocking his head to one side, taking a little anticipatory breath before delivering a good line, and then, flashing the tight little grin that invites the audience to share his good humor and well-being.

The Republicans, who are outstripping the Democrats in the use of high technology, presented Bush and Reagan through artful films about their careers. Although entertaining, the movies were not a patch on the old-fashioned stem-winding speech that Ted Kennedy gave Democrat Walter Mondale in San Francisco. But then Reagan used to introduce movies, so perhaps it's natural that a movie prefaced his appearance. Whatever the means of bringing him on, the jubilant Republican convention, at the sight of the beaming president, launched a chant of "four more years!" Every three or four lines they gave him thunderous ovations.

1988: One more for the Gipper

NEW ORLEANS — In a night of histrionics, President Reagan and a supporting cast slipped between real and reel life in a production that aroused a wildly applauding crowd, sent the old trouper temporarily into the wings and set the stage for Vice President George Bush.

From the Republicans' viewpoint, it couldn't have been better. Editorials called it the passing of the torch. It was more the handing off of the football, an image underscored by one speaker, former professional quarterback Jack Kemp.

With helmet hairdo, barking in his high-pitched, signal-calling voice, Kemp recalled for the crowd the role of George Gipp, played by Reagan before he left Hollywood for Washington. In that film, Coach Knute Rockne, sending Gipp into the game, says: "They'll give you the ball. You just run with it!"

And, Kemp related, "Ronald Reagan looks at Rockne and says, 'How far, coach?' " Thus do old athletes, sitting around, swap stories about their past exploits. But suddenly Kemp had ceased talking about the Gipper and was telling of the day Ronald Reagan had carried the ball for Rockne.

And then, reverting to reality, looking at Reagan far across the convention floor, Kemp said, "Mr. President, we all know what happened eight years ago, when America gave you the ball." Thanking Reagan for his legacy, Kemp promised, "And we just want to know that we're going to take it and run with it, and we're going to win in November."

Even Reagan did a reprise of his best-known role. "But George," he said to Bush, "just one personal request" — the crowd fell silent in interest — "Go out there" — and Reagan cut his eyes just a fraction to the left as if asking if he dared go on — "and win one for the Gipper!"

At those last words, his voice dropped almost to a whisper so that for an instant he was someone, an aging aunt or uncle, telling a wondrous fairy tale and as well, right at the close, the dying Gipper making a last request of Bush. The crowd cheered, and the 77-year-old president flashed a pleased little grin, a small boy who pulled a cookie out of a jar and got away with it. With backs running this way and that through the speeches, the convention seemed to be Monday night football.

The evening was an actor's dream. When Reagan and the first lady entered their box overlooking the convention floor, the audience erupted into a prolonged ovation during which the band played "Hail to the Chief" again and again. The speeches were, after all, in praise of him, and when time came for his turn at the podium, Reagan managed the enviable feat of introducing himself through a half-hour film recapping his career. When the lights in the Superdome went up, Reagan strode slowly, bulky chest out, squared shoulders back, across the platform and stood under the long, thunderous ovation as if abashed and awed before the Niagara waterfall beyond his power to affect.

Speaking more in sorrow than anger, he referred to Democrats as "our friends" or simply, "the other side" of the once worthy party of Franklin D. Roosevelt and Harry S. Truman, now gone to seed. Noting that "we need someone big enough and experienced enough" to negotiate with Mikhail S. Gorbachev, he said, alluding to Democrat Michael S. Dukakis, "This is no time to gamble with on-the-job training."

Citing his administration's successes, he drew loud applause when he said softly, "and George was there," thus brushing off with one sweep the chant — "Where was George?" — the Democrats had launched in Atlanta.

He had seen Bush up close — "someone who's not afraid to speak his mind and who can cut to the core of an issue," he said, thereby providing, Republicans may hope, a blanket defense for Bush's silence on his conduct during the Iran-Contra scandal and the administration's other unmentioned contretemps.

Indulging in a metaphor, he said, "We lit a prairie fire a few years back ... fed by passionate ideas and convictions, and we were determined to make them burn all across America."

There is a lot of brush to clear at the ranch, Reagan said, "But I want you to know that if the fires ever dim, I'll leave my phone number and address behind just in case you need a foot soldier."

The delegates applauded wildly this heartening, if somewhat elegiac notion, of Reagan returning like Arthur from Avalon.

"Just let me know, and I'll be there — as long as words don't leave me and as long as this sweet country strives to be special during its shining moment on Earth."

Some 200,000 balloons cascaded from the ceiling, even drifting onto the stage where Ronnie and Nancy, children in a nursery, began catching them and propelling them into the crowd. Then they left, looking back, flinging up their right hands in farewell — the sort of a triumphant closeout of movies we used to see, everybody living happily ever after.

1992: The Comeback Kid

As the Democratic Convention recedes, what stands out, a monadnock in a pitchy plain, is Mario Cuomo's speech nominating Bill Clinton for president.

Not until Cuomo came to the rostrum was there a sustained, moving affirmation. He mesmerized them. Earlier, Barbara Jordan wondered if Democrats had the stuff. Jackson preached.

Opening, Cuomo declared: "Tonight, I will have the great privilege and honor of placing before you the name of the next president of the United States, Governor Bill Clinton of Arkansas!" That stood on its head the old style of rambling on about "a man who..." then, at last, bawling a name to nobody's surprise. The directness of it riveted the delegates. Lest it seem the mere quick fulfilling of an obligation, Cuomo bugled Clinton's name 24 times thereafter and extended his own credibility to a character reference for Clinton. He validated him. Watching TV, the Clintons cried.

Cuomo's speech, 17 minutes in rehearsal, ran half an hour with applause lines, about the length of Clinton's benumbing nomination of Michael Dukakis four years ago. In a touch, Cuomo covered an epoch of opposing views, recalling that in 1984, while President Reagan was extolling the shining city on the hill, "some of us tried to convince America...there was another city, where people were struggling, many of them living in pain."

We are in "more than a recession," he said, and then, without tagging it an impending depression, he planted the idea: "Our economy has been weakened...by 12 years of conservative Republicans' supply side policy. In fact, supply side was just another version of the failed Republican dogma of 65 years ago — then called 'trickle down' — which led to the Great Depression."

His words bespeak the man. Mulling them for days, awakening at night to make notes, Cuomo wrote in longhand. He shunned the polarizing words of abortion, gay rights, and school prayer, but spoke of the Republican attempt "to tell us what God to believe in, and how to apply that God's judgment to our schoolrooms, our bedrooms, and our bodies."

The resonant voice, a rich-timbred Wurlitzer, can go from bass to crooning tremolo. The gestures are of a maestro. His language is pictorial. He sees children "growing up familiar with the sound of gunfire before they've ever heard an orchestra." He evoked the "quiet catastrophes," of a father, nearly in terror, laid off at 50, thinking, "What if I'm struck by cancer? What about the mortgage? What about the children in school?"

His face is cartoonish: big lower lip; heavy black brows; dark protruding, stabbing eyes, cupped in pouches ample as a Pullman's shoe hammock; a lavish nose seeming less so as age furrows the face, making ugliness arresting. Always there has been manliness.

Debt and deficit, he said, hang "like great albatrosses around our nation's neck..."

He noted parades to celebrate troops returning from the Persian Gulf and then envisioned another joyous parade, led by Bill Clinton, to rival anything imagined by Charles Dickens, "through cities and rural villages where all the people have safe streets, affordable housing, and health care when they needed it..." He went on enumerating blessings over which he "wants to sing... to clap my hands...to shout out our thanks because President Bill Clinton helped us to make the greatest nation in the world better than it's ever been.

"So step aside, Mr. Bush," he pounded. "You've had your parade. It's time for change — someone smart enough to know; strong enough to do; sure enough to lead. The Comeback Kid. A new voice for a new America!"

So he put the Arkansas governor into nomination for president.

One day the Democrats may wake up and nominate Governor Cuomo. Simply say: "Here's Mario!" He'll take it from there.

1992: Play It Again, Gipper!

Those who love words had a feast listening to the Republican National Convention in Houston. Ronald Reagan was at his mischievous best in playing off the words with which, in 1988, Lloyd Bentsen admonished Dan Quayle about being no Jack Kennedy.

Reagan set it up deftly, marvelling that he had seen eight decades of history, which somehow sounded even more impressive than his being 81. He remarked, cheerfully, that any day he woke up was a good day. The Astrodome's thousands roared with laughter. They felt, eating up the sight of the rugged, ruddy face with two spots of pink high on the cheek bones and the little black peeping eyes under heavy brows that Ronald Reagan would go right on living, returning every four years to hearten them, and, even after he leaves this world, he would come back, when needed, from Avalon.

So having reminded them of his antiquity, Reagan remarked that the Arkansas governor was presenting himself as Thomas Jefferson. With that, they began to chuckle, knowing what was coming, cheering each phrase, reaching a long crescendo on the one as Reagan said slowly, relishing every word of the punch line, "I knew Thomas Jefferson, Governor. He was a friend of mine. And you're no Thomas Jefferson!"

It was superb, right down to addressing Clinton as Governor. That gave Reagan's remarks an air of detachment. Use of his name would have made the attack personal. Turns out that GOP Chairman Rich Bond had used the joke a day or so before, and his audience responded with such hilarity that Bond realized it would be even more apt coming from Reagan.

Of course, Clinton regards elements of his program as Jeffersonian, but he didn't dwell on the sage as did Jerry Brown, who discovered Jefferson during the Democratic primaries and misquoted him nearly every time. And then, two nights later, accepting the nomination, Quayle reminded Clinton that he was no Ronald Reagan. It helped that he could ride Reagan's coattails.

Reagan was woefully wide of the mark when he said that Democrats don't understand the principle so "eloquently stated" by Abraham Lincoln: "You cannot strengthen the weak by weakening the strong. You cannot help the wage earner by pulling down the wage payer. You cannot help the poor by destroying the rich. You cannot help men permanently by doing for them what they could and should do for themselves."

Even as Reagan delivered it, I wondered how Lincoln could have indulged in sloganeering that expresses the core of the modern GOP. The statement didn't seem Lincolnesque. Next day, word came that scholars have long considered it a fake. "If we ever hear the Democrats quoting that passage by Lincoln and acting like they mean it," Reagan said, "then, my friends, we will know that the opposition has really changed."

And we'll know Lincoln probably never said it.

George Bush, accepting the nomination, closed with a quote he thought was from Harry Truman saying his speech, more than a political call to arms, was a new crusade to keep America safe and secure. Turns out that Truman, issuing the call in 1948 for the new crusade, was repeating for Democrats the challenge Franklin Roosevelt had given them in 1932.

Neither FDR nor Truman, being thorough Democrats, would have thought much of Bush. And there's little in Bush reminiscent of Truman. That fighting cock of a man didn't need handlers to encourage him to get in a campaign mode to battle the Republican Congress in 1948. He didn't "give 'em hell," he said later. "I just told the truth on 'em."

The Arkansas Express

President Clinton stirred the Democratic convention to an ovation Thursday by pledging to balance the budget and do it in a way that preserves Medicare, Medicaid, education and the environment.

And, alluding to the vetoes with which he withstood a Republican Congress, he declared, to ever-mounting applause, "And as long as I am president, I will never allow the Republican leadership to use the blackmail threat of a government shutdown to force these burdens on the American people.

"We didn't let it happen before and we won't let it happen again."

On Clinton's four-day, 500-mile train trek through five Midwest states, his acceptance speech was a kind of work in progress. Four aides worked on the speech's midsection while the president shaped the beginning and the end.

On the journey, Clinton was as jubilant as a boy who finds a red bicycle Christmas morning. Between each city, he took a stand, mike in hand, on the train's platform and continued communicating with passing America.

Spectators who gathered by the rails to watch the train pass were startled to be hailed by the president. One such moment, recorded by the Chicago Tribune, began with Clinton calling: "Hi, folks, hi. Nice garden!" To others he called: "I like your dogs! ... " "That's the biggest satellite dish I ever saw! ... " "Be careful, don't fall off that platform! ... " "Nice bikes! ... "

Each day he announced an initiative to correspond with that day's theme. At Kalamazoo, Mich., it was $1.9 billion to clean up two-thirds of Superfund sites and 5,000 old industrial sites. It reminds you of the train that chugs each Christmas through Southwest Virginia while Santa Claus throws candy to children along the way. Democrats should invite Clinton to fling candy this year.

His aides feared the president's voice would give out, but after plunging into the crowds he emerged refreshed. In his stem-winding delivery, Clinton was at his robust best. A tender moment occurred Wednesday night after a helicopter deposited him on the University of Illinois ball diamond.

On the platform, Hillary, grinning, extended her arms about belt-high as if welcoming a child bringing home from school an "A" paper. Clinton spread his arms wide, his face exultant at what he and she had done. Chelsea watched their beaming togetherness. As he and Hillary faced the crowd he said, "I think she did a great job, don't you?" Clinton said it as if she had baked a great cake.

Chapter Six

Jefferson and Others

A Patriotic Symbol

If Thomas Jefferson came back, former Gov. Colgate W. Darden Jr. once observed, "he'd have a hard time getting around the state without being hanged!" A revolutionary, Jefferson had a quaint notion people were born free and, to govern themselves, they'd best be taught to read, write and reason.

So, returning, he would be elated at the sight of children, black and white, going to school. In his day there was no system of public schools. To teach a black child to read was against the law. Jefferson's great dream was to create schools throughout Virginia. He made a bold move to do so during the American Revolution.

While Washington was fighting, Jefferson was writing a revolution, revising Virginia laws. "Our Revolution," he wrote, "presented us an album on which we were free to write what we pleased." The time to fix rights in law, he said, "is while our rulers are honest and ourselves united" and while people were attentive to their rights.

A committee set out in 1779 to write reforms in the laws. The others quit; Jefferson kept at it. By far the most important bill was one to set up a system "for diffusion of knowledge among the people," he wrote in 1786 to George Wythe at William and Mary College.

The bill envisioned a system of public schools topped by a national university. "Preach ... a crusade against ignorance, establish and improve the law for educating the common people," he wrote Wythe. The tax to support the schools would be a fraction "of what will be paid to kings, priests, and nobles who will rise up among us if we leave the people in ignorance."

Large land owners defeated the bill three times. A tax to educate the electorate they deemed bizarre. Had the General Assembly heeded his plea, Virginia would have had a literate population that could have withstood the pull to secede from the Union. Without Virginia and its generals, the Confederacy would have had to give up the Civil War. Jefferson turned to creating the University of Virginia, "the last act of usefulness I can render." With Virginians migrating to the western frontier and to eastern cities, Jefferson saw the university as a way to restore Virginia's vitality.

Writing to John Adams in their old age, Jefferson recalled the failure of the General Assembly to adopt his bill for public schools. "I have great hope," he wrote "that some patriotic spirit will call it up and make it the keystone of the arch of our government."

A patriotic spirit, Colgate Darden fought to keep Virginia's schools open during the Depression in the 1930s. Then, as its president, he revived Jefferson's university, which was lapsing into a country club. He set in motion advances that lifted it to national eminence.

In 1963, Darden led in reopening schools closed in Prince Edward County by Massive Resistance to desegregation; and then, to begin his last great service, he served on the State Board of Education. With Lewis F. Powell Jr., he began working to equalize opportunities so a child would get a good education wherever he or she lived, just as a county gets good roads no matter where or how poor it is.

In 1968, Gov. Mills Godwin appointed Darden to work on a commission to revise the Virginia Constitution. There Darden continued the drive to equalize schooling. Drawing phrases from Jefferson's bill for diffusion of knowledge, Darden proposed adding to the Virginia Declaration of Rights a resolution that Virginia achieve an effective system of education assuring the fullest development "of those talents which nature has sown so liberally among its people."

Elsewhere in the Constitution, a mandate guarantees a quality education for every child. As the 1969 General Assembly debated his bills, Darden consulted with legislators much as Jefferson had done. Norfolk Sen. Stanley Walker recalls that Darden was on the phone daily, saying "don't let them forget" this or that in the bills. "Sometimes he called me out of committee. All along, I sent him the drafted language."

The bills passed as Thomas Jefferson's spirit walked the Capitol.

TJ Lives

Writing from Philadelphia to his daughter Maria at Monticello, Thomas Jefferson asked for signs of spring. "Not a sprig of grass grows uninteresting to me," he cried in a phrase that takes wing.

That sentence, note, does not open with the great puffed-up "I" pronoun. He stresses what interests him — "a sprig of grass." The self-effacing "me" brings up the rear. His plea to Maria denotes his insatiable curiosity. In another letter, he confides, "I have a canine appetite for learning."

He instructed his university to follow the truth wherever it led. He wrote: "There is not a truth existing which I fear, or would wish unknown to the whole world." The locomotive of that sentence is "truth." It is almighty, god-like. And there again, in Jefferson's bow to truth, is forceful negative phrasing — "there is not" — to express the positive.

His admirers wonder how he would view today's issues. Not one exists on which he hasn't touched. Daily he wrote a dozen letters that fill 100 volumes. How would he regard feminism? His makeup had no sense of male superiority. His program of reading for his daughter would daunt today's collegians. In 1771, he figured at 14-to-1 chances she would marry a blockhead "and that the education of her family will probably rest on her own ideas and directions. ... With the poets and and prose writers I shall combine reading in the graver sciences."

Some critics mewl that the Declaration of Independence contains no startling new thought. Its object, Jefferson said, "was intended to be an expression of the American mind." Like the pet mockingbird that rode his shoulder singing, he blended the best of what was in the air into something better.

The other founders rose to great utterance. Jefferson stayed at a high pitch. Lines spring from his correspondence. Writing Edward Carrington, he mused: "If once the people become inattentive to public affairs, you and I and Congress and Assemblies, Judges, and Governors shall all become wolves."

He moved from designing a plow to playing the violin — which ought to shame our lame lament that there's so much to know we need learn less and less outside a speciality. Jefferson suffered no fences. He roamed without hindrance in arts and sciences. Since the engine of creative thought is the power to generalize and associate the dissimilar, Jefferson's delving in all branches heightened his reasoning when dealing with one.

Science discloses the inter-relation of things, and Jefferson's habit was to treat the universe as a vast, interlocking, challenging conundrum. Monticello, bespeaking his mind, harmonizes a horde of details. He hoped it would remain in constant revision "as architecture is my delight and putting up and pulling down one of my favorite amusements." Sometimes it seems that every line he wrote was creative. His sentiments march in marble around the Jefferson Memorial in Washington, D.C. Often they move visitors to tears.

The founders' brilliance in governance was the sort of flowering that visited other nations in arts and sciences. At their head was a one-man Renaissance. In 1960, after touring Monticello, testing every gadget, President Harry Truman gazed at its white dome. "I don't see how he can do and be so many things," he murmured.

Along with genius, Jefferson was born with a robust body, which he respected and exercised. He did things immediately after he thought them through. He had exquisite taste, faith in fellow Americans, abounding joy in the universe, and a sunny outlook. "My temperament is sanguine," he wrote John Adams. "I steer my bark with Hope in the head, leaving Fear astern. My hopes, indeed, sometimes fail, but not oftener than the forebodings of the gloomy."

Faced with a problem, he struck for the ideal, which, after all, is the most practicable approach in being not for the moment but all time. In his 80s, Jefferson built a university. He sited it, designed buildings, hired workmen, supervised construction, recruited teachers, drew the curriculum, scheduled classes, and, as rector, wrought the regulations. He drafted Presidents Madison and Monroe to serve with him on the board of visitors.

To the end he was a revolutionary. Too ill to join citizens of Washington celebrating the Declaration of Independence's 50th anniversary, he penned a final flaring of hope that it would be a signal to the world persuading people to throw off their bonds: "All eyes are opened, or opening, to the rights of man. The general spread of the light of science has already laid open to every view the palpable truth, that the mass of mankind has not been born with saddles on their backs, nor a favored few booted and spurred, ready to ride them legitimately, by the grace of God ..."

"Let the annual return of this day forever refresh our recollections of these rights and an undiminished devotion to them."

On the evening of July 3, Jefferson roused himself to ask, "Is it the Fourth?" He died at one o'clock in the afternoon of the Fourth.

In the afternoon of the Fourth in Massachusetts a dying Adams said in his last words: "Thomas Jefferson lives."

As he does. Look about you.

Hi! My name is...?

Throughout Southside Virginia, people recollect with joy Gov. William M. Tuck (1946-1950) who never ever forgot a name.

Frequently, an admirer would ask if Tuck remembered his name, at which the governor would rise slowly, lifting his arms high, like a majestic elephant trumpeting his delight, his mind, meanwhile, more sensitive than the most sophisticated computer, searching the recesses of his memory. So when he brought down his hands on the man's shoulders, the name rose, magically, to his lips, and one more soul went away consoled that he was remembered by Bill Tuck.

One time Tuck was with a neighboring state's lieutenant governor when a constituent confronted that worthy with a dare that he didn't know his name. The lieutenant governor turned to an aide and snapped, "Tell this damn fool his name! He don't know and I don't know either."

That wasn't Bill Tuck's style. He was shocked at the official's insensitivity to the man's appeal for confirmation of worth. A man's name, his most cherished — sometimes only — possession, deserves remembrance. A kindness in Tuck, as well as the pride of an old pro, impelled him to dredge up the name, embrace the bearer and set him at ease, at pride, remembered by the mighty Ajax of political wars.

One time a man, feet apart, chin raised, challenged him at a county fair, as if Tuck were the weight and age guesser, and said he bet Tuck didn't know his name. The hands rose high in the air, a smile wreathed the governor's jovial face, but, for once, the infallible memory faltered, failed to offer a clue, at which, Tuck shouted, as a crowd gathered: "Don't know your name? Why I could pick that face out of the multitude on the peopled plain at Judgment Day and name it!"

All the while his ears were fanning the crowd, flapping, testing, turning intently this way and that to pick up a hint, and, just as he concluded his response, Tuck heard, way out on the fringe, somebody yell, "That oughta tell ole Fred!" And that turned the key in the gates of recollection and the full name came flooding back to Tuck so that when his hands came down on Fred's shoulders, with such force as to almost buckle his knees, Tuck called his last name as well as his first and then inquired politely after the health of his wife, Sallie. The crowd roared with applause.

And Fred, face flushed, strutted off as if he had done it all.

Thirteen years after his death, anybody who ever met Bill Tuck remembers his name.

Listen Closely

"Most of us are 18, " said the valedictorian, a petite girl with an easy smile and hazel eyes, but serious now. "We're graduating from high school. So what does that mean?"

Her father, former Gov. Linwood Holton, listened closely. And later he told a reporter that watching her at graduation exercises in May 1970 for Richmond's John F. Kennedy High School, he thought of the September morning four years before when he and she had walked toward the entrance.

"It means we are adults, voters, leaders of today," the valedictorian told her peers. "We're becoming society. We are society. We've got the whole world in our hands. What can we do about it?"

As the two approached the school, a photographer stepped forward and snapped the picture, seen next day on front pages across America, of a Southern governor escorting his daughter to a public school that was 92 percent black.

"We as today's youth realize that there are many problems in this world yet to be solved," said the valedictorian. "Each of us has his own special interest and through these interests we can improve life through society."

Other Southern governors sent their children to private schools, and the Richmond School Board told the Holtons that, living in Capitol Square on state property, they could send their children to any public school they pleased. They accepted assignments to heavily integrated ones. "We told them," said the governor, "our children are going to do what the law says for them to do."

"Open housing holds a special meaning for us because we

know it can work," said the valedictorian. "Therefore it is our opportunity ... to prove the success of open housing by promoting it, live it, practice it, preach it. We can make favorable changes in this world merely by spreading the news of our experiences."

"Accompanying the children to school wasn't unusual," said the governor. "We'd been doing that for years. Even during the campaigns I'd go down with them some. I took her to school the first day in the first grade. We walked eight blocks, and I watched her cross the street and go up the steps into that big schoolhouse. So it was perfectly natural for us and the children. When a child gets into a new situation, she gets an assist from her parents."

"Cancer is another problem that affects all of society," said the valedictorian. "'Every day people we love and admire are struck by this crippling disease. Even Virginia's former Lt. Gov. Sargeant Reynolds ... was deprived of his life at its most productive and vital stage by cancer. Is it to remain that way? Each of us can make some contributions ... from crusading for a charitable organization to researching a medical cure."

At John F. Kennedy's entrance they were met by the colonel of the Cadets Corps, a tall black youth in resplendent white uniform. "Governor," he said, "we're delighted to have your daughter at this school, and she will be welcome here."

"Criminal justice is yet another problem in need of transition today," said the valedictorian. "A rich man walks away from a crime, and a poor man serves years in jail. It's not fair, and we can change it. There are many opportunities for changing this system, but the important thing is: Get involved."

"I just can't tell you how much it meant to me and to her to be met at the door by that senior," said the governor.

"Just as we have faced challenges in the past, we shall encounter in the future many, many opportunities for transition through social advances," said the valedictorian. "Of course, we know that we can't solve all of the world's problems, but each of us should strive individually to help find solutions for some of them."

"The experience was rewarding for all three children," said the governor. "Without their saying anything about it, you could see their confidence growing."

"If we bear this in mind and remain certain of our goal to produce some beneficial transition in some field, years from now we will be able to look back on our lives and be proud to live, " said the valedictorian, Virginia Tayloe Holton.

A Clarion Call

As a boy, encouraged by his mother, Gov. J. Lindsay Almond Jr. read and memorized passages from "Plutarch's Lives." He cherished the story of stuttering Demosthenes, "who put pebbles in his mouth to rage against the sea and build a great voice."

Young Almond declaimed not to billows but to turkey gobblers, he told me. "My mother raised Mammoth Bronze, the nearest things to wild ones. Unless the turkeys were observed acutely during laying season, crows would find and break up their nests. I would follow the flock into the forest.

"They were very alert and didn't want to disclose their nests. Sometimes they would sit in the woods for hours, the sunlight beating down on the sheen of their bronze feathers, and I'd keep an eye on 'em and declaim to the trees.

"Out in the forest alone, with no one to interfere — the turkeys didn't object, but sometimes a squirrel barked at me — I'd declaim "The Drummer Boy of Waterloo" and old songs, like one that began "She was born in old Kentucky/where the meadow grass is blue/There's the sunshine of the country/in her face and manner, too.' "

He went with his father electioneering around the county and at 16 began making speeches for his father's favorite candidates.

Patrick Henry was his idol. His liberty-or-death speech surpasses Churchill's rousing ones during World War II, Almond said..

Henry delivered it on March 23, 1775, to the Virginia Convention in Richmond's little St. John's Church.

And Almond, at my urging, delivered it one day to a tape recorder in his office. As he emoted, a crowd gathered, unknown to us, in the outer office.

Noting British troop movements in America, Almond-Henry declared, "Has Great Britain any enemy in this quarter of the world to call for all this ac-cu-mu-la-shun of navies and armies? No, sir, she has NONE. They are meant for US! They are sent over to bind and rivet upon us those chains which the British ministry has been so long forging."

(At this point during the broadcast a week later, WRNL Radio received a call from a bewildered listener who had just tuned in. "Is Lindsay Almond declaring war on Great Britain?" he asked.)

In dashing to the phone the listener no doubt missed the passage in which Almond declared: "We have done everything that could be done to avert the storm which is now coming on. We have pe-ti-SHUND. We have re-MOHN-strat-ed. We have sup-li-ca-ted. We have pros-trated ourselves before the THRONE!"

He caressed each syllable of the long words and deepened his voice at THRONE so that the listener well nigh saw the hateful thing.

"They tell us," continued Almond, "that we are weak ... but when shall we be stronGAH!" He poured strength into the last syllable. "Will it be next week, or next year? Will it be when we are totally disarmed and when a British GYAHD shall be stationed in ev'ry house?"

Now Almond-Henry was launched into the peroration: "Gentlemen cry peace, peace — but there is no peace! The war is actually begun! The next gale that sweeps from the north will bring to our ears the clash of sounding arms! Our brethren are already in the field! WHY STAND WE HERE IDLE?"

He uttered each of the last five words as if it were a question standing alone, stark, with the longest pause before "idle." The silence put a searing condemnation on that final word.

Now he was building again: "What is it that the gentlemen wish? What would they have? Is life so de-AH or peace so sweet" — he fairly hissed sweet — "as to be purchased at the price of chains and slavery?"

Nearing the top now he shouted: "FOR-BID IT, AL-MIGHTY GOD!"

And then climbing rapidly to the last peak, he cried: "I-know-not-what-course-others-may-take" — Almond actually said "m'take" in his rush to the summit — 'BUT AS FOR ME-E-E," — he was shouting now — "GIVE ME LI-BER-TE-E-E OR GIVE ME DEATH!"

Almond was leaning back in his chair when a burst of applause erupted from the audience lured by his clarion call throughout the third floor of the Capitol to eavesdrop in the outer office.

"ENCORE!" they yelled.

Opening Books — And Doors

Around Patrick County word was that young Jerry Baliles was the only person who had read every book in the public library. "That wasn't true," Gov. Gerald L. Baliles said the other day, "but I read most of 'em. When I was 7 or 8, my grandparents would come up to my room to cut out the light and say good- night, and then they'd come back a few minutes later and pull back the covers, and I'd be reading with a flashlight.

"We'd come in from working in the fields and my grandfather would take a nap after lunch and I'd slip off under a tree and read a book until they'd come yelling to take me back to work. I was the only one in the county for whom the bookmobile made a special stop, thanks to a charming, wonderful person, Lady Louise Clark. She promoted the tour of the bookmobile and generally paused at country stores or gas stations. The closest one to us was about a mile and a half away but the bookmobile stopped on the road in front of our house. I guess she just took pity on me, lugging books home in my little wagon.

"A borrower could take as many as 15 books, and so I'd get my brother and a friend and go through the shelves and pick up 15 for each of us and walk out with 45 books for the next six weeks. My grandfather didn't like television, which, in a way, was good for me; it gave me more time with books. In reading, you conjure up the scenes from the words. It requires imagination. With television, your mind is not stimulated to that degree.

"What did I read? Everything! I read the Leatherstocking Tales and biographies of the early presidents and explorers,

Hannibal crossing the Alps, a great many South Sea adventure stories, with freighters going to Shanghai. I was aboard. Geography fascinated me. When I read about a strange place, I'd pull out a map and find it. It helped me understand politics later, gave me a sense of the movement of peoples, tribes, nations."

So it was his experience with opening doors through books that piqued the governor's interest when, inspecting a minimum-security prison, he noticed a television set by each bed. "How in the world do you keep peace and quiet in here?" he asked the warden.

"Television's a privilege," the warden said. "If you want TV, you have to get an earplug."

"If television's a privilege, why not say that an individual, if he wants television a month, has to read a book a month?"

The warden laughed. "Yes, I guess you could, but half these guys can't read."

"Why don't they go to class for remedial programs?" the governor asked.

"There's a thing called peer pressure. If an individual tries to better himself, he is, in some instances, called a sissy and browbeaten."

So on the road back to Richmond the governor sketched on a yellow legal pad the idea for a program to encourage prisoners to learn to read. The key to motivating them, he said, is that they'll do something if they think it will enhance their chances for parole. And so he proposed that anyone who was illiterate would be allowed to learn to read and that it would be factored into his qualifications for parole. Those who could already read could work one-on-one with those who couldn't. He persuaded the General Assembly to appropriate $1 million for the program and sent out a call for volunteer teachers.

"If it works, you may find a way of breaking the cycle of recidivism," Baliles said. "Many prisoners, who are jailed repeatedly, can't read and write well enough to function on the outside. If a person can't fill out a job application or follow simple instructions, it's unlikely he will be able to obtain or retain employment. So he resorts to the one career option that doesn't require a job application. He commits a crime and goes back to prison — and that's costly to us in terms of tragic consequences as well as just finances."

He reverted in his thoughts to the boy reading in shade and laying aside the book to go back to work: "In those hot fields, looking up at airplanes flying over, I'd vow that I'd be doing that one day. And now, flying across the state, I look down, especially in rural areas, and wonder if some child down there is looking up and making the same vow that I did."

Run For Office? Never!

Driving away after covering in a Richmond hotel a luncheon speech in 1950 by Ohio Sen. Robert Taft, I paused to offer a ride to three black youths at the bus stop.

They waited tables at the hotel while attending Virginia Union University. Taft was campaigning for president, striving to win the Republican nomination at the 1952 national convention in Chicago.

The jaunty young man at my side was troubled by Taft's speech.

"You heard it?" I asked.

"I always listen." he said. He was a chemistry major fascinated with current events.

Once the tables were cleared, waiters could go to the locker room; but he always stayed "to hear what was said without waiting to read it in the newspapers. It's interesting."

How had Taft disturbed him?

"He was telling what he felt he had in common with most people in the South. He let them know that a vote for him was for what they hold dear. He said that the states should be left alone to deal with problems without any interference from the federal government.

"Despite changes taking place all around the country, he was telling them things were going to be all right and not to worry if he became president. There would be no change."

It struck me the student did a better job conveying the core of Taft's message than I had done in a great deal more words.

"If it troubles you, why don't you do something about it?" I asked.

"What?" he asked.

"Get into politics. Run for office."

"Never! No way!"

"Why not?

"Because politicians talk out of both sides of their mouth and it appears to me that many of them are crooks. They won't tell the truth. That's not for me."

We reached Virginia Union. As the three were walking across the campus, I called to the young man hungry for the truth. "What's your name?"

He turned, smiling.

"Doug Wilder," he said.

L. Douglas Wilder, serving in the Korean War, won a Bronze

Star for clearing a bunker of North Koreans. At home again, he went to law school, won a race for the Virginia Senate, and then won again for lieutenant governor and won election as governor in 1989.

Years later, recalling our conversation of 1950, he said he hoped young peopole were not as dissuaded from politics as he had felt. "Luckily for me, you and then other people asked that rhetorical question which I often use with youths: Why don't you run for office rather than criticize and complain?"

But sometimes, he said, he had a sense of deja vu, a feeling that things were much as they had always been.

"Now and then Virginians change," I noted. "They did when they elected the grandson of a slave to be their governor."

Chapter Seven

Of Maestros and Minstrels

Well, Hello, Louis

Stripped to the massive waist with its sagging brown folds, a large white handkerchief tied around his head, Louis Armstrong peered into the mirror as seriously as an artist about to do a self-portrait. He was a day shy of 65.

The night before he had been up until morning, blowing the trumpet at the Virginia Beach Dome, ballooning like a genie out of his small shoes, performing four encores of "Hello, Dolly," his shoulders flopping on the last one like a wounded bird, his great mouth shouting out every fourth word between fast mops of the handkerchief, his whole face shaking on the final note as if it would fall apart.

Even in the Dome, however, there had been a sense of an easy pacing of himself when he shuffled to the back of the stage to pick up another handkerchief, as casually as a man walking about the living room after a long day, never lifting his feet from the floor, just sliding them along, an old bear roaming around at the rear of the stage.

In the shadows, his face went as impassive as an old coconut, his eyes mere dumb dark spots, his mouth a wide, sad fold, but then the spotlight fell on him, and the face split and spilled again the milk of human kindness in the great, white grin as he moved forward and raised the rich orange horn to his lips.

"I have my rest," he said, looking in the mirror, spreading the white lather over his face. "I go through the same routine. I gotta go through this shaving every day," he said, enjoying the shaving, "even when I'm home." He dabbed on more lather, and considered, briefly, why people were so fond of him.

"I'm so fond of people," he said. "I always give 'em a show.

139

You know —" he turned from the mirror, the lather still on one cheek, and spreading his arms wide, one hand still holding the razor, he roared in that gravel voice: "HERE WE ARE, FOLKS. LET'S KEEP 'EM ROLLING WITH SOME OF THE GOOD OLD GOOD ONES!

"All over the world it's the same. A note's a note and don't need no interpreter. That's the way it is in Africa. In Leopoldville they stopped fighting four days to dig our concerts. They even gave us a concert.

"Even behind the curtains, no different. People are all the same. If I had 10 billion dollars, I'd be the same. I wasn't brought up on caviah-h-h and never had a steak until I came North. But my soul food will always be with me."

He turned from the mirror again, and, in a list that became a litany, he said: "Red beans ... ham hocks ... pig feets ... greens-s-zzz ... grits-szzz ... rice-s-zzz. There are places, they don't know what soul food looks like. I go along — steak, chicken, chops, lobster, fish — for the sake of my stomach. It's filling. But twice a week, I've got to have some soul food. My wife don't care for it. She worries about her weight, but I can blow it down.

"And then, too," he added, "I always have my SwisKris — " and he paused to hand me a green-bordered tiny packet of a powdered laxative — which I pocketed and still have in a bureau drawer somewhere. "It works," he said.

Half a century ago, Armstrong began playing in New Orleans when the superintendent of the Waif's Home gave him a bugle. That led to a cornet in honky-tonks, on boats and at funerals, and that to the trumpet after he joined Joe "King" Oliver in Chicago.

"Couldn't nobody get me outta New Orleans except the King. When I got off the train in Chicago, I was late, and he had gone back to work. I was scared and started to go right home, but a redcap put me in a cab. When I got out of the cab, I would hear the band playing so good, wailing so high, that I said: "Man, I ain't gon' go in there. That band is too good for me!' But someone told Joe I was outside, and he sent for me, and said, 'This is your place, come on in yere'."

Friday night he had sung a hit from the late 20's — "My only sin is in my skin, to be so black and blue" — and as he shuddered comically and walled his eyes, the audience laughed, but with him, not at him, because long ago the trouble ceased to belong to any one man and became everybody's, and it was a relief to find that somebody was still left who could laugh at it. What about all that, Louis?

He wiped a final dab of lather off his face. "It ain't for that," he said. "I just go on and do the tune. Musically, I do it. Music is a wonderful thing. You saw them little kids come in last night after the show. That's why I 'preciate music. It's nice you can still be around. Not many has the chance to meet two or three generations and still have a ball."

Making Music With Her Hands

To awaken a person to classical music, persuade him or her to attend a concert directed by JoAnn Faletta. A friend did that for me.

Faletta, who gives herself wholly to the music — swaying one moment, Ariel flying along a cresting wave, then Prospero commanding the tempest — achieves a visual dimension not often seen.

My wish was that when she took the Virginia Symphony to Carnegie Hall that the staging be rearranged a bit. Let the 85 orchestra members sit in the pit — raised a few feet — and bring Faletta stage front to face the audience while she conducts, treating all to the bewitchery of her leading the orchestra with all her body and mind.

Even without that complete exposure, New York critics found it superb, as did 1,000 Virginians who attended. The airline added flights.

"Every orchestra, when it's ready to prove itself, must go to Carnegie Hall," Faletta said before the performance. "This is the first time for most of them to play there. Artistically they are playing at a very high level. I never would have believed when I came five years ago it would sound as it does today. So they really are ready!"

She glows at the challenge.

Striding into the office, she is a crisp, young executive. But answering questions about her symphony, she's the artist conducting conversation as she would an orchestra.

During a concert, she noted, "We can't say a word to each other. All of it is through signals, gestures, eye contact, motions, body language. For two hours we are talking to each other constantly without saying a word. I can think of no other situation where a group works together and doesn't speak."

No wonder when she talks, her hands and body are moving, eliciting response. She leans forward to tap a finger on the table, touches it with the tips of four fingers, lifts her hands in a gathering motion, extends them, thrusting away. She leans back, nods, sways, pushes her right hand in her black curls. Her eyes squint in amusement. Her lips purse in mischief.

Of Maestros and Minstrels

Amid the torrent of words, the reporter is caught up with the shifting play of her features, the smiles, a rare grimace, the lifting of a shoulder, an eyebrow arched, a shrug, a knitting of the brow, a flashing gaming grin.

She pauses, raises an eyebrow, and he blurts: "Did you ever take acting lessons?" She laughs. She's been accused of talking with her hands, she says, "an Italian family thing."

"All of you moves," the reporter notes.

She holds stock still, arms locked at her sides to stay motionless, but as she talks, conveying feeling for the symphony, eyelids widen and the big, dark eyes roll like the large shooter marbles of childhood.

"You know what I think it says? I think in talking about music, even though I've been conducting now 15 years, it's still for me very exciting. I hope I feel that way when I'm 90."

The reporter hopes the board extends her contract 'til then.

"It's almost overwhelming to be in front of an orchestra. The collective years of their study is mind-boggling. If you added up all that time just in learning instruments, it would be hundreds of years.

"We've been very lucky. The chemistry between the musicians has been beautiful. They work so well together. They respect and appreciate each other's talent.

"And when we're on the stage at the Carnegie, I think that somehow our audience will know that. Besides the artistry they hear, they will be able to see a group of people of all ages with one heart and one soul — and that's unusual."

In 1985, Faletta was commuting between New York, where she was a Julliard student, and the Denver Chamber Orchestra, which she led — "a crazy and wonderful time." She entered the Stokowsky Conducting Competition, survived the winnowing of 250 contenders and won when the five finalists conducted at

Carnegie Hall the American Symphony in selections from 10 master works.

"I was in a little bit of a cloud the whole time. I realized afterward how it was an official stamp by the judges that a woman can conduct."

It was, she says, "a turning point." As a prize, she conducted the American Symphony in a concert at the Carnegie and then became associate conductor of the Milwaukee Symphony. Now at another turn she will go to the Carnegie with the Virginia Symphony. She has conducted there several times, "but this one means so much to me — my own orchestra, in which I take great pride and with which I have worked a long time."

In a full house at the Carnegie everything came together. It couldn't have turned out better. Fully a third of the audience was from Virginia, a vote of love and confidence. The reviews were glowing.

"In Hampton Roads, when I talk with businessmen, the heads of corporations, and speak at civic clubs and schools, we find a much higher interest in the Virginia Symphony. We hope many more people are beginning to realize what an extraordinary orchestra they have."

A Vote for the Real Elvis

A pollster at the post office asked, as I tottered out from mailing my income tax, for which Elvis I'd voted in the balloting for a new stamp.

Of Maestros and Minstrels

"Neither. Who's winning?"

"The young one," he said. "Nobody's voting for old Elvis."

I wheeled, went inside, and asked for a ballot with the two Elvises. A pleasant clerk helped me vote. I haven't been able to vote alone since we were put at machines. What threw me this time was a line of tiny squares in which to print my name. I went about it with the care of a talented chimpanzee, murmuring to my tutor, "What ever happened to the secret ballot?"

She pointed out that I need sign it only if I wished for more data on Elvis. So I quit midway and she showed me where to mark the ballot for the elder Elvis. "There!" she said as I finished. My vote went to old Elvis because of a moment remembered from his last concert. Baggy-eyed from taking uppers and downers, bloated from dissipation, he moved, encased in leather, as if he were in a diving suit 20,000 leagues under the sea. But the voice was there. The tumultuous applause, the fiercest fix, energized him. When an ovation thundered on, he glanced sideways at somebody offstage in the wings, his lip curling in an insolent grin that said, "I still have it!"

Elvis was on TV Friday night in "forgotten" tapes, including his first. At 18, just out of high school, he went in a shop and recorded for his mother "My Happiness."

"When the skies are gray, not blue" .... it begins. The record is tinny, his voice high-pitched, but a time or two it verges on deepening into his signature sound. Home movies showed his mother, ample, soft-faced, yet enduring in her large features. His father's face seemed anguished. Elvis had a twin who died. To think of a pair opens a vista down a path not taken. Film of Elvis entering the Army, being examined, boarding ship, shows him edgy as any recruit, all the more under the unrelenting lens.

Emceeing the documentary, his former wife, Priscilla, showed commendable restraint. On film she was a dimpled, dark-haired 16-year-old left behind in Germany when he returned home after a year or so in the Army. Now she is thin-faced, severe, her red hair cut short.

A clip with Milton Berle depicts Elvis in a slow, stylized, funny strut singing "Hound Dog." It drew 700,000 pieces of "pan mail." With Sinatra, he compensated by mimicking the astonished skinny crooner. "Everybody was hollering because I was wiggling my legs," he said after censors cut film below his waist. Asked if the crowd's hysteria invoked his responses, Elvis said, "I'm aware of everything I do at all times. It's just the way I feel."

He broke into a chorus as if he were shot from a cannon.

"This is a real, decent, fine boy," said Ed Sullivan, putting his arm around him. "We've never had a a pleasanter experience than we've had with you." But many disagreed. The stress was intense. An early band member said: "If he didn't sleep, we didn't sleep. We'd walk him down the road to wear him out." Later, drugs took over. His momma died while he was in the Army. Had she been there when he returned, he might have done better:

"... any place on earth will do,
just as long as I'm with you, my happiness."

Used Up

Three days ago, if you had asked me who Jerry Garcia was, I'd have said, instantly, a defensive lineman in the National Football League, probably with the Green Bay Packers. Garcia already had cast his sway over a cult of music lovers into their fourth decade, a mix of all sorts in their 20s, 30s and 40s.

Since his death from a heart attack in a drug rehab center, those in their 50s, 60s and even antic 70s are aware he led the Grateful Dead. The group developed a way of attracting a family of followers ranging from hippies of the 1960s to coat-and-tie careerists of the 1990s.

The band was lavish in playing long after other bands would have shut down. One devotee spoke on public radio of its creating "a moment that went on five hours." Another noted that the Grateful Dead had given 10 benefit concerts for the schools of Marin County in California. Admirers speak of the music's optimism and spontaneity.

Instead of banning taping equipment at concerts, the band installed recording "trees" into which deadheads could plug recorders. Brisk trading of tapes assured that at each arena not a seat went unsold. One who has kept attuned to music since the mid-1960s said that unlike bands that distort sound through heavy-handed amplifying, the Grateful Dead sought clarity.

"The crowd," he said, "wasn't disruptive. Fans were laid-back listening and communing. They just kind of hung out, a hippie version of a cocktail party. The band was nearly a backdrop in the stadium. The focus was more dispersed than it was when everybody was riveted on the Rolling Stones."

What with drugs, endless concerts and partying, riding buses with little sleep, no exercise, it was not a healthy lifestyle at best, and if a person became inured to the worst, it was destructive.

"Where a normal person had 10 or 20 parties a year, the band had that many in a month. Garcia wore out his body; he used it up."

One fan said that Garcia's withdrawal to a rehab center was a message to his followers. It was belated, tragically. Other rock stars are discovering that use of drugs is disastrous. One after another is cleaning up, and their performances are as good or better not only in technical proficiency but also in creativity in going in new directions, he said.

Aerosmith, enforcing all-clear tours even to roadies who set up the stage, "is at the top of its form." Eric Clapton is having his greatest success. Mick Jagger is as fit as an aerobics instructor. Younger groups who haven't cleaned up are "degenerating into mush."

As are some young fans. Ambushed by the myth that drugs are hep, they come to grief. An abbreviated life is a horrific price for artificial stimulants in a phony setting. Even as lifespans rise, some youths, blinded by glitz, cut theirs short. It mocks the sweet music.

Towering Violinist

Violinist Yehudi Menuhin, 52, played in Norfolk this week and received the sort of stormy ovation he has been drawing since he made his debut at age 10 in Carnegie Hall — crashing, standing applause from the first floor, with muffled bravos from the gallery, like the shouts of lost souls wandering around Dismal Swamp.

Standing in front of the orchestra, waiting to begin, holding the bow lowered in his right hand, a sword, the violin in his left, a buckler, he looks like D'Artagnan of the Three Musketeers. After the concert — Brahams' Concerto in D Major for Violin and Orchestra, Opus 77, which has the violin taking on the whole orchestra, D'Artagnan fending off the Cardinal's Guards — a member of the orchestra approached Menuhin reverently back-stage and said, "It was a pleasure playing against you, sir."

But then because the stalwart figure is so ruddy and broadchested, you think of a Viking, and a prow of a nose, a big, uplifting chin, and brilliant blue eyes. He towers on the stage. About him is an air of command, enough quiet confidence to encompass the company.

At the start of a passage, only a few seconds along, Menuhin stopped, lowered the violin, murmured to Conductor Russell Stanger, plinked the violin string three or four times, as if setting a pitch, and then nodded to Stanger, who had the orchestra begin again. Most of the audience and some among the players concluded that an instrument in the orchestra had been off-key. Anyway, all recovered nobly.

In the first movement is a cadenza, rife with double stops, and during these runs of simultaneous notes, the Stradivarius seemed to be answering Menuhin, on its own.

Backstage he accepted congratulations, signed programs and beamed about him like a child on Christmas morning. Gone was the giant; instead, he was almost elfin, scarcely taller than two or three children among the group of admirers. Many performers hurry away; not Menuhin. He stood at the door of his dressing room and listened, laughed and answered questions until the last fan left.

Was the unabashed response of the Norfolk audience unusual?

"Not in my experience," he said. "I enjoy the give and take, perhaps because I've heard so much Indian music, in which the audience participates.

"I must say," he added, smiling, a look of mischief about his eyes, "the atmosphere in this hall with the audience, wrapped up in the music, is something you don't sense when you walk down the main street."

Audiences differ, he said, and cited two, back-to-back, in Fargo, N.D., and in a suburban town near Chicago. The suburbanites drew up in station wagons, and the farmers came in old cars.

Which did he prefer?

"The farmers!"

They appreciated, he said, the unpredictable, "because they live with the weather and still have contact with nature." He had the feeling that the suburbanites, whose world runs on schedule, "would have liked to switch the dial."

A high school student, Chris Wall of First Colonial, asked him his favorite conductor.

"You put me on the spot," protested Menuhin, smiling, and then listed several: Zubin Mehta, Colin Davis, Furtwangler.

What was his first musical memory?

"Let me see now," he put his hand to his brow. "When was it?"

He paused to autograph an album, and then said: "I know .... my mother singing. And then, right after, and then, I, singing. At the age of 2, 1, 3..."

When did he first hear the violin?

"When I was taken to concerts, at 3 or 4."

And when did he first wish to play it?

"As soon as I heard the violin, I wanted to play the violin."

How much does he practice?

"I like to practice a minimum of two hours a day, and very often more."

Does he enjoy it?

"I refuse not to enjoy anything. I must enjoy what I do."

An admirer pressed forward to thank him and marvel at his

"wonderful family," which includes two sisters, Hephzibah and Yaltah, both fine pianists, and a fledging pianist in his 16-year-old son, Jeremy.

"It's a nice family," said Menuhin.

Had someone been off-key during the brief interruption in the concert?

"The A-string peg slipped on my violin. The weather here is drier than my violin has been accustomed to."

Outside the rain was pouring, and had been, all evening.

A Brave Van

A 156-voice choir and an 88-piece orchestra performed Saturday at the funeral in Fort Worth, Texas, for Rildia Bee O'Bryan Cliburn, 97, the mother, best friend, manager and first teacher of pianist Van Cliburn. He won the heart of America when the Soviets judged him best in the 1958 Tchaikovsky competition in Moscow.

A memorable sight was roly-poly Nikita Khrushchev rushing toward the tall youth with a dandelion puffball of blond curls. That the Soviets hadn't rigged it for one of their own astounded us. Thanks to their appreciation, Van Cliburn became an idol of even those of us whose musical taste stops at "Chopsticks."

Not long after conquering Moscow, he came to Norfolk — and came on stage in a rapid stroll, leonine head slightly back, riding broad shoulders, hands big as fielders' mitts. He sat well back from the keyboard, tails from his formal suit dropping straight behind him, folded wings on a stately insect, a praying mantis. He ate up that piano.

He drew a standing ovation and a second crowd at his dressing room. Inside, he had time for one question: his first musical memory. "When I was 3, I remember playing the piano, but before that I remember hearing music. I don't remember any day in my life there wasn't music. When I was 5 I told the family I wanted to be a concert pianist."

His mother, he said, had worked on a committee to bring Rachmaninoff to Shreveport. "I had heard his recording on the phonograph, you know, the old Victrola. Even then I knew, I could feel his great presence."

Soon after Rachmaninoff's visit, the child announced at lunch: "I want more than anything else to be a concert pianist."

The family pooh-poohed the notion. His father wanted him to be a doctor. His mother, whose own parents forbade her to become a concert pianist, "wanted me to be whatever I wanted to be."

After the Norfolk concert, Van Cliburn went out to sign autographs in the admiring throng, talking easily, looking down from a great height with amused blue eyes. In the dressing room, his mother recalled how she first heard him play. "I dismissed my pupil for the day and went in the kitchen, when I heard the piece being played again — it was Crawford's 'Arpeggio Waltz' — and I went back in to tell the boy he could go, and it was Van."

She told the 3-year-old: "It shows talent that you have the ear to play by rote, but you can learn to play yourself."

And proceeded to teach him.

In the eulogy Saturday, broadcaster Paul Harvey said that, before going on his most recent concert to Denver, Van Cliburn prayed as usual with his mother, but for the first time she added to the prayer: "God make Van brave."

With such a one, he couldn't help but be.

Velvet Voices

Mel Torme dropped by Richmond the other day, still whispering melodies as he did a half-century or so ago. They called him then the Velvet Fog, for his huskiness. I thought it was Velvet Frog. Boyish Torme had — and has yet — a sunniness about him, all scrubbed, but with a wide smiling, big-lipped mouth and slightly pop eyes that lent a froggy cast, albeit handsome. Sometimes my mind makes up its mind on impressions that don't jibe with reality, no matter how hard I argue with it.

Torme lifted his voice just above a whisper, a confidential cooing, a murmuring, half-singing, half-talking. Which is why he is still around.

Time's scythe is severest with women vocalists, such as Carol Channing, who belt out every note at their utmost. Their day is short. A talk show amateur tried to imitate Channing. Her voice is in such ruin that nearly anybody can offer a reasonable facsimile. But a viewer who admires her yet was wrathful that any ego-struck ham would dare to offer a reprise of her in decline.

As Macy's recent parade was forming, a TV camera lit on her face and it blossomed in a great glowing sunflower of a smile as she threw a kiss at the lens with both hands and flung wide her arms — still "Hello Dolly!"

Ethel Merman's trumpet of a voice when young could raise the quills on a porcupine; but she stayed beyond her prime. She flung herself into a score as of yore but the trumpet had become a shrieking steam calliope. On a high note, the house vibrated with her vibrato; but to the end she was game.

Best at seeming to sing was that old sweetheart, Perry Como. With a chorus swelling behind him, he would jerk his head or tilt his chin and you would swear he was going all out. Oh, he sang "Old Black Magic" full tilt, but it was a tour de force. Usually he was a hum-along.

Near the end of his skein, Como walked on stage for a PBS show. That's all, just walked, but that slight, jaunty, tousled gent with the dancing eyes, crinkly smile and courtly gesture drew a standing ovation that usually ends a concert. All without a note! The ultimate for a silent singer.

Some songs perpetuate the singer. Bing Crosby gradually faded to only an annual Christmas show, bantering more with his family than singing, except for "White Christmas" near the end, which welcomed home GIs.

Frank Sinatra does more stamping around than singing, as in "New York, New York, " where he can shout the lyrics. Tony Bennett excels yet at "San Francisco," which should assure him the key to that city though he may misplace the key here and there in other songs.

Best of them was Nat King Cole. His voice, were he here, would be as strong as ever; but he died of throat cancer from smoking. That habit perhaps exposed some of the tension beneath his smooth, effortless style as he wrought his charm on a segregated society. No one, old or new, can ever touch King Cole.

Cool Duke

"I've been listening to you 40 years," said the bespectacled man, handing Edward Kennedy Ellington a program to sign.

"Oh, good, don't stop now," murmured the Duke.

154

Of Maestros and Minstrels

It's not likely there'll ever be a time when someone isn't listening to the music of Duke Ellington, as they did Saturday at the Virginia Beach Dome. The band came on first, and then the Duke, in a casual, royal stroll. He always comes on quiet. He was cool before teen-agers found the word, not the cool that is blase, nor bored, nor scared, but the cool that is aware, the quiet aliveness of a man of 67 who is watching, weighing, savoring every note.

It's the cool of a man who can brush the piano keys with a touch light as dust and direct his big, driving band with a raised eyebrow, a lift of the chin, a soft finger snap ("Don't push it, let it fall"), a glance.

Backstage at intermission a fan said the musicians must be highly disciplined. "The one thing we don't have is discipline," said the Duke. "The idea is to try to create something they enjoy playing. Then you don't have to worry about discipline. It's a very American spirit, freedom of expression."

At one point he stood to the side, a trifle slumped, arms hanging loosely, and directed the band with slight movements of his body, a boy riding a bike, no hands. He knows it so well, and the big band is so responsive, that he has refined directing to quick abstractions, touching just the essential points. His conversation, too, is light satire, aimed mainly at himself, occasionally at the passing scene, but never at the expense of the person to whom he is talking.

Last year, the Advisory Board of the Pulitzer Prize Committee rejected a unanimous recommendation from its music jury for a special citation for the Duke. Two jurors quit but Ellington sighed: "Fate's been kind to me. Fate doesn't want me to be too famous too young."

"You can't allow yourself to be overwhelmed by this negative business," he said backstage. "Without optimism, what you do is nothing."

His dress, too, is always cool and blue. In the concert's first half, he wore a dark-patterned blue smoking jacket, and in the last, a luminous, powder-blue sport coat and slacks and dark blue shirt. He was all elegance, and has been from the time he was 15 and worked as a soda jerk in Washington, D.C. They began calling him 'Duke,' he said, because he was so "prideful of the stiff, starched uniform I used to wear on my job."

When Ellington sat down at the piano near intermission and played "Mood Indigo," and led the band with occasional quick, slashing, horizontal strokes, the white cuffs flashing, he was like a painter, an old master, successful, sure of himself, brushing in the design and the figure, and the band before him was both palette and canvas. Color runs riot in his music.

When I mentioned that to him, he leaned forward, intently, and said, "My first recognized talent was painting. When I was in high school, I won a scholarship to the Pratt Institute. I was very good, I confess it. I admit it."

But music had him. The 15-year-old soda jerk took to sitting in for a piano player who generally faded around midnight. By 16, the Duke had such local renown that "I had to study some music to protect my reputation.

"The things I wanted to do weren't in books, and I had to ask a lot of questions. I was lucky enough to always run into those who had the answers."

There's money in music, he said, "but I have fun, and that's the main thing," and by fun he means: "If I write something tonight I have to hear it tomorrow, and so I keep a band so I can play it."

And Saturday night he played the new, "Ad Lib on Nippon,"

a tone poem from his tour of Japan, and his old compositions called standards because they are just that, high marks against which other musicians can measure: "Sophisticated Lady," "Don't Get Around Much Anymore," "I Got It Bad (And That Ain't Good)," "In a Sentimental Mood," "Do Nothing 'Til You Hear From Me," "Caravan," "I'm Beginning to See the Light," "Satin Doll," "I Didn't Know about You..."

"I have relived my life," announced a middle-aged man, as the audience was leaving.

My wish was that the younger ones, and especially my own, could have heard the artistry of it. My only regular, continuing concern is to put them next to the best, the genuine ones.

"I'd like the teen-agers who go for that mop-haired music to hear you," I told the Duke in parting.

"We're here!" said someone, and I turned and saw three of them, sunburned, gangling, grinning: Dale Wiley, Peter Pastore and Mark Nemuth, all of Richmond. I said I thought their set preferred the wailing guitarists.

"Are you kidding ...?"

"They're all fakes ..."

"Nothing but chords ..."

"I'm almost ashamed of the teen-age population ..."

"No band on earth can or ever can or ever has been able to play like this one ..."

Take the A-Train!

Chapter Eight

On and Off the Field

Two Foes Fell

Joe Louis came along and from the first big bout we knew he was special. Every generation or so produces such a fighter, and seldom two together, which promotes arguments as to how Jack Dempsey would have done against Louis and Louis against Ali. Those who have seen all three lean to Louis.

So well-proportioned that though he stood more than 6 feet 1 and weighed 190, he looked lithe, even slight, dismantling the opposition, shuffling, left foot edging forward, so that the feet, nearly flat to the canvas, were platforms for the big guns that would set loose a barrage, the lethal, left jab – give him just this much of an opening, they used to marvel, holding their hands about six inches apart, and that was enough – and if not that, then the crunching straight right.

More of a boxer than Dempsey, who wasn't much more than a brawler, not so swift of foot as Ali, Louis had hands – oh, those hands – faster than those of any other heavyweight ever, earning him the sobriquet Brown Bomber, a name menacing, smacking at first of race; but his sheer ability silenced any talk of a white hope. Considerations of race were pointless when those short piston strokes worked. Two foes fell, the other one was Jim Crow.

And then, fighting against Max Schmeling, Hitler's ward, the Black Uhlan – what a Black Uhlan was nobody explained - Louis became, in a sudden twist that could happen only in America, the white hope and demolished Schmeling in their second encounter with such furious efficiency as to mock the master race.

After each fight, brought to the mike, he'd say, deadpanned: "Hello, Mumma." That was all. His fists did the job, and then, in the ring, he said what counted most. His words, when he chose to say more to the public, were like the left jabs, short and to the point. "We'll win," he said, of World War II, "because we're on God's side" – not, presumptuously, that God was on our side, but, precisely, because a democracy had chosen to line up right.

Once I interviewed him no more than three minutes, as long as a round. He had checked out of his room, on his way to referee a wrestling match; but he stopped in the hotel lobby in Norfolk. In his good-natured voice, bass viol deep, he said he'd talk until his ride showed.

When did he first aim to box?

"Back in '32. I was 17. I was taking violin lessons – my mother made me – and a friend talked me into going to the gym. I watched him train, and I liked it better than the violin."

What else did he do as a boy?

"In Detroit? I worked mostly on an ice wagon, when I was 16 or 17, carrying 25- and 50-pound blocks."

Before that?

"In Alabama my mother had eight children, and when she remarried, my stepfather had eight, and we all lived under one roof. My mother and father wouldn't leave us at home and we played in the cotton fields. We had a beautiful time in Alabama."

His mother kept a sharp eye on him?

"I think she raised us pretty good. She took a strap on us now and then. We moved to Detroit in 1926. My older brothers and my father went two years ahead of time."

How was Detroit?

"Not too bad. Not too good a school. We scuffled. We were welfare. But I paid it all back."

Could he recall his first bout?

"I sure can. I boxed an Olympic champ and he knocked me

down five or six times, maybe more than that. I didn't do good for a long time, but I finally got myself together."

What fight pleased him most?

"The second one with Schmeling. Because it was more than just another prize fight. It was country against country, race against race – super race and all that junk."

His hardest fight?

"That first one with Billy Conn. He was a good boxer, and he moved around a lot. He was an outstanding fighter, that's all. I couldn't do a thing with him."

What was his greatest strength?

"I imagine my mother. She was with me all the way."

In the Chrysler Museum is a black granite bust of Louis by artist Ruth Yates, donated by the Dudley Cooper. Photographer S.H. Ringo persuaded Louis, during his foray into Norfolk, to pose alongside his likeness, a pair of stone faces. The sculpture's nose and mouth had been rubbed bare, a curator explained to Louis, by children patting it.

A faint smile appeared on Louis' impassive face. "How 'bout that!" stone face said softly.

Ah-LEE! Ah-LEE!

In the Hampton Coliseum the pre-fight entertainment consisted mostly of estimating how far away the television screen was (a football field's length, the man on my right judged) and its size (15 chairs across the bottom, somewhat larger than the huge Stars and Stripes spread overhead, he decided), but, anyway, peering that distance was like looking from the back wall of the dining room, through the hall, to a home movie screen at the far end of the living room.

The Coliseum has housed a variety of extravaganzas, from Mickey Mouse to Lippizans, but Monday night the huge oval had something of a cockpit's closeness, a club fight's atmosphere mainly because of the cigarette smoke. It hung like a pall over skirmishing armies, and steadily thickened to the point that the color screen took on a mellow brown quality, as if time already were tinting the scene for history.

The arena darkened and Muhammad Ali came into focus on the TV screen to proclaim in an interview that although men, like trees and houses, grew old, and he was not what he had been, he was what he was and that was enough to dispose of Joe Frazier. The Coliseum roared and continued the din when Ali appeared on TV in the ring in a white-trimmed red robe, fit for Santa or Old King Cole. Frazier, white-robed, climbed through the ropes to boos.

Through most of the bout, however, the sentiment, at least among those who had no bets, surged back and forth between the superbly conditioned athletes who withheld nothing. The crowd noise in the Coliseum drowned the announcer's voice through the early rounds as Ali jabbed at the rooster-bobbing Frazier who kept coming, as if wound on a perpetual motion spring, taking three and four and more licks to land one.

Long ago, when Ali was Cassius Clay, he sang that he floated like a butterfly and stung like a bee, a light-hearted accurate simile disclosing a poet in the pugilist. Monday night the trouble was that, except for the first round or two, he didn't float but let Frazier bring the fight to him on the ropes where Ali relied on speed of hand and head, which did not suffice.

Frazier slammed lefts and rights to Ali's body with the slick thud of a sledge smacking into a clay bank and the crowd whoofed at the blows. But in the ninth Ali landed three successive rights so that even the black youth two rows up, who had money on Frazier, shouted "Boom! Boom! Boom!"

"Saved by the bell that time, Frazier," a son of Ali yelled.

In slow motion, on instant replay between rounds, Ali, loping across the ring and extending the right full length thrice, could have modeled for a Grecian medal, the discus thrower. But Frazier kept boring through the bee-stings – once he purposely dropped his guard and took several, disdainfully, to the face – and in the 11th he connected with a roundhouse left that knocked Ali bowlegged, and for the first time as Ali staggered back drunkenly, the crowd sensed that he could lose.

"Get on 'im, Joe! Gi'e it to him!" screamed the youth two rows back. "I want to see you nail him BAD!"

Frazier crowded forward, flailing away, and someone was chanting in anguish, "Ah-LEE! Ah-LEE! Ah-LEE!"

But in the 15th in a last spirited effort, Ali came out in a flurry, whereupon Frazier loosed another sling-shot left that dumped the challenger on his back and halfway through a somersault so that his dove-white shoes flashed ceiling-ward, high above his head.

"Dat's de fight!" yelled the young two rows back, "Whoo!"

By four, Ali was on his feet, seeming as stunned by the fact that he had been decked as by the punch itself, as if it were a role he did not know how to play.

Frazier came pounding forward - "He can't take it!" someone screamed - and Ali fell into a clinch. "Turn 'im loose and DANCE!" implored an Ali backer.

"Clay don't wanna turn 'Im loose!" called a Frazierite.

163

The round – and fight – ended.

"Whupped 'im!" said the youth two rows back. The referee made it unanimous.

"I told you he wouldn't fight!" yelled the youth, to nobody and everybody.

And on my left an Ali fan said, in disbelief, "Frazier took him, sonovagun!"

As the crowd crawled out of the Coliseum, like drugged bees, the post-fight analysis continued on the screen. The great majority of the fans, Howard Cosell assured us, had taken the fight in its stride. His fellow commentator, Burt Lancaster, remarked that the world had just seen two great fighters, two men of great character, because if they didn't have character, they could never have gone beyond the early rounds.

And over and over, in slow motion, as the commentators jabbered, the screen continued to replay the knockdown, Frazier launching a wide-swinging, crunching left, as if slinging a stone, his fist looping high and finding Ali's jaw and coming down, his body twisting with the effort, nearly to the floor, and Ali going back, back, back, tumbling to the canvas, and his huge sneaker-feet, pallid, clown-white, propelling high over his head, tossing surf, and then Ali getting up slowly, only to be tumbled again, as if the camera were intent on his taking a shattering fall, over and over, for every taunt he had hurled in society's face.

Spectators milled in the lobby. In one group an African-American teenager re-enacted round by round the highlights for three other youths and a man in his 50s. He re-created the fight, down to Ali's crumpling fall, and the man laughed softly at the excitement of the youths, one of whom, his hands shoved in his coat pockets, did a continuous up-and-down jog, and two others, as the script demanded, portrayed either Ali or Frazier. After the second run-through, one yelled, in ecstasy, "I'm not going to work in the morning! Ain't no way I can GO to WORK!"

They moved, finally, across the nearly deserted parking-lot, falling against each other, waving their arms, laughing, a wavering, staggering knot on the vast, paved, arc-lit stage.

Enduring in Style

It was almost impossible for anybody to hate Arthur Ashe Jr. What a strange — and wonderful — warrior he has been against injustice! Surely none has been any more patient, calm, composed — or more dedicated and unyielding in principle than Ashe when he took a stand. His face had a watchful, even slightly plaintive look, as if he expected the worst but was confident of doing his best with whatever came his way. In rare smiles, he seemed most vulnerable. And after Ashe worked out a burden privately, he felt compelled to share his discovery with the public. He was self-effacing, almost reclusive, but he felt a duty to try to right a wrong even if it took a trip to South Africa to expose apartheid.

In tennis, Ashe came of age in the era of the brat. To rev up, some players flew into rages that would disgrace a 4-year-old. He never threw a racket, railed at a ref, cursed a fan, or gloated over a foe. Win or lose, he commended his opponents. He never alibied. He found fault in himself, not the stars. Captaining a U.S. Davis Cup team, troubled at the behavior of John McEnroe and teammates, he warned them to shape up or he would forfeit the match.

Ashe needed no spur to whip up his play. He had been steeled to endure raw slurs. At his core, under disciplined control, he was cold as ice — dry ice. No wonder, fiercely focused under calm demeanor, going all out all the time, Ashe suffered three heart attacks, the last within a few days of his death Saturday from AIDS-related illness.

To understand him, go back to when he arrived at the summer tennis clinic operated in Lynchburg by Dr. R. Walter Johnson. Startled at the frail, thin 10-year-old, Dr. Johnson thought the boy had rickets. But under a rigorous regimen and endless practice, the child became a lithe, gliding panther. Most beginners move out of position to avoid using their backhand, and they shirk from work on their serve. Untiring Ashe turned those usual weaknesses into strengths. When he won the Wimbledon Championship against Jimmy Connors in 1975, the thunderbolt of a serve that whistled past Connors began back in Lynchburg, Va. Johnson taught Ashe that his behavior had to be impeccable, more so than that of white players. Keep your cool and keep your eye on the ball, he commanded. And Ashe's father told him, "You don't get nowhere by making enemies."

Remember, Johnson said, when the referee errs in a call against your opponent, correct the mistake. Which, years later, is what Ashe did in a match with John Newcombe. The reversal cost him the point, the game. Ashe remained serene — much more so than he would have been had he let it go.

Gentle Ashe was beau geste.

To spare his daughter embarrassment, he kept his AIDS a secret more than three years, but when word of it got out 10 months ago, he turned with more than even his usual vigor to educating the public. He had become ombudsman for the world, going to jail in his waning hours for Haitians, making a video for AIDS victims, urging visitors at his bedside we must do more for Somalia and our uneducated youth. His zeal while dying wound up as a legacy on which his daughter can draw. The private bout that became public took a turn back in armoring her through life.

Friends bade him goodbye in a memorial service Wednesday in Richmond and in the near-silent passage Tuesday night of 5,000 as he lay in state, a slight, even boyish figure, in the Governor's Mansion. Behind the casket were two silver, flower-filled trophies; above him was a portrait of George Washington in buff and blue uniform.

Most mourners wore Sunday best; some came in work clothes. A jogger, slightly abstract, showed up in shorts and T-shirt. A young woman left three roses; a child placed a worn tennis ball on the floor. The swift-moving line was of all ages and walks of life, black and white. They were solemn, sorrowing. Some bowed heads at the casket. Many cried. A tall, rugged man said, "God is stronger than AIDS, brother."

Others saluted, said, "So long." A few blew kisses. Some pushed kin or friends in wheelchairs. Parents rolled months-old babies in strollers. Several visitors, leaving the room, turned and waved goodbye. A woman said, softly, "Go in peace, Arthur."

Quiet Trailblazer

Getting Arthur Ashe across the color line and into his first major tournament resulted from the earlier efforts of three men: his coach, who was a black physician in Lynchburg; a tennis official in Norfolk; and a former governor who was president of the University of Virginia. All that was left for teenage Ashe to do was win the tournament in Charlottesville. Which he did.

In 1953, when he was 10, Ashe began spending summers in Lynchburg at the home of R. Walter Johnson, a general practitioner. A former college football star who once scored eight touchdowns in a single game, Dr. Johnson taught basics in tennis and character to black youngsters on a court built alongside his house. He also used his money and rare donations to "send many a black kid to college — not just those interested in tennis — and he financed my education in Geneva, Switzerland," said his younger sister, Dr. E. El-Dorado Johnson of Lynchburg.

A dozen aspiring tennis players (Althea Gibson was among them) were also under Dr. Johnson's tutelage, she said. When he ran out of room at his house, he placed them around the neighborhood. Of Ashe she said: "He was well-mannered, quiet. He was just class." And he was cool. "That was the first thing my brother instilled in students: 'Don't lose your cool.' He had a saying: 'Those whom the gods would destroy they first make angry.'

"They had to hold their emotions in check because then they couldn't play on the white courts. My brother insisted that they make good grades in school. He had a dress code. They had to be clean when they went on the court, even here in Lynchburg. He financed all of Arthur's tennis trips, and he got him a scholarship at UCLA. He was like a father to him, really. They respected each other."

In 1959, watching the National Intercollegiate Championships in Charlottesville, Dr. Johnson asked if his proteges might enter the next year. While other officials stood perplexed, E.T. Penzold of Norfolk spoke up: "I see no reason why they can't play."

Penzold was president of the Middle Atlantic Lawn Tennis Association. After Penzold's death in 1970, Dr. Johnson recalled:

"He provided us that winter with forms to qualify, and he suggested we look beyond Lynchburg for talent by building our own national intercollegiate competition and bring the best to Charlottesville — which we did — until finally we brought Arthur Ashe. Mr. Penzold was a very great man."

Penzold consulted with the University of Virginia's president, former Gov. Colgate W. Darden Jr. The two studied forms and bylaws. There was no rule against blacks playing. It hadn't crossed many people's minds that blacks would take up tennis. But there was resistance within the community to admitting blacks to what had become the occasion for luncheons and parties. Darden and Penzold discussed how to prepare for the breakthrough, but they never wavered in their determination that blacks would play.

Lucy Penzold recalled frequent telephone conversations between her husband and Dr. Johnson, some of them for as much as an hour, on how his team should train. And E.T. told her, "Arthur Ashe is going to win this tournament."

"Everybody had such high regard for him," she said, "and he was so impressive on the court, and the kids all liked him."

And in Lynchburg, E. El-Dorado Johnson said, "That was the very beginning. That was the first time Arthur was allowed to play (with whites), and he won."

Giving His Utmost

If you don't give a fig for football, a game that would given you some sense of its allure was Sunday's between the Denver Broncos and Oakland Raiders.

The only player I know on either team is Bronco Quarterback John Elway. For the the 32nd time in his career he led the Broncs from seeming defeat to a resounding fourth-quarter victory. In wrapping up the win for his team, Elway also made it possible for the Miami Dolphins to make the playoffs leading to the Super Bowl.

The Dolphins have a fine quarterback in Dan Marino who led them in a 41-22 victory over the St. Louis Rams, but, because of the whimsical standings in the league, victory over the Rams wouldn't have mattered had Denver not defeated the Raiders. In an elegant double negative, Denver fullback Keith Byars said of Elway, "I can't think of no one else I would want in there with our fate in his hand than No. 7."

And I can't think of no one else who could better have expressed gratitude than did Byars. Elway is a wonder in bringing a team from one end of the field to the other in the waning minutes. Under circumstances that seem to scream in tension, he moves with a detached, almost vacuous expression. His mouth dropped open slightly, he has the somewhat distracted air of a preoccupied man who has picked up a swatter to smack a fly.

His teammates go about their business in dogged certitude that if it is possible to bring them back from the brink, John can do it. Elway has that arm with sniper-sight accuracy, and if there's an opening, he can dive for yardage or seize any other opportunity to win. Foes feel that when Elway is on the field he is a constant threat to reverse a game to his favor. He has never enjoyed the luxury of throwing to a super receiver. In Sunday's game he distributed passes among eight teammates. He makes the best of what's given.

What is his secret? Serenity from having pulled off the impossible so often and pleasure in the game even in the shadow of defeat. An extra dose of vitality enjoyed by great champions. Makes no difference to viewers whether the Broncos make the playoffs or the Super Bowl. Elway will give his utmost, which is quite enough to expect on an afternoon, no matter the standings.

My colleague Fred Kirsch was explaining football to a friend from Australia as they watched the Bronco-Raiders set-to. Keep your eye on Elway, Fred advised. He has the habit of coming through at the end. Sure enough, Elway did for Fred. There couldn't have been a better introduction of football to a visitor from Down Under.

Stan The Man

Each of the two major baseball leagues announced last week its most valuable player. My all-time most valuable player is Stan Musial, though I couldn't give you, off-hand, a single statistic from his many records on the diamond as a right fielder and, near the close of his career, first baseman. The play that gets my vote for Musial was one he made off the field.

The insight into that play and Musial's character comes from a colleague, Frank Callaham, who started newspapering, as I did, with the Lynchburg News, although Callaham is some 25 years behind me on the base paths.

Musial's team, the St. Louis Cardinals, came to town for an exhibition game with its farm club in Lynchburg. The city's mayor, the Rev. Dr. John Suttenfield, seized the chance to take with him to the game an invalid child from his congregation at

Fairview Christian Church. As with many preachers, nearly every minute of Suttenfield's life was a ministration to others.

The boy, 9, had a wasting disease, but scarcely a shadow of it fell across his bright, eager face. He loved baseball, especially the Cardinals, and, most of all, Musial. He kept up with him through the sports pages of the Lynchburg News. Suttenfield brought his friend to the ballpark in an ambulance. While the boy watched the Cardinals warm up on the field before the game, Suttenfield went down to the visitors' dugout. Some of the major leaguers, he figured, maybe even the great Musial, would sign a baseball for the child.

But, absorbed in warming up, the players turned their backs to the minister, indifferent to his low-keyed request, and he went back up in the stands to his place beside the boy. Suttenfield, who had played baseball as a catcher with Lynchburg College and local teams, and later at Fort Story, where he was a chaplain during World War II, knew the game well.

A boulder of a man with a deep, resonant voice, he thought it a sin to be downcast for long by a rebuff. He rallied his feelings and heightened the boy's anticipation of the game by naming the players warming up on the field below them and discussing their skills. He got out his camera to get a snapshot through which the boy, during the few remaining days, could recall this day with friends who had joined him at the game.

Suttenfield arranged them so everyone would be seen clearly, and he was about to say cheese and snap the shutter when, behind him at his shoulder, a cheerful voice asked, "Mind if I get in the picture?"

Suttenfield wheeled — and faced Stan Musial with that quick, sharp-edged, deep dip of a smile. Musial knelt beside the boy, put his big hand on his frail shoulder, and Suttenfield took the picture. The photograph would give the boy something to pore over, reliving it, memorizing every detail, and show vistors. Musial answered his fan's questions and drew him out about his own views. It was a good 15 minutes of satisfying chat, after which Musial signed and gave the boy a baseball. And then because the St. Louis Cardinals were coming out for the first inning, Musial went down on the field, and, during the game, knocked the hide off the ball.

Without a warmup.

His Airness

Outside Chicago's United Center is a statue of Michael Jordan, a little larger than life as usual, rising, streaming upwards in the air, a breaching whale, his arm lifted to dunk a basketball and win again.

Inside that arena Friday in the waning skin-tight fight for the NBA championship, the whale rose and at the height of his leap, his foes' faces at about his knees, Jordan, arms outstretched, seeming ready to make the game-winning shot, shifted his aim and flicked the ball to Steve Kerr, near the center of the floor. With five seconds left, Kerr sank a 17-foot 3-point jumper that gave the Chicago Bulls a 2-point lead en route to a 90-86 victory that clinched the Bulls' championship.

That shot said a lot about Jordan and his Bulls. Coach Phil Jackson called it a "redemption shot" for Kerr, who had been outplayed most of the way by John Stockton. Despite Kerr's earlier lackluster play, Jordan called beforehand for him to do it. In a timeout, with 28 seconds left and the game tied, 86-86, shrewd

Jordan foresaw Utah's strategy that John Stockton would leave Kerr to double-team Jordan. Be ready, Jordan told Kerr. He would, Kerr promised.

But Kerr admitted later, "I was asking myself, " 'Will I?' "

"If he missed that shot, I don't think he would have slept all summer," Jordan said.

It is rare enough to call one's own shot as Babe Ruth foretold homers a time or two; but to call for a shot from a slumping teammate in the last-gasp finish with the championship at stake showed Jordan's confidence in his judgment and, down deep, Kerr's ability. Kerr came through. It meant as much to Jordan as if he had done it.

After an earlier playoff game with the Miami Heat, when Jordan scored 50 points, one of his teammates grumbled that no one else had a chance to shoot. But, truly, through most of the games Jordan had to carry the team with the help of Scottie Pippen. They make a remarkable tag team, Coach Jackson noted.

Saturday night, cradling the Most Valuable Player trophy, a grotesque cup that means so much, Jordan said he would share it with Pippen.

"I'll keep this," he said. "I may give him the car."

Management is considering breaking up the Bulls. But ousting Jackson means Jordan and Pippen will follow. Still, Jordan held up six fingers to the roaring crowd, promising a sixth championship. And when he calls a shot, he usually makes it.

Dream of a Team!

Did something the other evening I hadn't done since childhood. Fell out of bed. Or, rather, off the sofa. It hurt. I was stretched out, watching a game between the Detroit Pistons and the champion Chicago Bulls, the Bulls being led by Michael Jordan, a team unto himself.

Jordan has sangfroid.

But at the moment, the Bulls were behind by a point. Then, suddenly, smoothly, I blended right into the game, a startling change of venue, as they say. One minute I was on the sofa, supine, with heavy, drooping eyelids, and the next I was running around the basketball court, shouting, "HEY, MICHAEL! OVER HERE! I'M IN THE CLEAR!"

Nobody seemed to notice the introduction into the game of an inept figure clad in street clothes, dashing around bellowing, waving his arms. The refs didn't blow a whistle. The fans didn't boo. Jordan, his head swiveling at my shout, directed a stare my way. And his arm, like a frog's tongue flicking out to pick up a fly, threw the ball in a straight line at me. I caught it!

Such is his influence on us team-mates that I didn't even think about not catching it. WHUMPF! It landed in my midriff and I grasped it. And, inspired, put on a demonstration of dribbling of which I had no idea I was capable.

At no other time have I been able to bounce a basketball twice on the floor, but out there with the Bulls, who stood, mouths agape, I ran in figure eights and dribbled the ball behind my back and through my legs, and shouted, "One-two-three-O'Leary!" as we used to chant as children.

And once I bounced the ball from shoulder to shoulder, smiling and bowing, while the crowd roared. But Jordan, beset by five foes, shouted at me: "GO FOR THE BASKET, GUYBO! GO FOR IT!"

"MISS IT!" the Pistons shouted.

"SINK IT!" yelled the Bulls.

Which, glowing with pride at Jordan's trust in me, I set out to do. I was making good time, on the long journey toward the other end of the court, when, lo, my trousers fell down around my ankles.

And I was reduced to leaping along with two-footed jumps like a state fair contestant in a sack race.

The crowd was standing now, cheering at the mad spectacle. There danced before my eyes the headline that would surely appear next morning on the front page:

FAN SINKS SHOT, WINS GAME!

And then, no doubt, just below it:

LOSES PANTS

They would have to get that in.

But no time to waste on idle speculation. Keep moving to the basket.

Hearing Jordan shout, "SHOOT!" I raised and aimed the ball, which all of a sudden seemed heavy, pig iron, and getting set for the shot, crouching for one mighty final bound, I tripped.

And the ball went bouncing ahead of me as I fell to the hardwood floor.

KABLAM! And, the next second, I was lying on my back, looking up at the trainer, who was slapping a wet towel on my face, when suddenly he faded and in his place was the chocolate Labrador retriever, licking my mug.

And right behind the retriever, Gin was bending, concerned, toward me.

"WHY ARE YOU ON THE FLOOR?" she cried.

"Get back in the stands where you belong," I said, "and take this dog with you."

"WHAT HAPPENED?" she pleaded.

"I let down Michael Jordan," I said.

Angel on an Angel

Never have so many and women been convinced that a female's rights had been abridged as when Codex swung out and bumped or brushed the filly Genuine Risk, who was about to take the lead at Pimlico. If there's one thing that can put women's rights across the finish line, it's what happened Saturday at the Preakness. At least that's the impression I got from the person seated across from me at the breakfast table.

"Did you see what happened at Pimlico?" she asked in a stern voice.

"No," I said, "I was away from TV."

"You should have made it your business to see it," she said. "That other horse bumped the filly and his rider hit her in the head with his whip."

"That's no way to treat a lady," I said.

"That filly has the sweetest disposition," she said, "and he just intimidated her."

(From her tone, the filly could have been one of her best friends.)

"So what do you think?" she demanded.

"I didn't see it."

"That never prevented you from expressing an opinion before. You didn't see 'Death of a Princess' either, and you're full of opinions about that."

"That's a horse of a different color," I said, "And it involves freedom of the ..."

"And THIS," she said, "Involves encroachment on the rights of a female who has excelled in a male's world and was about to win again. All you males stick together."

"Please remember, " I said, "that Angel Cordero was riding that horse. Unfortunately, I was elsewhere. Had I been in the saddle, it never would have occurred, I assure you."

"You ought to be ashamed," she said, "To make light of an injustice."

In truth, the idea of that little filly being bullied is well nigh intolerable. To appease her, I called Baltimore and talked with Larry Lewis of the News-American who had watched over closed circuit in the press box the replay of the incident. Writers from around the country were just about unanimous that Codex bumped Genuine Risk, and many seemed to think that when Cordero looked over his shoulder and saw the filly coming, he veered out and may even have struck the filly in the face, with his whip, Lewis said. He certainly was waving the whip in front of her. American Sports Editor John Steadman wrote that there definitely was a foul and that Codex should have been taken down, disqualified, that is. Genuine Risk was robbed, Steadman concluded. On the Baltimore Sun, racing editor William Boniface chided Codex (or his rider) for an "ungentlemanly display of poor manners." Sun writer Bob Maisel said there could be no doubt Codex "interfered with her stride just as she seemed ready to take the lead."

There'll always be a lingering doubt as to whether Genuine

Risk "wouldn't have made the lead and kept it just as she did in the Derby, if not forced to alter course and be steadied just as she was doing her best running," Maisel wrote.

So the controversy, like the one surrounding the "long count" when Gene Tunney whipped Jack Dempsey, will continue. Because she was wronged, the filly will gain even more fervent admirers in a race that will, like the chase around Keats' Grecian urn, continue to be run through time.

However, when I reported to her most fanatical supporter, I merely read the reports from Baltimore writers.

"So what do you think?" she challenged.

"There's one lesson we can draw from all this," I said. "When you're in a tight race, get Angel Cordero to do the riding."

A Big-Mouthed River

Leland Thomas fell in love with the Elizabeth River when his father took him fishing at age 2. "I don't know why he waited so long," said Thomas, who will be 90 'fore long. He no longer fishes, except in memory, which is vivid.

"I have wanted to say something about this small river for a long time," the Portsmouth resident noted. "It has touched the lives of more West Norfolk people for a longer time in more ways than any other body of water nearby, even than the mighty Atlantic Ocean."

His father, Andrew Tilden Thomas, first took him fishing in 1905.

"Papa was a real fisherman. With never-ending patience he

could sit for hours with his homemade hand line in his hand, never getting a bite; but he always said, 'They will bite on the next tide.'" That first morning they set out before breakfast in a 16-foot skiff to catch the first incoming tide which brought the fish — "or so Papa would say. But that day the fish never heard Papa. We fished 'til about 2 p.m. and I was very, very hungry."

His father rowed to Craney Island where Captain Frank Ashberry protected oyster beds. All Frank had left from breakfast was cold bread, cooked atop the stove, and black molasses. "That was my first experience learning that when you are hungry anything will taste good."

The Elizabeth, a tidal river, is only two or three miles long, he noted. Its branches are longer than the Elizabeth River itself. At one end, toward Norfolk and Portsmouth, are the Western, Eastern, and Southern Branches. Toward Newport News the Elizabeth joins the Hampton Roads.

"So it is a small river. My fifth-grade teacher, Miss Louise Poindexter, said the Elizabeth is the only river in the United States named after a woman, and it is all mouth. It was named for Queen Elizabeth. I have heard she could out-talk kings, princes, and princesses, so maybe my teacher was correct." (She erred. The river was named for Princess Elizabeth, daughter of King James I. But grant Miss Poindexter some poetic license.)

The Elizabeth fed more West Norfolk families than all the area's food stores put together, including those run by Parsons, Blanchard, Davis, Ayers, and Adolph Bloom. "Between West Norfolk proper and Craney Island was Loves Creek, so muddy you could walk its length barefooted at low tide and catch all the fish bait you could use in a day's fishing: hard and soft crabs, alewives, and gudgeon."

On high tide, Loves Creek offered two swimming holes where most West Norfolk boys learned to swim before daring to try the Elizabeth River, Thomas said. "On the first high tide of the day following the first low tide, most families that had a boat went fishing in the Elizabeth for such varieties as croakers, trout, spot, perch, black Wills, butters, and hogs, including the unwanted toads and eels.

"At night, when you could get a rod and reel, you could fish off the West Norfolk Bridge under a light and catch large trouts and rock-fish. So many fish were chasing elwys and fish bait attracted by the light, that I have dipped them up with a shrimp net.

"The Elizabeth River floats the U.S. Navy's biggest battleships and carriers, but the fish have gone. Where to, I wonder. And I often wonder if boys now days, with expensive rods and reels and costly fish bait and fancy boats, have as much fun as we did in the early 1900s. The Elizabeth, my river I call it, wasn't mine entirely. It was every West Norfolk boy's home base, a paradise for good times. It was where we learned to swim, fish, catch crabs, and wade in mud up to our knees that stuck so tight to our feet it would pull our shoes off, if we had shoes to wear."

Chapter Nine

Ya Ol' Contrarian

Stockdale's Questions

My favorite candidate for vice president is Adm. James Stockdale, who ran with Ross Perot four years ago. That rough-cut old man's first words in debate in 1992 are memorable.

"Who am I?" he cried. "Why am I here?"

Some pundits dismissed him. To me he was an intelligent, decent man of integrity and dignity. Those questions have plagued us ever since Adam and Eve woke up in the Garden.

The admiral's answers were: one, he was a friend of Perot; and two, Perot hadn't been able to find anyone else who would run with him. You try to do even out-sized things for a friend and for your country.

As vice presidents go, some of us would prefer James Stockdale with his white thatch and wide grim mouth from which issued blunt, unprogrammed words. No need to feel sorry for that old bear, who limps from torture he endured in Vietnam.

Much of the way in the debate, Dan Quayle and Al Gore smacked of small boys scrapping in the dirt over which had the better old man. Stockdale seemed to be an amazed Everyman, the American of strong convictions but of little experience in political combat. Every now and then Stockdale came through with untutored eloquence.

After an exchange between Gore and Quayle on the abortion issue, Stockdale declared, "I'm for a woman having the right to choose. PERIOD!" The audience, expecting more, waited in silence until stocky Stockdale shouted again, "PERIOD!" At another point, when Gore and Quayle were bent on outyelling each other, Stockdale said, "I think America is seeing right now the reason this nation is in gridlock."

Pundits dismissed him as lacking the stuff of a vice president. Few vice presidents can match Stockdale's challenges in keeping "civilization" alive in a prisoner of war camp. One thing he'd have been able to define — the difference between what's right and wrong in public life, which seems to escape some of our congressmen.

So many of the country's major problems — even war resulting in heavy losses of lives — stem from some of our representatives' reluctance to face and tell the truth. You get the feeling Stockdale could bring it to their attention.

My flashback was triggered last week by a television replay of Stockdale's debut in 1992. He was smiling as he posed the two questions, and the crowd enjoyed his self-deprecating humor. Some pundits missed it.

His cockleburr questions will stick in the public mind after utterances of other vice presidential hopefuls are forgot. Ross Perot promised to pick a great American as his running mate — and he did.

I'd have voted for Admiral Stockdale and been proud of it.

Trying to Civilize Huck

They're trying to civilize Huck again just as Miss Watson, a prim maiden lady, tried at the start of "Adventures of Huckleberry Finn."

"They" have been trying to curry him since his birth in 1885 when the Hartford, Conn., library banned him. Now "they" are parents in a Texas town who demand that Huck be combed out of the curriculum so children can't read his adventures. Poor souls, they don't know better, which is how Huck, an instinctive humanitarian, might put it. Those adults have been denied the joy — and enlightenment — of reading the greatest American novel. Even Ernest Hemingway, who couldn't abide competitors, conceded Twain is champ. Maybe because he was dead.

"All modern literature comes from one book by Mark Twain called 'Huckleberry Finn,'" Hemingway wrote. "If you read it, you must stop where Nigger Jim is stolen from the boys. That's the real end. The rest is just cheating, but it's the best book we've had. All American literature comes from it. There was nothing before. There has been nothing as good since."

Nor will there ever.

Omitting that, Hem faltered.

My debt is to Miss Minter, who read a chapter of Huck each day before recess. To get an extra chapter, we'd give up recess. (Nobody, not even parents, meddled with Miss Minter's fifth grade.) In Texas, the deluded parents, white and black, decry the use of the "N" word. They couldn't have read the book or they would understand Twain wrapped in that one hate word an indictment of the bigots and racists from whose foul mouths it issued.

In a society of legalized slavery, Huck accepts Jim, a runaway slave, as his equal. The two innocents float on a raft down the Mississippi toward freedom. Each time they go ashore, they encounter inhumanity: a blood feud that kills a boy Huck's age; a lynching; a duel when a cool aristocrat slays a drunken fool; two swindlers who con a town and conspire to sell Jim into slavery. A gripping, rolling panorama unfolds the ills of those times — most of which plague these.

On TV a Texas school teacher, who happens to be black, defended the book. It is, she said, a legacy of freedom of speech.

After Huck and Jim escape the parasite pair, lawmen come long side the raft and demand of Huck whether a runaway is aboard.

"Who's with you?" one called.

"My Pap. He has smallpox!" Huck said. They fled.

Every constraint in Huck's upbringing commands he betray Jim. Instead, he lies to save his friend, deciding, "All right, I'll go to Hell!" That cry, a great preachment of loyal brotherhood, should be explained to misguided students. Huck and Twain side with the angels. The protesting parents, in pitiful ignorance, pour souls, abet bigotry.

GI Guy

A friend drafted me to talk at a church supper. The congregation, he said, was a mite conservative. Bulletin notices testified to its work for the poor. The pastor was a delight; my remarks humdrum. Closing, I lauded their concern for the wretched, among whom Christ, were He here, would be.

In a question session, somebody was troubled by federal spending on such untested schemes, he said, as summer jobs. As am I, I told him.

An arms race broke the Soviets and strapped us. Some observers, I noted, would leave people to pull themselves out of misery. Amid free enterprise, they believe "they govern best who govern least."

Then something hit me.

In 1939, I recalled, the National Youth Administration paid me 30 cents an hour writing in the University of Richmond news bureau for an ex-newsman. I never worked harder or learned more. Or found a better friend.

Drafted in 1942, I lived nearly four years on government issue among the best men I ever met. Back home, I relied on Harry Truman's GI Bill for tuition to finish college, then used $25 a week toward a year's "on-the-job training" at The Lynchburg News.

The GI Bill took me and Gin to Columbia University. We settled in a veterans village. The GI Bill gave us $105 a month. We paid $33 rent. A dollar leased two cots, a table, chairs, ice box, stove, heater.

We splurged $50 for a red-gold cocker spaniel. Gin taught in Nyack. I wrote as a stringer, 30 cents an inch, then full time for The Journal-News. With Uncle Sam undergirding us, we were happy.

Later, in Richmond, as I reported for The News Leader and she taught, we used a GI loan at 4 percent to buy a house. That one supplied a down payment for a second home for our growing family, then a third dwelling when we moved to Norfolk, she teaching, I writing for The Virginian-Pilot. A picnic, all along, with the GI Bill and Gin.

How could I oppose federal aid for summer jobs that might inspire some youth as I had been moved in 1939 by dynamic ex-newsman Joe Nettles?

Applying five years late for medicare, I found I was qualified as well for Social Security. Leaving the federal building's crowded elevator, I blurted, startling a crowded elevator: "Thank God for Franklin Roosevelt!"

FDR, I told the audience in church, ran for the presidency as a conservative. To right a capsized economy, he tried an array of ideas. Truman's GI Bill unleashed energies that fueled prosperity and shaped lives. Lyndon Johnson freed slaves at the ballot box. Other presidents helped, too.

Can the government no longer lend a hand? I asked. Can a deficit-ridden nation manage to help our grandchildren as we were helped?

Thinking back, I said, I feel compelled to assume whatever burden needed to enable a government to do for those coming on what it did for us — and pray it works. "I'm a GI boy!" I exclaimed.

In the rear, an old, old man arose and shouted, "Here's another GI boy!"

Well, two remembered.

The Bells Toll For Thee

Amid Christmas chimes, a death knell is resounding in Virginia for five men slated for execution. When the toll is done by Dec. 18, Virginia could lead the Western world for executions in 1996, says Amnesty International. Virginia Is for Lovers, it seems, could become, momentarily, Virginia Is for Vengeance.

Two of the five December executions have occurred. In all cases, petitions for clemency have been sent to Gov. George F. Allen. So many executions in a row this season, he told The Richmond Times-Dispatch on Nov. 29, will not be easy for him nor for others, especially, he said, for the survivors of the murdered victims. Nor, one might add, will it be easy for the one executed, nor for his kin, especially if the sentence seems unjust or the trial unfair.

Ya Ol' Contrarian

What should be pondered along with guilt or innocence is whether some are executed while others who have committed similar crimes are not. It's an issue of disparities arising from whether the accused has been represented adequately or been dealt with fairly by the courts. Among inconsistencies, a study by The Virginian-Pilot's Laura LaFay discovered, the nations federal courts have reversed 40 percent of death sentences because of constitutional problems. But in Virginia, the U.S. 4th Circuit Court of Appeals has reversed only 7 percent.

Foes of capital punishment, Gov. Allen said, could learn from his three years administering it. "It's something probably that you don't understand fully unless you have that responsibility in your own hands," he said.

Bells tolling death throughout December, mingling with bells pealing for the birth of a child, are something from which we all, including the Governor, could learn. One question is whether the State should be entrusted with the God-like power of imposing death. But since the State has it, most folks would urge that every effort be exerted to assure a just system.

And if there is doubt, then, in the game of life as in baseball, the tie should go to the runner. After death by lethal injection, if new evidence casts doubt on the call, no replay, instant or distant, can help. The State's power to kill its citizens doesn't extend, in case of error, to recalling life.

Troubling aspects beset the first two deaths. On Nov. 19, a lawyer for Ronald Bennett released a videotape of the key witness recanting testimony that had implicated Bennett. Then she recanted the videotape. The governor permitted the execution to take place Nov. 21.

Gregory Warren Beaver, executed last night, had two court-appointed attorneys. One was disbarred in October for neglecting four clients. The other, a part-time prosecutor, was running

189

for election in an adjacent county while he was defending Beaver. This poses a question of conflict of interest.

On Nov. 7, Gov. Allen gave clemency to Joseph Patrick Payne, who had been convicted of slaying a fellow prisoner. Court-appointed attorneys had failed to call a dozen or so witnesses in Payne's behalf. The prosecution's key witness, Robert "Dirty Smitty" Smith, had been given a 15-year reduction of sentence for testifying against Payne.

Payne's second attorney from a Washington, D.C. firm, Paul Khoury, found four jurors who said they wouldn't have convicted Payne had they known all the facts. Gov. Allen had Smith submit to a lie detector, and then spared Payne. Khoury worked nine years without a fee for Payne. To save him, he told LaFay, was like trying to move a mountain. His success may stir other firms to level mountains, pro bono.

Hearing a funeral bell, poet John Donne reflected, "Any man's death diminishes me because I am involved in mankind.

"And therefore," he said, "never send to know for whom the bell tolls; it tolls for thee."

Donne's advice in the 16th century still applies, as it did last night when the bell tolled for Gregory Beaver.

Oh Say, Can't You See?

A trend surfaced in the state Democratic convention at Virginia Beach when the chairman asked delegates to stand during the singing of "God Bless America," Is this the beginning of a move to supplant "The Star-Spangled Banner" as our national anthem?

If so, it ought to be resisted. Suddenly "The Star-Spangled Banner" became especially dear to the heart. Formerly one sometimes thought of it mainly as being especially hard to sing, particularly that portion around the rocket's red glare and then again at the land of the free, when one's voice seemed required to soar as high as a rocket.

If the notes of our traditional anthem are demanding, then the words are vivid, the entire song being one long question as to the state of the nation, a kind of reminder that we ought not to take it or our freedoms for granted. The anthem is a challenge. The song is filled with one lovely or striking image after another: dawn's early light, twilight's last gleaming, rocket's red glare, bombs bursting in air. The dominant image is of the rippling red and white stripes and blue field with white stars over the breastworks of Fort McHenry.

Not to be disrespectful, but the image aroused in mind by "God Bless America" is of ample Kate Smith, God bless her. I admire Kate Smith. She's as wholesome as whole wheat bread. Not only is her voice robust and appealing, but also her personality is such that I don't feel uneasy in her presence. With Frank Sinatra I'm thinking constantly that I shouldn't be enjoying this fellow's singing so much. But in her buoyant optimism, jollity, and courage, Kate Smith embodies qualities we like to believe are part of the national character.

Still, "God Bless America" doesn't rank with "The Star-Spangled Banner" as a song to stand up for. "God Bless America" is triumphant, even somewhat complacent, about our national situation. "The Star-Spangled Banner" calls for self-searching about our country. Peril impends. In a touch of piosity, "God Bless America" invokes a blessing. "The Star-Spangled Banner" sounds an alert.

And I don't feel up to standing for more than one song. If we stand for "God Bless America" as a stand-in national anthem, pretty soon righteous masters of ceremonies are going to be hauling us to our feet for "America the Beautiful" and then "America," and before you know it we will be jumping up for "Old Cape Cod." To back up a bit, the song "America," which begins with the words "My country 'tis of thee, sweet land of liberty," appeals to me, perhaps because we sang it in kindergarten.

Never before or since have I been so nearly undone by a song as I was on the Sunday after President John F. Kennedy's death when, for our first hymn, the congregation in church all of us, children and adults, stood and sang "My country 'tis of thee." That moment, all across the land, it was a national anthem. We were one.

It's How You Play the Game

How strange to find oneself pulling for another country's team to beat the entry from the United States in the Olympic games. My wish is that 12 players from some little nation will knock off our Dream Team of professional All-Star basketball chumps. When it comes to sportsmanship that Dream Team is a nightmare, swaggering around bragging.

Up until 1992 our Olympic teams of amateurs from America's colleges lost a game now and then. It lent suspense. And last week the Dream Team barely beat, 96-90, the Select team of collegians aiming to win gold medals in the World Championships this summer in Puerto Rico. That's more as it should be.

But in 1992, bowing to hysterical fans, we abandoned the amateur standing and went professional in choosing our Olympic team. When it defeated the Cuban entry 136 to 57, Coach Miguel Calderon Gomez said, "As we say in Cuba, you cannot cover the sun with your finger."

The 1992 team won by an average of 43.8 points. Third country players asked, shyly, like kids on a playground, for our players' autographs. In talk last week among our players, Karl Malone said: "If we have a chance to beat a team by 40 or 50, I promise you we'll try to do that. We've already talked about it, and we know 10 points won't do it. It's got to be a bigger double-digit thing."

It matters not whether you win or lose, it's by how many points you smear the smaller foe. Asked if any other team might offer competition, Charles Barkley said, "The women's national team, that's about it." He is called "Sir Charles" more for his sometimes overpowering presence on the court, certainly not for any sense of noblesse oblige or respect for the foe.

In 1992 the world's best basketball player, Michael Jordan, didn't care to go to the games in Barcelona. He had experienced Olympic play and he wished to give others a chance. He also had led the Chicago Bulls to another NBA championship and he wanted to rest and play golf. Answering the fans' demand, he relented, but it was a relaxed Jordan who let other players, notably Barkley, put on a show.

Jordan, who walks on air instead of water, won't be in Atlanta. His mind is focused on the next NBA season, which is where Scottie Pippen's thoughts should be after his spotty play last season. Only so many games are left in Jordan's legs – and not many more in Pippen's. Here's a dare that might tempt Jordan, who can't resist a challenge. Let the other countries draw lots to see which one could claim Jordan as a temporary citizen for a berth on its Olympic team. Now THERE would be something worth watching and cheering.

A Real Crime

Word went out this week that "Godfather III," the third round in the continuing story of a dynasty of gangsters, will feature John Travolta. We may as well brace ourselves for an outpouring of guff. I don't mean the movie. If viewed as entertaining trash, that's not much worse than the ordinary soap opera on television.

What is revolting is the rhapsodizing of the reviewers who treat these "Godfather" films as if they were "King Lear" or "Oedipus Rex." The Washington Post's critic, for instance, wrote last November that "Godfather II" "represents the most satisfying and significant television event" since "Roots."

When it's over, he wrote, viewers "will all feel the sense of accomplishment one gets from making it through an epic – in this case an epic of depth, intelligence and shattering emotional peaks."

I found it nothing more than an epic con, a phony romanticizing of crime, a slick glorifying of violence. It was another shoot–'em–up, a cops and robbers story with one set of robbers whitewashed to play the cops.

Reflect a minute. Did the Godfather (Marlon Brando) or his youngest son (Al Pacino) order any act of violence without some rough justification? Even the climactic shoot-out with the Godfather's family contesting the other four gangs arose because Godfather Brando had refused to join them in dealing in drugs.

Gambling, yes, and "even women," said Brando, but no drugs, never. Clean crime was his aim.

Yet, seldom in the two movies did the criminal operations – gambling, prostitution, loan sharking, or their victims – intrude. The dons squabbling over the business might have been trading in cornflakes for all the attention the goods received.

It was crime sanitized and elevated to a corporate level, relieved of unsavory detail that would have made the characters despicable in the viewers' eyes. The Mafia Story was treated as deferentially as "The Forsyte Saga."

In the portions depicting Godfather I as a youth (Robert De Niro) and as an old man (Brando), the Godfather killed an extortionist preying on shopkeepers, rescued a widow from an unscrupulous landlord, and ordered the beating of thugs who had brutalized a girl. Why, he was a regular Robin Hood!

A preface to the two films offered viewers the message that they presented "a realistic depiction of the self-destructive effects of crime and violence."

To the contrary, the "Godfather" pictures are no more baleful than fairy tales, not nearly as grim, in fact, as Grimms. Madison Avenue couldn't have done a better job of prettifying and ennobling organized crime.

Heroine

Of course, Shannon Faulkner has, thus far, the right to go to The Citadel. And it has the right to treat her as it does any other cadet and shave her head as a new recruit. If it chooses to be so stupid.

195

If it does give her a knob haircut, the picture of shorn Shannon will appear the next day on the front page of every newspaper in the United States and on TV. Talk shows will talk of little else. Overnight, she will become a heroine inspiring other young women to storm The Citadel's gates.

In shearing her, The Citadel, producer of governors and 40 percent of South Carolina's CEOs, will appear an anachronistic institution lacking compassion, common sense, and the vision to change to meet the needs of the modern military. And The Citadel will have violated its own grandest tradition and that of other service academies.

Implicit in their image is a chivalric mission to defend the weak, especially womankind. Their medieval towers are redolent of knights riding to the rescue of maidens fair. Each knight might beseech a lock of his beloved's hair, but not the entire scalp. They put women on a pedestal, not in a barber's chair.

To exclude women is to ignore the demands of the Army, Navy, Marines, and Air Force, which are rapidly expanding women's roles in national defense. Why, the modern-day Citadel alumnus may expect to find himself working beside those mysterious creatures and even have to take orders from one, the likes of which bore him into this world. Many a Citadel graduate, intent on a military career, is likely to leave the school's monastic surroundings with a blind spot about women's abilities. Moreover, he will have been deprived on the campus of women's keen intellect, which in many respects is superior to that of men.

That was evident after the admission of women to universities where many male students had scoffed at the notion of women in their midst. But professors found that the presence of women lent a lift to discourse in formerly all-male classes.

The contention that women don't have the stuff to endure discipline at The Citadel overlooks their fortitude in undergoing without fanfare the much harsher strain of bearing children.

The revealing novel "Lords of Discipline" by alumnus Pat Conroy suggests that the enlightening influence of women will enhance, not impair, the way of life at The Citadel.

Shame on You!

Never was Shannon Faulkner more vulnerable, more appealing, than she was Saturday in quitting her 2 ½ year battle to become the first female cadet at The Citadel. From public reaction, one oft-repeated sentence sums up the sentiment of both sides: "I'm glad she's leaving." It served alike for those who had been sympathetic to her plucky pursuit of an impossible dream and to those exulting that The Citadel will remain a male bastion.

To those of us rooting for her, some scenes during her five days as a cadet sully the scutcheon of that peacock-proud institution. An air of protective gallantry toward women by the military is a tradition as old as any in The Citadel's history. There is a saying, originating in the ancient British military, of the necessity of being "an officer and a gentleman."

They may become officers one day; many have much to learn about becoming gentlemen. On the last day there were the resounding cheers that arose at word that Faulkner was leaving. How she had yearned to be one of them! How that must have wrung her heart if she heard them!

During a break near the close of her first day in the corps, the

197

cadets gathered, chatting, in two large, closed circles, while she stood alone. Not one had the manhood or courtesy to walk over to her. In years to come, when they are truly men, no longer callow kids, some may rue that they lacked the compassion and grit to extend kindness to an individual. For that, loving and caring for one another, is the basis for civilization that sets us apart from barbarism. It is the first tenet to be taught at any institution of learning, military or civilian.

Citadel President Claudius Watts said early he didn't know whether the other cadets would ignore her. "I cannot legislate friendship. I cannot legislate respect," he said. "She can earn my respect. She obviously believes in what she's embarked on, and she should get credit for that. I don't agree with her position."

The president was so focused on what he deemed he couldn't do — a simple order or two down the line would have done wonders — he missed, apparently, what The Citadel command should have done: instruct its young charges in civility and a sense of humanity. With all that drilling and spit and polish, what The Citadel needs is a woman's touch, some feminization among those grim battlements, some training in sensitivity for all its troops. Without women around to exert subtle guidance, men tend to become self-centered, stodgy.

"I don't think there is any dishonor in leaving," Faulkner said. "I think there's a disjustice in me staying and killing myself just for the political point."

No dishonor for her. She leaves a lesson for the occupants of The Citadel, if they but look.

Chapter Ten

Making Progress,
Confoundit!

You Rang?

One thing making it harder to communicate is that telephones no longer ring. They murmur. What in the name of Alexander Graham Bell — whose very name has a ring — does AT&T have to gain by producing phones that won't ring? They tinkle. If you are three paces away you can't hear the phone. It whispers.

Has society become so refined it no longer can endure the sound of a good, honest, forthright, Fourth of July ring from Mr. Bell's invention? You would think that somebody in AT&T would recognize that in manufacturing mute phones they are running into a dead end. Somewhere along the line it is going to occur to people there is no point in having a telephone they can't hear.

The other week the phone at home lost its voice entirely. Its inner works malfunctioned. Such is my innate confidence in modern technology that I assumed my hearing was failing. I phoned a friend and asked him to call me immediately, then, hanging up, I put my ear on the phone like an Indian, ear to the ground, listening for buffalo. Nothing! The buffalo weren't running. Mr. Bell's set was kaput. I reported its failure to a pleasant consumer comforter. "And, please, ma'am, when they send the repair man — or woman, whichever — please have him or her bring along a phone that truly rings and not just trills. Bring one that may be heard not from just three feet but at least three rooms away. A phone whose ring is so penetrating it reaches the the ears of the householder in the field across the way throwing a ball to a Labrador retriever.

"A ring so imperative it would start booted firemen sliding down poles and jumping on the backs of siren-screaming fire trucks. Bring one that can be heard from one Alp to another. Have the black phone set on a two-foot tall stem upon a base so heavy that the phone won't be falling over all the time and hurting itself. Have a two-foot cord attached to the receiver which you hold to the ear while you grasp the phone with the other hand and speak into a cup of a mouthpiece."

The customer comforter laughed. "I don't think they make them that way anymore," she said. The trouble began when the company marketed a phone, all colors of the rainbow instead of basic black, that could be cuddled in one hand against one's face. A princess phone, it was termed. It caught on with consumers after actress Jean Harlow — or maybe Carole Lombard — appeared on film immersed in suds, phone in hand to her face. Ere long, the old business-like black phone was gone. To fit the intimacy of its frilly, pastel replacement, the bell's decibels were lowered to the tinkle of a tete-a-tete.

The repairman gave me a number through which to order a phone that would ring its head off.

Just Add Water And Stir

Sometimes things in the news make me feel like an alien, just landed. And they are not necessarily major findings in the headlines, either. More often, a minor item will touch on a change in lifestyle.

The other day, the head of a Boston nutrition clinic observed that the microwave has revolutionized children's meal patterns. It used to be that your mother wouldn't let you near the stove, said Johanna Dwyer. Now, she said, children can prepare their own food.

That children are fixing their own meals in a microwave oven startled me because one such oven is sitting unused in our pantry. Been there five years, and I haven't touched it. Nor do I intend to. Even if it means ending a sentence with a preposition.

The microwave oven arouses in me the superstitious dread that the Indians felt when they first looked at a compass wiggling around or saw themselves in a mirror. They wanted none of it.

I could identify, in boyhood, with women who had a nice, new electric stove on which to set a vase of pretty flowers while they were cooking dinner on an old wood or coal-fed range. For one thing, the food tasted better coming from the old-fashioned iron-bound stove, especially the biscuits.

The women felt that the heat blasting away in the cavernous old number was, somehow, steadier, more reliable. And the food seemed more substantial. It was well done, by George, after passing through the fiery furnace.

You can write it down pretty much as an abiding principle that every time-saving advance in the mechanics of daily life means a lessening in its quality. Today's waffles emerging from electric irons — made of aluminum, plastic, and alloys — cannot compare to the crisp, brown, thoroughly baked waffles that came out of the old cumbersome, heavy metal irons turned by hand over an open flame.

Even soaked in country butter, churned on the premises, and heavy cane syrup, that waffle from hand-turned irons was crunchy to the last bite.

It is not so much my own deprivation that I mourn — I can recall perfectly the waffles' taste and texture — as it is the loss of the experience to younger generations. Not even when, describing to them those waffles of yore, I break down and start sobbing, can they comprehend what they have missed.

Another thing is, I just don't have the patience to master the new techniques. Were it left to me, we would still be starting automobiles with a crank. So I stand in awe of these children, scooting items in and out of microwave ovens. Of 407 youngsters, ages 9 to 15, surveyed, 74 percent said they decide for themselves what snacks to eat and 65 percent said they choose what they eat for breakfast.

Forty-six percent of those questioned by the Gallup poll said they pick their own lunch, and 27 percent chose their own dinner. But 50 percent of all of them said foods that are good for them don't taste good. And another survey of 5,043 youngsters showed only one in three said they eat the right kinds of food very often.

Another difficulty is, as a recent study for the Center for Science in the Public Interest discovered, processed foods for children often are low in nutrition. "The same companies that sell healthful foods for adults foist fatty, salty, sugary foods on our children," the study said.

Where is the progress in progress, one wonders.

Dishpan Hands

Washing dishes by hand is fast becoming a lost art.

The advent of the dishwashing machine in the early 1930s started the decline of the manual art, and the post-World War II super-duper washers and dryers hastened it.

Why, if you have an expensive washer, you give a dirty platter only a swipe, and the jet stream scours it clean. You'd best check behind less costly machines for tiny residues left on the crockery.

But next to the electric light, dish and clothes washers are the 20th century's greatest inventions. Spacecraft don't stack up against machines that freed women from drudgery at sink and washtub.

That liberation assured them time to unite and march for equal rights and other just causes. Man walking on the moon was nothing to women walking out of the kitchen.

But when machines took over, couples no longer had quiet moments chatting as one washed the dishes and the other dried. You put your motions with the dishes on automatic drive while your minds free-wheeled over the day.

Amid these hectic schedules for couples, how ironic that one of their rare, intimate interludes during the day occurs during what used to be deemed an irksome chore.

It is not generally known, but I was one of the world's great dishwashers — still am after a holiday feast. I take over at the taps. My finishing school was with a nasty-tempered KP pusher called Ornery, but never to his face. Every World War II mess hall had a pusher who made sure no man loafed at whatever job he was assigned.

If the pusher wasn't wrathful by nature, he soon formed that habit bossing men, few of whom felt they were serving their country with distinction by washing dishes, mopping floors or cleaning grease traps.

Once, our outfit pulled 60 straight days of kitchen police. We had finished training, and while the Army pondered where to send us, it put us on perpetual KP. All the GIs had it, save Sgt. Maypop, who stood between us and the pusher when that mad monitor seemed about to commit mayhem. "Don't yers mind, men," Maypop said. "When yers gets out yers can get a job in any kitchen in the country."

That was Maypop for you — sunny-side up no matter which way the eggs were turned. Pots and pans were especially daunting. They just kept coming, an endless assembly line. The cooks fancied themselves chefs, and with so much manpower at their bidding, if they made the merest mistake, instead of rinsing the pot, they flung it at the KP to scour again. The two of us frenzied slaves, no matter how fast we moved, were behind.

And fell further back, when Ornery stopped to check our handiwork. He would select a pot from the leaning, towering pile, run his index finger over its shining interior, and, if in passing, he felt the tiniest, well-nigh microscopic fleck, he would order us to wash it again.

Not just the guilty pot but the entire pile that we had done. Which explains why, on Thanksgiving, before the final hot rinse, I run an index finger around the inside of the pot.

Scrub-A-Dub-Dumb

How reassuring to find that one's perplexity in trying to cope with modern gadgetry is shared by a multitude. A chorus of me-toos greeted a recent column on how difficult it has become to operate showers in new hotels.

In the place of the laughably simple old-fashioned contrivance of two faucets — one for hot water, the other for cold — hotels have installed a single huge dial, which turns one way for hot water, the other for cold, and, moreover, pulls out or pushes in to change the velocity of the stream of water. In some mysterious maneuver, which varies among hotels, one may stop and unstop the tub.

The line between cold water turning to hot, as one revolves the dial, is so thin that even after one has mastered the mechanics of the apparatus, it takes longer to set the water's temperature than it does to take the shower.

It is as if manufacturers wish to stay abreast of changing technology by making the taking of a shower as complex as the launching of a spacecraft. I doubt that former astronaut John Glenn can get into such a shower with confidence that he knows how to work it.

Among those agreeing with my thesis is J.W. Smith of Richmond. He reported that, on a vacation trip to Myrtle Beach, S.C., he was able to get the shower started but couldn't figure how to turn it off. I know precisely how he felt. In a new hotel, not only was it impossible to turn off the shower, but I couldn't unstop the tub either, so that Gin found me on my knees with a glass frantically bailing water from tub to sink.

"Shall I bring you your celluloid duck?" she asked.

"Run find a bucket," I shouted. "It's gaining!"

The trend to make life difficult has also overtaken manufacturers of television sets and electricians who install light switches. In the same hotel — so swank that the tooth fairy left a tiny chocolate mint on each guest's pillow — I had one dickens of a time finding switches on lamps, so cleverly were they hidden in recesses around the base.

The floor lamp defeated me completely. There simply was no way to turn it on. Neither was there any sort of button or switch to get the television set going. Preparing to ring the desk, I noticed inconspicuous buttons above the bed's headboard, and, punching them, brought the lamp and the TV into play simultaneously. It would not have surprised me more if a boxing glove had shot from the wall and slugged me in the kisser.

The next week, arriving in Pennsylvania at the reunion of my old Army outfit, I came upon Jack Norris of San Antonio, Texas, who remarked that he had not been able to turn on his room's television set.

Through four years, from Abilene to Okinawa, Norris helped me fix all manner of straps and buckles and uncooperative equipment, so it seemed only fair to examine the set, not that he expected a solution from the most inept guy in the company. So I looked it over and pressed buttons to no avail, and had the phone in hand to SOS the desk when, glancing at the wall, saw the obscure little panel of buttons. I pushed one; the set came to life.

Norris was astounded, not so much at the method of turning on the set as my hitting upon a solution. No point in telling him it was a second effort within two days.

Major Appliance

To some economists, things ought to be built to wear out so as to create a demand for more things. They call it planned obsolescence. My conviction is that anything that costs more than $100 is supposed to last forever. If it don't, it's a failure of capitalism. Imagine my surprise when our kitchen range, bought in 1964, became arthritic. After only 30 years of service, that stove had proved to be a lemon. I was of a mind to call the Better Business Bureau.

Lemon or not, it had to go, old love spurned. So we bought one from a firm that has supplied our other appliances and excels in making repairs, which I don't. My mechanical ineptitude is renowned. Recently when I bought a hammer at the hardware store, Phil the owner almost fell apart laughing, asking, "Is this the first one?"

At the appliance firm, the salesman was a pleasure to deal with, as were the two deliverymen who shoved the new stove into a space I'd have sworn it couldn't fit. It amazed me, too, that the gleaming range was far lighter than the old ironclad it had replaced. In this Plastic Age, I'm a baffled, bellowing, left-over dinosaur. Of even greater concern was an envelope, stuck to the stove, containing a set of instructions labeled: DO YOUR PART.

Do my part, indeed! It reminded me of the Christmas dawn, with the boys eager to run to the tree, when I discovered that dotty old Santy hadn't included batteries for the electric train.

Paying thrice as much for the new stove as the one purchased in 1964, I figured I'd done my part. Had I been a seer on the order of Henry Ford or Harvey Firestone, I'd have bought TWO stoves in 1964 and stashed one, unused, on the front stoop, with a vase of flowers atop it, as a long-term replacement for the one that just failed.

The do-your-part packet held a flange or hasp or some such gadget along with a cartoon of a stove tipping over under the weight of a child standing on its open door that had been pulled level with the floor. That the firm was bent on recruiting me, as the last nut in its assembly line, violated the Wagner Act. Shoving its duty onto the consumer showed scant regard for free enterprise. A repairman, dispatched to my rescue, burst out laughing at my plight. "Are you a writer?" he asked, in a sympathetic tone that made me grin.

Working with a power drill, he removed the stove's door, a step quite beyond my ken. The safety device couldn't be anchored to the tile floor, so he devised an ingenious way to attach it to the wall behind the stove. Da Vinci couldn't have done better. Working back there, he discovered that the clock on the dash was on the blink. He'd come back with a new one soon, he said. He made it look easy. But if the Lord had left me to build the Ark, the animals would be swimming yet, two by two.

Jack 'Em Up

In an anniversary review of the American automobile, my first proposal is that manufacturers raise it a foot and a half off the ground, as it was at its birth.

That way, to get out of the car, you wouldn't have to plant your feet on the ground as if bracing to jump over the moon and grip the door frame with both hands and wheeze and heave and pull and throw yourself around, a sumo wrestler trying to extricate yourself from quicksand just to dismount from the car.

What in the name of Henry Ford possessed designers in Detroit to lower the chassis so close to the ground as to make the vehicle more of a glorified skateboard than a full-grown automobile? Henry Ford put the American motorist on a throne. From that perch he or she could survey all that moved in his or her realm. You could open the door and step upon the running board and then put your foot to the ground without strain and greet earth-bound commoners with the grace and dignity of royalty descending among them.

Approaching the car, preparing to board it, you could see at a glance clear through the underside of the car to the daylight on the other side. You could notice immediately on a hot August day if a chicken had settled under the car, in the shade so as to escape the heat of the sun. That way, knowing full well the chicken was under there, you were not traumatized and scared out of your wits when you turned the key in the ignition and pumped the gas and set off thereby a sudden cackling, flapping of wings, and ruffling of agitated feathers as if the engine had somehow been replaced with a chicken coop.

Also, sitting high behind the steering wheel, you had a clear view of what was ahead and on both sides as the car chugged along, so you could give the right of way to a slow-going turtle or a flock of fledgling bob whites scurrying across the road. And if the creek rose during a cloudburst and submerged the road, the car's chassis cleared the tide and brought you to safety. You could, in an emergency, jump a curb in town without raking the bottom of the car and tearing up the transmission and who knows what else.

In a pinch, you could pack six persons in the two seats in the interior and put four on each running board rimming the sides. Do you know any car today, except an eight-door stretch limousine, that can convey 14 passengers? In the old days, the ordinary auto could do it. That, then, is the first of the six-part series to revamp the motor car. When and what will the next one offer? No telling!

Ignition and Liftoff

One hoists oneself into a rental car as if climbing into the cockpit of a stealth bomber to take it on a flight at thrice the speed of light. There ain't a confounded thing on the entire dashboard — or console — of a new car that can be identified readily. For 15 minutes I am slapping my hands around aimlessly like a chimpanzee looking for a lever that will produce a banana.

You wouldn't think problems would arise with a radio not much larger than a pack of cards. All it needs are two knobs, one to turn it on and off and control the volume and the other to twirl around the dial and offer, when pressed, AM or FM fare. The other day one had 18 knobs, buttons, switches.

I have driven to Roanoke with the radio tuned to deafening rock because I couldn't find how to change stations, reduce the volume, switch to FM or turn it off. And another day I left Raleigh early to reach home before dark so as not to have to figure how to turn on the headlights. Branded in my mind is my first encounter with an automatic seat belt. Oh, I had heard of them, but one does not expect to face such unsettling innovations outside the pages of futuristic journals.

So in an airport in Birmingham, I let out a shriek and bellowed, "YE GODS!" when what I took for the dreaded Malaysia noose snake shot out with a sharp hiss from somewhere above me, simultaneously gripping me about the waist and the throat. I felt like Laocoon struggling with two serpents that came rearing out of the sea to wrap him in their coils. Yelling in solitude induced in me the feeling that besets a tree when nobody is around to hear it fall. It is very well for science to proclaim that in such circumstances no sound occurs, but what does science know?

Most times I get away from home in a smooth launch, thanks to friends at a rental car agency. They rush out to greet me like the heads-up crew at Houston cheering an astronaut. Last week, after I had spent a frustrating 15 minutes trying to find the key to the car's gas-cap lock, Jennifer uncovered it when she pressed an orange button in the glove compartment. I wouldn't dared have pushed it for fear of being thrown 30 feet through the roof.

On another occasion, Jack explained that to turn the ignition key one had to press the foot brake — a device to prevent the car from being started by a child, which proved Jack was dealing with one. And one day Ann found me outside the car staring, befuddled, at a blank surface where the door handle should have been and alerted me to it at shoulder height instead of belt level. What does a carmaker create with such a change other than confusion?

I sat wondering another time how to raise and lower windows until Herman showed me tiny buttons to push in the left armrest. I drove off with windows rising and falling as in a clown car. And Herman, when I couldn't start the wipers, flicked them with a jigger on the steering column.

Arriving at home the other night, I couldn't find how to open the door from the inside. I blew the horn. Gin approached. "Dear girl," I said, "open the door from out there so's I can show you this lovely interior." Only after she opened it from the outside did I find the handle inside crouching in a slight indenture above the window buttons.

How handy things used to be when cars didn't try to be different.

Fill 'Er Up

Auto manufacturers ought to to agree on a simple dashboard. It'd do wonders for the national psyche. In 15 years, there has been a sort of explosion in complex jiggers on dashboards. Last week on a journey in a new rental car, I counted 14 buttons on the radio and 11 on the air conditioner/heater. How different things used to be. A child could operate the radio: one knob to turn it on and off, the other to change stations. About 85 miles down the road, I figured how to turn on the radio and, thereafter, hit a button marked "scan," and it bounced around stations at random.

I rented a car last week because (1) no fool would take the 17-year-old Pontiac beyond a 30-mile radius and (2) the rental office, a block away, is manned by a half-dozen of the most understanding people you could meet. They, as they put it, "look out" for me.

They look out not in the sense of a turtle trying to cross the Indianapolis Speedway on July 4 but as one looks "after" his brethren or sistren on this old globe spinning through the ether. (Yes, I know, you are grabbing the dictionary, which I just did, to see if it has "sistren." You'll find it marked "obsolete" for sisters; but this is a case of an outcast word regaining favor, since a masculine word no longer may stand for both genders.)

A month ago, I thought things had come to a pretty pass when, trying to open the door of a new rental car, I reached out, belt-high, and found no handle, nothing to grip. My hand just flabbed against the plain side of the automobile. Ye gods, I thought, how does one get in this jitney — through the top like a submarine?

I was standing, nonplussed, wondering if one were expected to use a can opener, when Jennifer rushed out from the rental agency and opened the car door from a handle set shoulder-high. So help me, had she not appeared, I'd be there pondering yet how to get in. The other day I drew a car so designed that you couldn't tell at a glance one end from the other. This time, Anne came running, crying: "No, no! You're trying to get in through the trunk. It won't work that way, try as you might."

She led me to the front door. Jack checked me out on the console as if I were preparing for a shot to Mars. I am particularly eager to learn the whereabouts of the light switch ever since, in Baltimore, I sat in a gas station 15 minutes searching for it only to have a mechanic, after five minutes, discover it on a funny-looking appurtenance curving up from the right side of the steering column. Never before had I seen a light switch on the right side. It had been one of the few instances where a left-handed person could shine.

Last week's trip offered the eeriest mix-up. Before starting homeward at midnight across an uninhabited stretch of Southside Virginia, I had asked a filling station operator to fill the tank while I bought milk and crackers.

After driving half an hour, I noticed the gas gauge was a shade above empty. In another 45 minutes, I reached a convenience store with a man in a booth. After dispensing $3 worth, the hose gagged.

The man, at my urging, dismounted and looked at the gauge, still at empty. "F I 'uz you, I'd top it every 50 miles, empty or not," he advised.

I stopped once again, found the gauge hadn't budged much above a hair, and decided either it or I was dysfunctional. In Norfolk next day, I asked Herman the mechanic to look at the immovable gauge. "Notice," he said, "that you have been looking at the empty warning, but the gas gauge is still at near full."

By George, he was right.

"I know how you feel," he said. "It confused me at first."

See what I mean? Understanding.

Getting the Scoop ...
No, not that kind

A year or so ago, maybe more, a manufacturer of laundermat detergent enclosed a little plastic measuring scoop in its box of soap powders.

How thoughtful of them to do this, I thought, upon finding the white plastic scoop tucked in the box. But, figuring they would only favor consumers with a single crackerjack prize in a soap box, I wished we had at least one more to replace the first one when it got lost. No need to have worried. In the ensuing months we have received at least 200 scoops. And when you consider their unceasing distribution throughout the United States and, for all I fancy, the known world, the time will come when we will have enough of these scoops so that, placed end to end, they would reach to Mars. And back, full of dust.

It puts you in mind of the lad who started a vast vat of oatmeal cooking but forgot, as it neared the brim, the magic word to turn it off. That porridge overflowed the pot and out of the chimney and down the cobbled street until the pot's owner returned and uttered the magic word. Villagers, armed with spoons, had to eat their way home.

I envision such a fate overtaking us with runaway plastic scoops, which are not nearly as flavorful as porridge. Why, you may well ask, doesn't the fool simply switch to a scoopless brand of detergent? Because, as is well known, I am a traditionalist. The brand of detergent that Gin brought home eons ago and taught me how to use in the clothes washing machine was the first of its type. As a matter of fact, she told me, "Now don't put ANY-

THING but this very soap powder in this particular washing machine!" — as if, left unwatched, I might dump EVERYTHING — tops, gyroscopes, feathers from pillowcases, galoshes, clothes pins, kites, garden hose, wagon tongues, straw hats, umbrellas, antimacassars, yoyos, as well as some really odd things into it.

"You'd think," I said, "I was a child."

"Yes," she said.

Even had she not forbade it, I'd never have selected any other kind of soap powder. I wasn't even sure, as varieties of detergents proliferated on the store shelves, that any other kind would suit our machine, and I had no desire to investigate. It rattles me to go down the aisle of liquids, powders, soaps, cleansers, all in bright day-glo colors clamoring, "Try me! Choose me!"

Anyway, even if it weren't, I am loyal to a fault. To this day, going into the store for toothpaste, I ask for Ipana, which is long gone but the tube I long to see.

"Eye WHAT?" the clerk inquired the other day, irritated at being confronted with a doddering dotard asking for something incomprehensible. "Eye WHAT?"

"PANA!" I shot back, a little irked myself at having to deal with a Visigoth.

"What is a PANA?" he asked.

"Spelled backward," I told him, "it is an ANAP!"

And turned on my heel. One day there'll be a mountain slide of white plastic scoops cascading upon us. Don't say you weren't warned.

Chapter Eleven

Pop Goes The Culture

Wrinkles in Time

Let us moan the demise of the seersucker suit. Oh, well, one or two seersuckers are lurking in stores on hangers on the backs of doors that never close. They will be uncovered years hence and deemed fossils.

So few seersuckers are in the wild. Mainly the breed is on the skids to extinction. Even in the Deep South, they are rare. My mind was on a seersucker suit on a trip to Alabama. Birmingham boasts a Rich's store. The manager said he hadn't been able to find a seersucker all summer.

I reeled. No seersuckers! Why, you knew summer had arrived when your father put on his blue-and-white-striped seersucker. Later, brown and white stripes came in vogue. Seersuckers came pre-rumpled. They had so many wrinkles when new that nobody could tell when they were wrinkled from wear and tear.

They were loose and they were cool, being run up out of cotton, and you didn't have to worry about their getting wrinkled when no room was left to add wrinkles. You have heard of wrinkle-free clothes? Original seersuckers were wrinkle-full. The cotton cloth had a puckery feeling you couldn't iron out even if you tried. So the first seersuckers were shapeless. They hung on you as if draped limp and loose on a newel bed post. All summer, men looked cool and frumpy and felt born free.

They hung on to shapeless jackets as if they were life preservers. Grown men couldn't carry security blankets, but the seersuckers served just as well. Harold Sugg had a brown and white striper of which he was inordinately fond. One day Sugg spilled homemade fig preserves on it. The cleaner couldn't remove the stain, so Harold said dye the whole thing.

"What color?" the cleaner said.

"Fig color," said Harold.

Manufacturers finally blended synthetic fibers with the cotton so that the seersucker could take a crease. Instead of a nice soft look, the seersucker took on a sheen, as if Simonized. They were, a farmer told me, "half cotton, half rotten."

Former Gov. Colgate Darden loved the wrinkles. He said they lent character to a suit much as they do to an old man's face. Traveling in South Carolina, he and two young state officials found a general store that sold seersuckers at $17 each. Darden bought two, satisfied they would last forever. One day his younger brother, Pretlow, bought him a new seersucker. The governor was aghast when he learned it cost $200.

And it didn't have any wrinkles, either.

Dapper Cappers

Internationally renowned hat designer Jack McConnell was at The Famous in Portsmouth, and I dropped by to see if hats are back. They are.

The place was thronged with women parading about like little girls playing dress-up. They came from deep in North Carolina and across the water from Williamsburg — all ages, all races — and for hours they tried different styles as if searching for an identity as well as a hat.

"That is more YOU than anything I've seen you in today," one woman cried to her companion, who was wearing a white cap adorned with a sheaf of bell-like blossoms that swept downward past her right eyebrow.

"When I get depressed," a customer confessed, "I buy a hat. It makes me feel better, and it's cheaper than a psychiatrist."

Nearby a woman wheeled and said, "I feel absolutely rich in this one!"

"All you need is a Rolls," someone assured her.

A clerk hurried by. "Do we have another nervous hat?" she called.

A nervous hat is a turbanlike toque, the shape of a pineapple, deep magenta in color. Two-inch antennas, tipped with magenta sequins, sprout from its surface. At the least movement, the antennas quiver.

Setting the nervous hat atop her head, a woman stared at it, a-tremble, in the mirror. "What is this doing?" she inquired. "Are we fighting each other?"

The more extreme a hat might seem to a male the more likely it is, once crowning a feminine brow, to make sense. A woman peered from under a sombrero. Clusters of yellow wisteria dangled from the brim. "Isn't that gorgeous," she said, staring at her image in the glass but speaking to a friend.

"That isn't a hat, that's a STATEMENT," the friend replied.

Presiding was designer McConnell, a six-footer who resembles a benign Vincent Price with deep, cultured voice to match. He wore an Oxford gray suit with black velvet lapels and scroll-like facings on the pockets and buttonholes. The pockets showed red lining. Asked if he had a hat, McConnell produced a Tyrolean, bought in Vienna, with a brush in the band.

"I venture to say it's the only one in the country, and it cost me a pretty penny." he said.

Younger people are wearing hats, he said, "maybe as a rebellion against their mothers who were not wearing them."

Around him women were buying hats ranging in price from

$100 to $150. "When people are down and the press is talking about hard times, that's the best time for millinery," McConnell said.

A woman, a hat set straight on her head, approached. "Is this right?" she asked submissively, childlike. McConnell tilted the hat at a slight angle. She looked in the mirror, smiled and departed. "A woman can never put on her hat like I can," McConnell remarked.

Women are more likely to temporize over hats than are men.

"A man buys the first hat he sees," he said. "The more a woman debates, the less successful her choice is likely to be."

One appeared in a hat, smoke gray and large as a shield. McConnell steered her to another."You see," he told her, "now your cheeks have an upward sweep."

She left, and he said, "I will never tell a woman a hat looks good on her if it doesn't. I will say the hat is pretty, but I won't say it's right for her, unless I agree. If she trusts me, she will never go out in something unsuited to her. It's a sense of knowing proportions. I can tell at a glance.

"Most women," he added, "stand too close to a mirror. Stand way back to see yourself as others see you."

A former actor on radio and off Broadway, McConnell began designing hats after serving with the Navy during World War II.

"I started making hats as a hobby while I was dating a girl who made them," he said. He rented a shop with a furrier on 57th Street, began filling orders for syndicates, then started his own national business. He has just completed a pre-Easter tour of 41 cities.

Women can become quite intense in their quest for the right hat. In Little Rock two women seized the same hat, and, vying for it, tore off the brim.

"That's when I leave the floor," McConnell said.

Someone called him. He turned to see a former customer. He held out his hands. "But where's your hat?" he asked. "Didn't you like it?"

"It's so admired," she said, "I had to put it in my will."

All Buttoned Up

Frank Sinatra advises in Esquire Magazine how to live and love, including how to dress in black tie. "For me," he confides, "a tuxedo is a way of life." For me, too, for a hectic hour or so, 1.4 times a year.

Here is Sinatra's dress code:

"My basic rules are to have shirt cuffs extended half an inch from the jacket sleeve. Trousers should break just above the shoe. Try not to sit down, because it wrinkles the pants. If you have to sit down, don't cross your legs. Pocket handkerchiefs are optional, but I always wear one, usually orange, since orange is my favorite color. Shine your Mary Janes on the underside of a couch cushion."

He's right about not sitting down, even if one is wearing only one's Sunday suit, much less a tux. Try to sit about an inch and a half above the chair or sofa, a feat of levitation induced by going into a deep trance. Not only does it save the crease, but the pants seat also won't wear out as fast.

Sinatra probably owns a tux. His very own. To buy one is wise, an idea that occurs to me 45 minutes before time to put it on, too late to rent one either. Lurking in a closet is an old-fashioned tux handed down the years by my father-in-law. On me, it drapes as if any minute it is going to fall off, or apart, but it is black, which suffices.

True, youths spend more dressing for a high school prom than Sinatra does for Broadway. They wear tuxedos run up on a rainbow and look like drum majors. For a foxy grandpa to go so bedecked would be fit only for the end ring of a circus with the other clowns. White shirts are *de rigueur.* Mine's faded blue, a hue so obsolete guests murmur, "Who's the gauche one in blue?" But a ruffle down the shirt front hides what are buttons instead of studs. The cuffs are secured by safety pins, when they can be found. More often, hurrying, one stuffs the cuffs up one's jacket sleeves. Soon they extrude as with the off-handed flourish of a Restoration fop. Bow ties flap away bat-like. A neighbor offers one, string or clip-on. I take the latter.

Sinatra's reference to Mary Janes, a little girl's buckle shoe, is a nostalgic touch, a nonchalant blend with younger generations. Face it, mine is an antic figure but most revelers are too transported with their own attire to notice yours. And if they break up in laughter at the rumpled apparition, then to occasion merriment is nothing to rue in a world so full of woe.

In a wedding with young ones dancing amid art in the Chrysler Museum's great court, I sidled inside, moving between pillars and around the jamming band, intent only on catching the shining bride's eye to let her know I cared and did. When she started to me, open-faced, laughing, I fled, taking care not to leave my Mary Jane on the wide, slate-tiled front steps.

Dancing Away a Dire Decade

Thoughts while strolling ...

What impressed me growing up about 10 years behind movie star Ginger Rogers was, well, her ginger.

The nickname Ginger emerged from a sibling trying to pronounce Virginia, but it fit her like the glass slipper fit Cinderella.

You felt it when she was battling her way through a dance routine with Fred Astaire in their lovely musicals star-studding the dark Depression.

Their light romances, all but one in the 1930s, were just right for those dire times.

Whole families flocked together to watch them. We didn't have money to fling on grim, life-like stuff. Gloom cloaked the streets outside movie palaces. We wanted escape.

Fred and Ginger obliged.

Astaire never found any partner to match him for airy grace. Everything he did we thought was effortless. He earned that state of grace in grinding rehearsals beyond our ken.

A winsome shade in top hat and tails, he dared her throughout the dance with one audacious move after another, and she, gloriously gowned, fought with furious, almost comic energy to keep up, matching him step for step, and in high heels and backward at that, her swirling figure fraught with frantic intensity.

The two first danced during a Broadway rehearsal for "Girl Crazy," a 1930 Gershwin musical in which she was starring. Astaire, then on Broadway with his sister, Adele, visited the rehearsal.

Producers were dissatisfied with the dance routine for "Embraceable You."

"Here, Ginger, try it with me," Astaire said.

Ginger Rogers died Tuesday and for now, anyway, she outshines him in the mind as they dance.

Lighten Up!

Santa Claus may be destined to be the Last Fat Man.

And even he is in danger of fading.

Fat men used to be all over the lot, delighting the eye. In the 1920s, men were more apt to be fat than not. Women were dedicated to beefing up anybody who weighed less than 295 pounds.

It was their mission.

"Thin as a rail!" women said of them, heaping homemade vanilla ice cream atop mince meat pie already rich enough to fill a regiment. "Land sakes!" they said. "Eat it, honey, ALL of it!"

Who could resist such blandishments!

To be stout was generally thought to be hardy as well as hefty.

And fat men were happy, year-long Santas, big round shapes, tipping about light-footed, brightening the landscape with their embonpoint, handsome fellows filling the air with the jollity of their laughter, pulling half dollars from vest pockets to scatter among children hoping for mere dimes.

I never met a fat man I didn't like.

It was a pleasure to be around a fat man. Still is, when you can find one. Shakespeare noticed it. He saw everything.

225

"Let me have men about me that are fat, sleek headed..." Julius Caesar cried. "Yon Cassius has a lean and hungry look." It is well nigh impossible, well-fed, to have a sour outlook. It is as if that extra layer or two of fat insulates a body from anger as well as foul weather. A buffer against ill humor. It buoys them up.

In the 1950s, fat men began evanescing. Replaced by wiry ones who ate bean sprouts, perpetually out of sorts from sheer hunger.

The nutritionists are even after Santa Claus, I heard.

Getting their hooks in the corpulent old elf through his missus.

"Sam," Mrs. Claus said just before he took off this year with his reindeer — that's her pet name for him, "Sam," even though he's no more Sam than I am — "Sam, I think you ought to give some thought to your weight!"

"Some WHAT to WHAT?" Santa said, startled.

"The nutritionist came by the other day. She said you are in danger of becoming overweight, eating cookies and milk as well as dark fruitcake, rum-soaked, on hearths all over the world."

"And if I didn't eat it," Santa retorted, "what would the children think? 'Tis better to give than to receive, I've found, and so should they. So should we all. My heart is so full when I start home, Cora, I can barely move."

"Are you sure it isn't your belly, shaking like a bowl full of jelly?"

"What a canard!" said Santa.

"The nutritionist said baby boomers are leaving eggnog by the fire."

"More egg than nog," Santa said. "Anyway, I'm more worried with the reindeers' condition. Donner has a bruised hoof.

Rudolph has the sniffles. I may tether Ellwood to the end of the sleigh, just in case."

"The nutritionist left you something," said. Mrs. Claus.

"What?" Santa asked, excited.

"A new Stairmaster," she said.

"STAIRMASTER!" Santa exclaimed. "I get enough exercise climbing down and up chimneys."

Spielberg's Salute

Kong is still king.

So I say after seeing "Jurassic Park," the film about the theme park that offers real dinosaurs in a fenced-in South American jungle. Huge predators, including a tyrannosaurus rex, break through the electrified strands and run amok, making, in the process, tons of money for Stephen Spielberg, who made the movie at a cost of $45 million. But I doubt Rex will be around as long as King Kong, a giant ape trapped on Skull Island and shipped by a showman to New York. The ape escapes and lays waste to much of Manhattan, a darn sight more difficult than trashing a jungle.

"King Kong," filmed with $300,000 in 1933, still runs on TV, next only in appeal to "Gone with the Wind." Still, "Jurassic Park" is a hit. Not long after it got under way Saturday, a child, 6, ran bawling up the aisle, his big brother right behind him, scolding him for being scared. A little later, when human visitors had escaped one dinosaur, another's tentacle come slithering into view. In the theater, a male voice behind us shouted, "Oh God, no!"

There are touches designed to ease tension, so it can be

ratcheted a notch higher. Near the opening, as a van is following the twisting road to the park, a huge gate rears into view. Just as I was thinking of the wall that had immured Kong, a visitor in the van mutters, "What have they got in there! Kong?" Muffled, uttered swiftly, it is almost a throwaway line with which many young people couldn't relate even if it were heard clearly; but, never mind, it is Spielberg's salute to Kong's creators.

And his work is not unworthy of comparison to theirs. Its ingenious, if far-fetched, premise is that genetic engineers use bits of vital matter from remains of prehistoric monsters to clone living counterparts. And it touches the question of whether humans should play God, introducing long-gone species into an unfit, contemporary ecology.

Modern techniques render the dinosaurs utterly realistic in motion. In one scene, a nasty, two-legged pair of them, sniffing and peering and bounding and skittering around a huge kitchen, search for their prey, two children, about the age of many of those in the audiences. The spectacle is a triumph of special effects. How they were achieved fascinates many young people. When King Kong loomed on the screen 60 years ago, it didn't interest us much to learn that five-story-high Kong was extrapolated from an 18-inch doll. Our eyes were only for Kong, all 50 feet of him, starting out as a god in his little world, trampling natives, hounding the movie crew that had come to film him, and, as it turned out, capture him and bring him, bound, to Broadway.

More incredible than effects was the shaping of the ape into a hero, smitten by beauteous Fay Wray. Pursuing her, he ransacks New York. Bedecked in blonde wig, she deserved an Oscar if, for nothing else, her incessant screaming as the great ape, wreaking destruction, bobbed up everywhere she went. She had found a friend. The ape had become enobling. At last, having obliterated an elevated train, he turns to the Empire State Building, the nearest thing to his jungle peak, and, clutching Fay, he climbs it. Straddling the top, roaring defiance, he bats at a wasp swarm of attacking biplanes. When he grasped one — it seemed about the size of an orange crate in his huge hand — we cheered.

But, bullets thudding into his throat, he is wounded mortally. Placing Fay on a ledge, he topples from the tower. On the street, the showman gazes at the fallen, tragic being. A police captain says, "Well, Mr. Denham, the airplanes got 'im." Showman Denham shakes his head.

"Oh, no, it wasn't the airplanes. It was Beauty killed the Beast."

Friends, don't talk to me of genetic engineering and special effects.

There was a story!

Chin Up

Of course, Jay Leno will succeed hosting "The Tonight Show" from which Johnny Carson retired Friday night after 30 years as king of late-night comedy.

Substituting for months as an apprentice prince on Carson's nights off, Leno already had demonstrated that the crown would fit. Elevating Leno, NBC chose well. Another candidate for Carson's throne, sardonic David Letterman, already had found in the late-late night spot the niche for his sharp-edged style.

Deft, witty Carson's supreme gift as host lay in listening, reacting nimbly to others' remarks, encouraging and setting them at ease, pointing up their performances for the audience. In his dry demeanor, modeled on Jack Benny's style, suave Carson was the ultimate straight man when working with other comedians.

Among the show's most pleasurable moments were those in which Carson watched with deep appreciation the likes of Buddy Hackett or Don Rickles indulge in outrageous buffoonery. When Hackett, eyes rolling like BBs in his baffled baby face, reached the peak of madness, Carson, doubled up in laughter, would duck behind his desk and emerge wiping his eyes. Carson not only shared the spotlight, he gave it up, hilariously — and the show was the stronger for his generosity. So was he.

Leno may not be quite as quick in rebuttal as Carson, but he conveys that all-important sympathetic interest in the guests. Leno also has a prow of a chin. Early in his career, he was advised to "do something" about that snowplow of a chin. Fortunately, he didn't. It is, in the end, an ingratiating chin. Nearly all the great comedians sublimated handicaps by reshaping them into distinctive traits. It was the very root of their humor. As children with impediments, they clowned for approval.

Sometimes the physical drawback was coupled with ethnicity, turned droll, supplicating. Jimmy Durante had his schnozzola. Laurel was thin; Hardy, fat. W.C. Fields had a klaxon-like bulb nose. Rickles' head is as bald as a bedpost. (Wearing a toupee, he didn't look funny, he looked ordinary.) Larry Storch's cartoonish features function as a mobile mask. Behind Jonathan Winters' vast cabbage face lurks quirky brilliance. Chaplin turned a slender frame into a wand. "My panache!" cried Cyrano de Bergerac of his white plume, but it was really his gigantic nose. Because of it, he honed his skill with words that enabled him to woo Roxanne through another man's notes.

With a stubborn decency, something of an oddity itself, Leno has that panache of a chin. Without it, he would have been almost handsome; but he wouldn't have been host for "The Tonight Show." His massive torso is topped by the huge mockup of a head, which wobbles a bit, now and then. Then Leno looks like a 10-cent store Buddha that, when tapped, trembled ever so slightly.

Carson eased up near the close — he unbuttoned his blazer — but he didn't relax standards. Among the last guests was Elizabeth Taylor who had rebuffed other bids to the show. The thought of the live audience unnerved her, she said. Carson was edgy, at first, endearing somehow in that virtuoso in his last show. Amid a routine, Steve Martin, that wild and crazy guy, grabbed Carson's hand and buried his face on his wrist and sobbed: "Don't go!" — at which Carson reared back, laughing. Two words, after all that time, were the best goodbye.

You say Tomato, I say Tomoto

Would it be pardonable, do you think, to say a word in support of Dan Quayle? They are after him again about his spelling. Signing copies of his book, "Standing Firm," — in which, I bet you 10 to 1, there isn't a single misspelled word — the former vice president was approached by a 5-year-old girl with two file cards to be autographed. Her name, her mother said, was Samantha.

"S-Y-M..." Quayle began, reciting the letters.

"S-A-M," he was corrected. So there's more hilarity over Quayle's inability to spell. You would think they were Noah Webster, all these people laughing. Forgetting that Americans are the most miserable spellers on earth. Half the population can't spell kat.

You want to see some sloppy spelling, read the letters of the founding fathers. In one letter, they'd spell the same word three different ways. Take your choice! The English language was cooling down, still soft and malleable, and nobody objected to variant versions in the spelling of a word. There was no just one way to spell a word. They were more interested, anyway, in what they were writing than in how it was spelled.

Get the words right, to the devil with the spelling.

Odds are that the rough version of the Declaration of Independence had more errors in spelling than hen tracks in a chicken run. Ben Franklin had to correct it. Washington, a notoriously bad speller, called him over and said, "Ben, in the name of posterity, bring this thing into some kind of conformity. If we must have misspelled words, let's have them misspelled the same way.

"Remember, if we do not hang together, we will most assuredly hang separately."

Washington was good at cooking up words, on any subject, that looked as though they ought to march in marble around a building. I'm grateful to Quayle for misspelling "potato," putting an "e" on the end, during the Bush-Quayle yoking. It just looked better that way. And, furthermore, that's the way I spelled it most of the time.

And "tomatoe," too.

But no more. There was such an outcry at Quayle's expense that it finally drove into my poor head: "You don't spell 'potato' with an e, you dolt!"

And I have not spelled potato with an e since.

Quayle was under heavy stress at the book signing, with 600 customers in line. Every one of them waiting for a shot at telling him what he did wrong in the campaign, while he nodded and smiled and gritted his teeth.

And they leaned over him and watched him form every letter. Further, what with the names of people these days, especially young girls — Debi, Debbi, Debbie, Deby — you have to be careful. So he looks up, checking, and says "S-y-m — " and every reporter in place legs to a telephone, writing SYM on a pad.

Of all the writers in Christendom, the worst are journalists, especially columnists.

The People's Princess

You remember, don't you, when we got up at 4 a.m. to watch the wedding of Lady Diana and Prince Charles?

A glass coach came rolling out of a fairy tale, and inside it was Lady Diana, princess to be, hid in a frothy veil and billowing gown that filled the coach — an explosion of white as occurs when a green comber hits a rocky shore and erupts into dazzling salt-white foam.

The glass coach seemed awash in blinding snowy surf. Then we saw her hand and caught a glimpse of wondering blue eyes. She alighted from the carriage. Her train kept unreeling behind her until it stretched as long as a townhouse plot. Thereafter the gown — an antique white that shone bright and pure in the sunlight — dominated the day's pageantry, an icy white comet standing frozen across the sky in mid-passage.

She walked St. Paul's long aisle — it seemed to extend forever — beside her father, who looked abash, marveling, as if to say, has it really come to this?

The archbishop read from Corinthians — faith, hope, love, these three — and she and Charles exchanged vows. The archbishop offered advice: Solve our economic problems but fail to build loving families and it profits us nothing. That, in short, was their assignment — exemplify marital happiness for the Commonwealth and all else.

Finally, the icy comet still frozen in the sky, the two made encore appearances on Buckingham Palace's balcony to the roar of a million throats. And just as they were going into the palace the last time, he slipped his arm around her and kissed her quickly.

The door — and the first chapter of the fairy tale — closed.

They brought her home yesterday from Paris. An honor guard met the plane and bore the casket to a waiting hearse. Another vigil, a sad one, is in motion.

There's no way to parcel the blame. Perhaps something of a generational gap obtained — she was 19 during the courtship and he was 12 years older and in tutelage from childhood to be a king one day.

Things had been better, lately, as they met on common ground in their concern for their two boys. And Diana had found romance and a role as Lady Bountiful worldwide.

Lord Jeffrey Archer spoke Sunday of her "great humanitarian, caring side" on NBC's "Meet the Press." She supported the AIDS campaign long before it was fashionable, he said, and then she campaigned for a ban on land mines.

"When she traveled to New York or Chicago or Los Angeles, she could fill halls that very few film stars could fill," he said. "It will be impossible to replace her. I mean, she was the brightest star in our constellation."

She was to host a charity function for the Red Cross on Oct. 9, he noted. "We sold out on day one and would have made vast sums because of her presence."

Moderator Tim Russert observed that many people in Great Britain's government took umbrage when, on a visit to Bosnia, she spoke out about land mines. They felt she had crossed the line from royalty into political decision making.

She didn't even understand the controversy that had been blown up out of all proportion "because what she cared about was saving lives, and she hated land mines," Lord Archer replied. Another of her roles, he said, was to introduce Prince William "to the real world, to show him that there's suffering out there."

Russert remarked that she wanted to be remembered as "the people's princess."

"She was that," Lord Archer replied. "She empathized with the young and the old. She literally touched them and they felt they were friends straightaway."

From political poles, conservative Republican Pat Buchanan and liberal Democrat Mario Cuomo found agreement in assessing the role of the paparazzi in the wreck that took three lives, including Di's.

There's no question the press has the right to follow a celebrity, Buchanan said. "They chase Diana because they know they can sell those pictures to the tabloids for tens of thousands of dollars and the reason the tabloids pay is because we want to see all those pictures of her down at Monte Carlo and on the Riviera and with her boyfriend and the rest of it."

To say the paparazzi alone are responsible wouldn't be proper, said Buchanan. "I think a lot of us are responsible."

"That's very close to the heart of the matter," Cuomo agreed.

"In the end, these paparazzi were paid professionals doing what the public demanded, and that is pictures of celebrities like Princess Diana, and so, to some extent, we're responsible."

Why are some films on television so ugly and barbaric? "asked Cuomo". "It's because people will pay to watch them. And so in the end we're a society, in large measure, that desires things that later we say disgust us. So to some extent we're implicated."

Russert asked if media groups should look at themselves and their behavior.

"In the end," Cuomo said, "the media's job is to give the people what they want. I think people should start talking for themselves about why tabloids are selling. Because we read them, because we love to read, especially, the ugly stuff.

"The pretty stuff is nice, the fairy tale was wonderful. The nightmare will get even more attention, and that's what people should be asking themselves about. What is this proclivity we have for negativism, for harshness?"

And so the question hangs with the white and icy comet in the sky.

Chapter Twelve

In The Public's Eye

Beginning Again

Yet again the family gathered around the flickering television set, and the national family, too, like cave people for warmth
and enlightenment, this time to view Richard Nixon's latest,
surely last, crisis. The gathering evoked the sense of other watches
and the thought that of the last four presidents, three — Kennedy
assassinated, Johnson undone by Vietnam, Nixon tripped by
Watergate — have ended tragically, only Ike departing happily.

During a two-hour countdown, commentators and congressmen speculated on how Nixon would go — with a forthright
statement of misdeeds that manfully, they expected, would free
the country of Watergate.

Reprises of his career aroused memories of the Pinocchio-
nosed young congressman: Ike clasping him to his bosom after
the Checkers speech, chortling, "That's my boy!" Nixon's daugh-
ters, gangling children then, big-eyed in a box at a national nominating convetion; Mrs. Nixon, tremulous, soft-eyed, smiling,
crisis-free briefly, standing in the middle of Pennsylvania Avenue after her husband's inaugural parade had gone by, seeming
as young as a college girl at a prom; Kennedy and Nixon in the
first debate that decided the series of four and the extremely close
election — Kennedy a flame, Nixon standing awkwardly, favor-
ing a hurt knee, a sick crane; Nixon, at airports, shopping cen-
ters, and auditoriums, delivering with head-jerking earnestness
the good, solid verities that Americans used to embroider and
hang on the wall and still hold in their hearts.

Now he was before us again, and except for one swift reference to wrong judgments, wrenched out of him, his address was

more of a last hurrah than a confession. On the scales in some viewers' minds were Watergate's transgressions. Against them, without acknowledging those imperfections, Nixon piled on his scales the splendid foreign-policy achievements, nuclear test ban, Mideast peace, friendship with Russia and China, and — a shot for the listening wives, mothers and grandmothers — the fact that their men weren't dying in Vietnam.

It was a greater tour de force than the Checkers speech, and even the commentators, with one exception, pronounced it good. Roger Mudd, larger-eyed than normal, going against his audience's grain, spelled out in a firm voice that Nixon had failed to address the issue that had divided Congress and country.

Gaunt, haggard, dark eyes staring, the President at 61 nevertheless displayed undimmed the remarkable stamina that has enabled him to rebound from defeats that would floor ordinary men. The performance guaranteed that in his next public appearance he would be cheered by a people who are, above all, forgiving and forgetting. Rather than even a last hurrah, the 16-minute spiel was but another beginning, in style and thrust, a fighting campaign speech. Even as the Presidential Seal was fading from the screen, there was an eerie — if illogical — feeling that Richard Nixon would be running again.

Missing McCarthy

Eugene J. McCarthy, who led a youthful army to the polls for the cause of peace 16 years ago, hasn't broken the habit of speaking his mind. At his home tucked into the folds of Virginia's

Blue Ridge Mountains, the former Minnesota senator criticized Walter Mondale and Ronald Reagan, defended today's youth from charges of apathy, and insisted Americans can still be rallied to bear hardships for their country.

Tall, patrician 68-year old McCarthy is silver-haired. The features aren't as arrowheaded-hard as they were in 1968 when he, while others quailed, challenged President Johnson for escalating the Vietnam War. But the mind is sharp. The lines sing and zing. The poet yet lurks in the politician. Of Reagan, he said: "He's almost like a person who just lives in clearings. He can be moved to another clearing and he's a different person almost — or at least he has no sense of what's in the jungle between the clearings.

"And it's not just with political issues, it's sort of intellectual. He doesn't see the contradictions in some of the things he says about religion. It doesn't seem to distress him at all. They say he sleeps well every night. "

Of the choice between Reagan and Mondale, he said, "It's hard to judge. Reagan is wrong on things he didn't know about and Mondale's wrong on things he did know about."

The pied piper who beckoned youth from classrooms to protest a war now journeys from college campuses to corporate seminars asking Americans to be their true, best selves. "We're the most over-transported, over-fueled, over-fed, over-advertised, over-salted, over-drugged, even to drugging cattle and chickens, over-corporated and over-armed country in the history of the world."

Since he left the Senate in 1970, McCarthy has written a dozen books, including poetry. In the 1968 campaign, aides, missing McCarthy, would find him in his hotel writing a poem.

He was reared in the town of Watkins in central Minnesota.

240

His mother was "quite amazing, totally unselfish, concerned about our health and education. She wanted us to read before we went to school." His father, "pretty independent-minded, was mostly a cattle dealer. He couldn't really work for anybody. To him there were two ways of doing things: the way people are doing them and the way they ought to be doing them."

Just passing a man harnessing horses, his father would criticize the way he had them hitched, not aggressively, he'd just say that's not the way to do it, McCarthy recalled. "Watkins was a good place in which to grow up. It provided a test of talents. All we needed were three good things: a good horn to determine whether we could play in the band, a good baseball glove, a good pair of ice skates. If there was talent that was wasted, it wasn't because there wasn't a marginal test of it somewhere in the town."

McCarthy played first base in a semi-pro league. When he was 16 on a summer job in a lumberyard, he read Charles Eliot's 5-foot shelf of Harvard classics "I'd had pretty good reading in high school but the Eliot books sort of pulled it together."

He earned his degree at St. John's University in three years and then a master's degree at the University of Minnesota. He taught social sciences in high school for five years and from 1940 to 1942 was professor of economics at St. John's. During World War II, he worked in the War Department's intelligence office. After the war, he taught at St. Thomas College in St. Paul. A history professor, Marshall Smeiser, recruited him into precinct politics. In 1948, McCarthy was elected to the House of Representatives. Re-elected four times, he then moved to the Senate for two terms.

The intensifying Vietnam War, with periodic collapses of governments in South Vietnam, alarmed him. In the Senate Foreign Relations Committee in August he heard Under Secretary of State Nicholas Katzenbach insist that Johnson had authority to follow his war course even without the Gulf of Tonkin resolution. "This is the wildest testimony I ever heard," McCarthy told reporters. "There is no limit to what he says the president can do. There is only one thing to do — take it to the country."

He had been moved, too, by Jean Larteguy's "The Centurions," about French officers who couldn't fight the war they faced in Vietnam and Algeria without it destroying their character and personality. "The same thing happened to us," he said. "So far as we know now our officers weren't affected particularly, but the men were. We couldn't fight that kind of war."

So he waged his anti-war run for the presidency in 1968 "partly for my own children and their friends," and also because "someone had to make a move so people who were against the war would have some kind of orderly way to raise objections. I wasn't going to let Johnson push me around. As a senator, I didn't think that one should. Whether you could handle him or not in a public contest I wasn't sure, but someone had to challenge the war and his concept of the presidential power."

Ignored by many editorial writers, he scored an unexpectedly high 42 percent of the vote in the New Hampshire primary compared with Johnson's 48 percent. Johnson withdrew from the race. Robert Kennedy made a feral rush into the fray. New Hampshire became the pivot on which America began to turn from war to peace. After a few weeks Johnson invited McCarthy to the White House. They faced each other across the wide gulf at the center of the conference table where the Cabinet met.

"He told someone later that he was surprised I was so restrained. I don't know what he thought I was going to do. I didn't make any powerful arguments, say, 'It's terrible what you've done, Mr. President.' And he didn't attempt to say, 'Look, I know stuff about this and we've got to fight it." It was a non-meeting.

"He talked a little about Bobby Kennedy. I didn't know quite what the message was — whether I should look out for Bobby or whether he'd been looking out for Bobby." McCarthy made a quick knife-like motion across his throat and added, "He didn't say anything more than that."

"By that gesture did Johnson mean 'He cut my throat,' or 'Cut his throat'?"

"It was just a warning, I guess," said McCarthy.

To compare today's youths with those of the "abnormal period" of the 1960s, he believes unfair. Instead, he looks to the 1950s for comparisons. "They may be misdirected now, but they are not apathetic. I find them more concerned than were those in the 1950s."

He is sanguine about the country's economic potential and believes people would be receptive to bold proposals. If, coming into office, "Reagan had said we had to be unselfish to shape up the country, the people would have responded, but he sort of drifted away," he said. "The country would have accepted some hardship in the name of fiscal responsibility if the sacrifice had been general. We could have had special taxes to pay bills and control inflation if we had done it across the board.

"There's also a moral aspect of how much we have a right to consume in our generation. People might be willing to give up some of their income, some of their work, so that 6 million unemployed would be absorbed in the working force — as we did in 1936 and 1938 with the 40-hour week and retirement at 65.

"I think we've been better off with Reagan than we would have been with Carter the last four years," he said. If Reagan had moved on some of the things he promised, such as reducing the bureaucracy, "I'd say give him another four years — but you don't know what he'll do."

A week ago, McCarthy drew laughter and applause in a speech to Virginia editors. Afterward, a young woman who had been a child in 1968 stopped by his chair and bent to whisper, "I like the way your mind works."

Another generation had discovered Eugene McCarthy.

Building Dreams

James Wilson Rouse, who twice changed the face of America, will receive the Presidential Medal of Freedom. Rouse, a daring dreamer and doer with a rollicking grin, relishes an exchange of ideas as his mind is working on how to put them into action. His gear is always in go. His regard for the underdog and his strength derive from roots in the Depression on Maryland's Eastern Shore.

"I had a very bad year in my life," he once explained. "My mother died in February. I was 16 in April and graduated from high school that June. My father died in August and the mortgage was foreclosed in October. I can remember thinking, 'This is tough, but this is good for me.' It's always stuck with me. I knew somehow that I was going through a period that was strengthening."

The boy from Easton, Md., devised the closed shopping mall. The Rouse Co. built four before many other developers caught on. In a second entrepreneurial leap, it built Columbia, a garden city between Baltimore and Washington.

When flight to the suburbs, which Rouse had helped trigger, left downtowns bereft of people, he sought to counter that by creating festival complexes in urban cores. In Boston, it was Faneuil Hall Marketplace; in Philadelphia, the Gallery on Marketplace East; in Baltimore, Harborplace. They checker the map.

In 1963, he failed to recruit a major department store for Norfolk. In 1979, he was vacationing in Sandbridge with Patty, his Norfolk-born wife. Civic leaders conferred with him there, and he agreed to try again in Norfolk.

Saltwater runs like blood in Norfolk's veins; and this time, through a festival place, Waterside, the city found its way back to the Elizabeth River, where it began. In Washington, D.C., he helped guide Jubilee Housing, fostered by the Church of the Savior. It renovates slum tenements and lives. Man, Rouse believes, is God's instrument in the continuing process of creation.

He founded the nonprofit Enterprise Foundation to help produce low- and moderate-income housing.

After that pivotal 16th year, he worked his way through the University of Virginia and entered the University of Maryland Law School in Baltimore. Paid to park cars, he learned on the job how to drive. While in law school he worked for the Federal Housing Administration in 1935. In 1937, at 22, he headed a mortgage department in a trust company. Three years later, he formed his own company in mortgage banking and moved into development. Of failures, he said: "All you have is an obligation to do your best, think your best, work your best and be faithful, hopeful and optimistic. Then failure doesn't matter."

Nader The Crusader

Consumer advocate Ralph Nader has come around again in shaping public opinion —— or maybe it is that Nader has never desisted, and much of the public has come around to him. Just now he is a spearpoint in the drive against congressional pay raises. Regard his crusades as you will, there is no mistaking his persuasiveness —— or durability.

Tall, gangling, he hovers over a lectern, a dark question mark, asking audiences to think. Untiring, he will talk an hour, answer questions another hour and, as the crowd disperses, crouch on the edge of the platform and hand out pamphlets to those who linger. At the close, there are still two or three, talking. The few who stay are the most committed, he figures.

On stage he is a brooding Savonarola lashing American industry and government for what he deems shortcomings. In interviews, he is lighthearted and boyish, laughing at inquiries about his work schedule, which most mortals would find unsafe at any speed.

It's fun for him. "I'm fascinated by the way organizations and humans behave in conflict situations – whether consumer, corporate or government – and that's always a process of discovery, which is often what keeps people interested in the human condition," he told me once during an interview.

The process began for him when, "basically, I had a lucky choice of parents. They had their impact on me very early. Well, that's what parents are for!" They were immigrants from Lebanon: his father, the operator of a bakery-restaurant in Winsted, Conn.; his mother, a teacher.

"My father believed he could be an active citizen and a businessman at the same time, even if he lost a few customers in the process of being engaged in community issues. So, as they used to say, when you went into the restaurant, you got a cup of coffee and conversation for a dime." His father tested in court a state law that required voters to register by party before a primary.

"One time, when I was about 9, I came home from school and my father said to me, 'Ralph, what did you do today, believe or think?' I'll never forget that.

"My mother taught us by indirection. Over a year, she would relate a historical epic chapter by chapter when we came home from school and each story had a bit of wisdom. One of her aphorisms was: 'I believe it is me.'

"The sense was that if you think something else is to blame for your not fulfilling an objective, it is much more constructive to put the burden on yourself, to recognize that you should have been able to do it regardless."

When he was 4 he wanted to be a lawyer and at 5 and 6 used to go to the courtroom in Winsted. Between Princeton and Harvard Law School, he became interested in probing the automobile's effect on America. "Once, driving alone, I saw an accident and stopped. A child had been almost decapitated in the wreck. The glove-compartment door was like a guillotine. The immediate impression was, 'How terrible!' But the secondary one was, 'Why did the compartment door have to pop open?' "

He kept studying the problem while he was practicing law in Connecticut. In 1965 he published "Unsafe At Any Speed" and in 1969 he founded the first of several consumer investigating groups. Where does it end?

"There is no end. The objective, I think, is to build a thick, not a thin, democracy. A thin democracy is one that can be manipulated. I'll tell you the sign of a thin democracy. It's when major institutional crimes are committed by government and then exposed and there is no public outrage.

"In this country we need hundreds of thousands of public citizens, generalists in society, who work to improve institutions of power, who try to take all these specialized activities and make some sense of them in terms of common purpose. Too many people are working on their littler nuts and bolts with nobody looking for the bigger picture of whether it translates into policies for transportation, health, peace, rebuilding cities, equal opportunity."

And where's the satisfaction for Nader? He spread his hands.

"The greatest reward," he said, "is the justice of the cause. there's nothing in the world more important than to be able to help your fellow human beings."

Billionaire Populist

Not since George Wallace ran as a third-party presidential candidate 25 years ago has anyone aroused a crowd as did H. Ross Perot, speaking Sunday to a packed Field House at Old Dominion University. They were ready. They applauded the national anthem and arose for a roaring ovation when pepper-pot Perot stood beaming at the lectern. Similarities of Wallace and Perot are striking — as are differences. Wallace's voice rose to a yammering yell. He shook his head to the side with every word as if he were a hound dog trying to rid his ear of a tick. His face a mask of hatred, he railed at federal dimwits and "pointy-headed pseudo-intellectuals." He split races and classes and excoriated both parties as not having a "dime's worth of difference."

Perot rears back and expounds themes, a teller of home-spun tales, a father who has $3 billion to prove he knows best. His lines crackle, a string of Chinese firecrackers. He pulls hearers together. He asked students to stand, saying, "We're all here because we love you and want to pass on to you the love we had in this wonderful country." He then sought "everybody who ever fought in combat" or had a loved one who did. By then, most were standing.

He seeks to exalt his hearers. He quoted a blue–collar "roads," rather than Rhodes, scholar. He depicted the media "sneering" at his followers ever getting enough signatures for his run for the presidency, adding, "We're the swing vote across the country. That's enough to get both parties to tap dance and chew gum for the American people."

Wallace would have relished that line! But racism stained Wallace's "message." Perot's is free of it. When blacks resented his addressing them as "you people," Benjamin Hooks and Jesse Jackson defended Perot. Few if any blacks were there Sunday, maybe because they feel he does not stress their plight. Perot would put us all in the same lifeboat, sinking.

Perot's continuing service is in riveting the electorate on the deficit. Used to be, he said, every other generation raised the standard of living. At the rate of the rising deficit, it will take 12 generations. As a group, he said, they had enough impact "so if you whisper, everybody in Washington will hear you." Clinton's operatives, he said, were attending his rallies — and he welcomed them Sunday. If they were there, they had no kind words to relay to the White House.

Perot did not mention the president by name, but his shots

were plain. He started a list of new phrases, saying "tax and spend" had become "contribute and invest," and the audience cheered and whistled as he declared, "Just call a dog a dog and not a canine!" — his voice flicking like the tip of a horse whip. Beyond the belt line, he said, there's an assumption that tax money falls out of the sky, "but it comes off the sweat of the brow of millions of hard-working people."

Vice President Gore didn't escape. Harry Truman, Perot said, had a staff of three, but Gore has 26 and a housekeeper paid $50,000 a year. A woman in California had told him, "I want that job!"

" 'Lady, I said, 'you'll have to get in the line behind me.' "

Sacrifices should begin at the top, he said. Congress should cut salaries and perks and reduce pensions to those of ordinary people. Perot asked for the line-item veto, first because the president wants it, and second "because I want to see what he'll do with it."

The crowd of all ages filed out, faces serious, intent. Many stopped to join "United We Stand, America . " Perot, the billionaire populist, it was plain, is here to stay,

The Noblest Career

Adlai Stevenson never was overly concerned about how a proposal would look to the electorate if he thought it made sense.

That was his attitude in campaigning against Dwight Eisenhower in 1952. Ike had been deemed invincible, but Stevenson's habit of taking forthright stands on controversial issues won him admirers. That he invariably picked the most sensitive places in which to bare his conscience nearly drove his aides to distraction.

That was a prime year with two top-notch presidential candidates. One of Stevenson's most celebrated stands was taken in Virginia shortly after his campaign opened in September. Ike had been ducking any mention of civil rights, much less a discussion. The question was whether Stevenson would touch the topic during a speech in Richmond. Another question was whether Stevenson could draw an ample crowd to the cavernous 5,000-seat Mosque Auditorium.

Riding in a motorcade through the city, Adlai was stopped by a large, determined party who told him sternly: "I like Ike!"

"So do I," shot back Stevenson, "but I hope you'll come and listen to me tonight."

Just before the candidate went on stage, an awed member of the Virginia House of Delegates, W. Griffith Purcell, motioned me to follow him backstage and along several turns in a long, dark hall. The ordinarily laughing, wise-cracking Grif was as mysterious and quiet as if he had seen a saint. Tiptoeing down a final length of hallway, he stopped and cracked a door, peered inside, and then gestured for me to look. I didn't know what to expect.

I peeped through the crack in the doorway. In a dingy, white-calcimined, cell-like room, Stevenson sat on a faded brocaded chair, his legs crossed, and studied his text. A naked light bulb hung three feet above his bald head. He was so intent on poring over the text and making changes that his features were seemingly drawn to almost a visible, physical, raindrop point of absorption. It was a monastic scene in the auditorium's dusty depths, highlighted by his monkish devotion to the text and Grif Purcell's reverent curiosity.

Stevenson stepped that night onto the lighted stage of a house packed to overflowing. It also was Richmond's first large-scale integrated audience. With almost saucy aplomb, he bowed and proceeded to give the audience his plea for civil rights for all, closing: "It will always be better to reason together than to hurl recriminations at one another. I should justly earn your contempt if I talked one way in the South and another way elsewhere." The audience interrupted 13 times with applause, and that line drew a standing ovation. That campaign of 1952 stands out like a beacon, and it is the loser that you remember first for his intellectual courage and for treating every audience as if it were his equal.

The jokes weren't quite as erudite in 1956, and he was not at such pains to hurl challenges in the very citadels of the opposition, but he hadn't changed. He showed it by advocating what was then a controversial proposal for a nuclear test ban treaty.

He insisted that politics was "the noblest career anyone can choose," and his practice did much to rehabilitate that calling in the eyes of the American people.

Historic Handshake

The question uppermost as Prime Minister Rabin and PLO chief Arafat met on the White House Lawn was not who would have Jerusalem but whether the two would shake hands. Specifically whether Rabin could force himself to take Arafat's hand. Given slight encouragement, Arafat would smother everybody there with hugs and kisses.

In a transport of joy all day, Arafat was the poor boy from across the tracks who finds himself, unexpectedly, in a birthday party among his betters.

Rabin, dour, moved through the procedures zombie-like, his voice a low, tolling bell. Asked beforehand whether her husband would shake hands, his wife said, "It would be hard" she said. And Rabin felt impelled to tell those back home, especially the hardliners, just how hard it was for him and them.

The two flanked President Clinton, a towering presence. As the final signature was being penned on the treaty, Clinton leaned over and whispered in Rabin's ear, then stepped back, leaving a space, motioning to Arafat, and, putting his arm around Rabin, gave the prime minister a nudge bordering on a shove. Arafat plunged forward, trembling in eagerness, arm outstretched. It was almost necessary for Rabin to extend his own hand to avert being speared by the onrushing Arafat.

So they shook.

When the two clasped hands, the audience gasped, then cheered. Somebody shouted, "Bravo!" Many were in tears. Ordinarily when the camera is on the president in a group, he experiences a ham actor's difficulty in getting his mouth just right for the scene. Most times, it's slightly ajar with a fixed, little wonder-struck smile as he looks around.

With all his being focused on getting the two old foes together, Clinton let his expression take care of itself. When the two clinched, briefly, Clinton raised his arms in a benediction, his mouth set in a firm, inch-long line, as if to say, "Now, that's done!"

He was not going to allow, at the end, any rebuff to sour the ceremony. He wanted every moment, every word to be right. The handshake signified, especially to the Arab world, nearly as much as the signing.

The aim was to get momentum going for peace to bring aboard Jordan, Syria, and Lebanon, rolling over extremists on both sides. During the day, TV flashed the picture from 15 years ago, of the three-way clasp of Anwar Sadat, Menachem Begin, and Jimmy Carter with his beacon-grin.

(Not a word of that treaty had been broken, which ought to reassure Palestinians, Carter told an interviewer Monday.)

The photograph of the new trio was just as impressive. Clinton is determined to put America's weight behind the drive and will pass the hat among the nations to help as Bush did for Desert Storm.

If Arafat was in perpetual motion, grasping all hands, Rabin, closing his mournful litany recital, delivered vivid lines to the Palestinians: "We are destined to live together on the same soil in the same land — we, the soldiers who have returned from battles stained with blood; we, who have seen our relatives and friends killed before our eyes...

"We who have fought against you...we say to you today in a loud and clear voice: Enough of blood and tears! Enough!"

Later, Arafat was asked if he ever doubted Rabin would take his hand. After a pause, he said, "A little bit. But I put my hand straight out, stretching."

Like a man reaching for a lifeboat.

Flirting With History

Signing 2,012 books, flashing nearly as many smiles, piling up votes for a presidential race come mid-November, Colin

Powell stayed 45 minutes overtime Friday at the post exchange across from the Norfolk Naval Base.

At 1:45 p.m. he set out, unfazed, for a grueling session at Prince Books on East Main Street.

"I don't cozy up to anybody," he said on arriving at the Naval Base. But a slight modifying of his views on some key issues this week seem designed to woo the Republican right wing. He is gearing up to run.

As an unending line wound around the huge post exchange and snaked past counters through its interior, few on the march for books seemed concerned with issues. They place faith in his character.

On a slight platform, he sat behind a large desk. On his left, two women opened books to the title page and passed them to him.

He scrawled his bold signature with his right hand, filling half the page.

With his left hand he swept the book to a woman on his right who passed it over to each customer filing by.

Powell managed to look up, catch the customer's eye, smile, and say, "How're you!"

"Thanks," they said.

"Run," they said.

Now and then the assembly line snarled. A kink occurred when Elizabeth Walker, a Virginia Beach sixth grade teacher in blue denim, asked Powell to sign under an inscription she had penned on a blank page: Keep striving to make a difference in one child's life.

To efforts to move her along, she cried: "My students are going to be very upset if I don't get this book signed!"

Reaching for the book, a smiling Powell said: "This lady looks like she might break up the place!"

Behind her, a Navy wife, Karen Cormier of Portsmouth, pushed a shopping cart with Breanna, 7 months, asleep in the basket, and Mandalyn, 2 years, sitting wide-eyed in the cart.

Flash bulbs flickered around Powell's nearly crew-cut head. Behind a rope, shoppers watched the panorama passing the desk. One tried in vain to photograph Powell from afar through the line. Seeing the woman's frustration, Beth Baker, a public affairs officer, took the woman's camera and took Powell's picture, close up. Others among the shoppers rushed to buy cameras and kept Baker busy.

Two men began uncrating books, stacking them for the handlers on the left.

Powell, smiling, arose, stretched, and took off his dark blue coat. The crowd applauded. Over his head a poster proclaimed, AMERICAN DREAM, AMERICAN HERO. His picture, smiling slightly, looked down on the scene. Powell, signing, propped a book under his right elbow.

Duncan DeGraff, Random House regional sales manager, began assisting customers along by placing his right hand under each one's left elbow.

Security director Charles Simpson assisted. Now books and buyers kept pace, parading before the general, and reached the end of the desk together.

Steve Kilroy stopped before Powell and raised a camera in his right hand, plastic bag uplifted in his left.

Better not try to take a picture through that bag, Powell advised.

"I hope you don't drive a ship!" he quipped.

Powell arose to push the desk forward to get nearer the people.

Bill Smullen, his executive assistant, conferred a moment

with him, then told a reporter the general was going overtime. The end of the line still was out of sight down the long aisle.

"These are his people," Smullen said.

The pace quickened, as many as six at a time moving nearly lock-step past the desk, as if the speeding production line were like the one that engulfed Charlie Chaplin in "Modern Times." Powell leaned forward across the desk, supporting himself on his left arm, a tired schoolboy working laboriously to cipher; he was unflagging in his drive to meet the demand.

Watching, Rear Adm. Jack Kavanaugh, chief of the nation's post exchanges, said, "I think he feels like he's home. This is the only military installation he visited."

The general arose, put on his coat, straightened up. He thanked Eileen Rowan, Sylvia Parks, Phyllis Quinsy — "My handlers," he said. He no longer looked weary. He and his entourage reached Prince Books on East Main Street by 3 p.m. People who had not made it through the line at the Naval Base showed up, jubilant, at Prince, escort Janet Molinaro was happy to see.

At both stops, the crowd was diverse in age, race and dress, a cross-section, it looked like, of the American Dream.

Powell signed until 5 p.m., his deadline, but kept on. He had resolved, at the last stop of his 23-city tour, to break the record of 60,000 autographed books. At 5:40 p.m., he signed 60,001. Wanda Chappell of Random House copped it.

And you think Colin Powell's not going to go for the presidency!

Twenty to 1, he runs.

Sing a Song of Tsongas

He looked like E.T.

And there was something extraterrestrial, too, in Paul Tsongas' call to raise taxes and make sacrifices when other presidential candidates were promoting tax decreases. And suddenly as Tsongas was withdrawing from the race at a news conference marked by grace, even those who had not harbored any notion of voting for him realized they would miss him. Many had sensed that impending void at the first news of his leaving. There had been something comforting about Tsongas. He was the conscience that made us feel better, even when we had no intention of heeding it.

The thin cipher of a face with heavy brows and highly mobile features — wispy hair, wide mouth, bulging eyes - worked as he talked in slightly slurred tones as a hand puppet, a Kermit the Frog once removed from us, struggling from the heart to reach us.

So that his insights, deftly composed, coming through a halting delivery were all the more arresting just as a lack of chrome, his unrelieved absence of cosmetic imagery, enforcing candor in look and word, became an offbeat charisma.

Many had a sense of his being a buffer between the blond, bluff bolster of Bill Clinton and the cut and slash of Jerry Brown just as Tsongas confided after their searing face-off in Chicago that he was set to jump between them.

He was, should the other two become unbearable, a kind of security blanket, one with which, if need be, Democrats could lose with honor.

And now with his family, he was saying adieu. In dark suit

with black-and-white-striped tie, his oft stray hair combed, he had it all together. He spoke of the press. "There are cynics in the group, but it is a cynicism born of idealism. The fact is that this country would be devastated without them. We are blessed. Without the diligence of the press there would be no America."

He had called the others who had dropped from the race. "Bob Kerrey was in Disney World," he said. The crowd laughed and he added, "I told him I would be there, too, at 3 o'clock. You can decide who is Goofy. I wouldn't be Grumpy, though."

To whether he had felt pressures from national leaders to step aside, he replied, "I sure did, a year ago." That drew stormy applause from fans crowding into the news conference. He corrected a couple of misstatements: "Molly is in the fourth grade, not the fifth. And the second is, I have three children, not four."

Of Niki, her face blurred with tears and pride, he said he had noticed "that half the young men in my campaign have fallen in love with my wife. I will admit I found that a great threat and I want to get rid of them."

To supporters, he said, "The message must endure. That is what I want you to take away. That is what this was about."

Of his sense of mission, after surviving cancer, to leave a better America for his children, he said he felt "deeply fulfilled. The obligation of my survival has been met." (A lasting image of the campaign was a TV commercial of his half-submerged, powerful shoulders thrusting through the water.)

Asked what he thought of people who insisted they were still going to vote for him, he thought a moment, then said, "Why not?" And added: "I hadn't thought about it, but it is an intriguing notion, and I thank you for bringing it up."

It had been "a great adventure," he said. "This is the way you affect your country. In this one year and 12 days, I think we

have done more than all the other years I've put into public service, and I'm proud to have been an American."

In the farewell there was neither a trace of E.T. nor a hint of
Kermit. Throughout he was presidential.

Let Dole Be Himself

Like the Humphrey Bogart he resembles, Bob Dole, leaving the
Senate to campaign full-time for the presidency, cracked a fissure
and let voters see the lava of emotion roiling beneath the crust. At
some point in a film, laconic, glittering-eyed, pursed-mouth, lean-
faced Bogart, given to snarling asides a la Dole, would break down
and offer a glimpse at the core. As often as not, it was sentimental.

Dole's farewell, critics agreed, was his best. Nor did anyone intimate it was an act, the charge brought against Bill Clinton
when he emotes; but if there were an Oscar for oratory, Dole
would have it for this speech.

Bidding his staff goodbye, he cried, it was reported, but not
in his speech. "I will seek the presidency with nothing to fall
back on but the judgment of the people and nowhere to go but
the White House or home," he said, his voice quavering on home,
as if he were about to join the jobless. "I will stand before you
without office or authority, a private citizen, a Kansan, an American, just a man ..."

At that his voice cracked, but he did not go over the edge,
which was well. It is one thing to choke up, manly even; it is
another, in voters' eyes, to weep as Ed Muskie did in the snow in
New Hampshire long ago.

Newt Gingrich was there, hovering over Dole's left shoulder, his rosy face floating balloon-like above the packed mass. Over Dole's right shoulder graven-faced Pete Dominici was nodding approval. Some regret the ceremony didn't occur at Dole's Kansas home; but it was better the voters see him tearing away from his beloved Senate.

When people speak of Dole's "dark" side, they cite the night in the New Hampshire primary in 1988 when NBC's Tom Brokaw asked Dole if he'd like to say anything to George Bush.

"Yeah, stop lying about my record!" Dole growled.

To me, it was a splendid, forthright response that enlivened the campaign, but many in the media were shocked. There is criticism, too, of his staccato, sometimes herky-jerky delivery. That traces to his war injuries, which left him with a nonfunctioning right arm and an awkward left hand that tires easily.

The Washington Post's David Maraniss reports that because it was difficult for Dole to take notes and then read them, he trained himself to listen to the classroom lecture and later, over and over, to the recording.

He began developing his own intellectual shorthand, written and oral, which sometimes led to the short-circuiting of ideas, making it hard for him to communicate to the masses, Maraniss observes.

The question is whether the GOP hard right will let moderate-conservative Dole go on his own. In the past, he was mindful, mulling over a hike in the minimum wage, that his father wore overalls to work. Or he recalled, pondering aid for the underdog, his 39 months hospitalized under government care. Dole, a child of the Depression, was not apt to forget the net.

The GOP extreme should understand that its hard-edged image can be a major drag if thrust on the candidate. Seeing what he endured and overcame from the war and observing his splendid record in Congress, the Republican factions had better let Bob Dole be himself.

Chapter Thirteen

The Produce Aisle

Daring to Perfect Perfection

Ah, Lord, now the scientists are tampering with tomatoes!

Going to mix up their genetics, pulling a gene from this or that vegetable, to improve that red orb, dripping with juices when plucked from the fields in July, as if it had partaken of the sun itself.

Improve the tomato?

How can one perfect perfection?

As it has been ever since Thomas Jefferson defied traditional wisdom and began eating what was then called the love apple from France.

Many asserted that they were poison, but Jefferson dashed that canard by serving tomatoes. Once tomatoes were tasted, nobody was going to believe that anything so good could be bad.

Most likely, it was the love apple, instead of the apple, that the serpent offered Eve. For centuries, cross-grained males have held it against her that she persuaded Adam to try it. Nonsense! She simply showed her good sense.

Some tomato!

If the scientists were bent on blending genes into vegetables, why didn't they start with broccoli? Enlarge the florets, shrink the stalks, make it taste like something else.

If the lab boys intend to hold onto their grants, they'd better heed my advice. But, no, they'll lunge ahead, and, in a year or so, call a news conference.

"Lady and gentlemen," the head scientist will start –he has spied a woman amid the press –"in studying tomatoes we naturally had to consume a ton or so, most of them in sandwiches, and while I'm thinking about it, let me urge you to spread the mayonnaise on the bottom slice of bread. If you put the mayo on top, the lettuce will get between it and the tomato, which is ill-advised. For the best effect, mayo and tomato must interface.

"This was our first discovery, three months into the trials, and it's a wonder nobody ever noticed it before, but that's science for you.

"Next, we pondered introducing genes from butter beans and corn into the tomato until it dawned on us that we would come up with succotash, which already is established as a dish into which you throw everything that's left over anyway.

"We started to lengthen the tomato's shelf life, but every time we'd set up an experiment, somebody would come up with the finding that we had done away with another bushel, and we had to send out for more tomatoes. We had a deuce of a time keeping a ready supply.

"Further, and this was a subtle judgment, after we learned that all winter long people yearn for tomatoes, it seemed a shame to deprive them of that almost unbearable sense of expectation. It rivals a child's waiting for Christmas.

"Even after it arrives, we are aware of the brevity of its stay.

"And while the tomato is delicious at any time, it is best in the sunny months, especially on hot days when nothing but the tomato, with its high liquidity and distinctive flavor, tempts the palate.

"When all else seems lackluster, a tomato sandwish –pardon, my mouth is watering –is easily fixed. Fling down two pieces of bread, spread mayonnaise, cut two slices of tomato onto the bread, clap the pieces of bread together.

"Done in four swift strokes! "Of all viands, it is the veggie–
or berry–that most engages consumers' minds and tummies; for
lady and gentlemen, the mind and tummy are intertwined. When
your mind is on a tomato sandwich, it is difficult to think of
anything else.

"In short, our over-arching recommendation is this: LEAVE
THE TOMATO ALONE!"

He overlooked one factor: the possibility that gene-splicing
may reduce the need for pesticides. Jefferson would welcome
that protection for his beloved love apple.

The Techtonic Tomato

The tomato sandwich is not by nature a safe one to put together and devour. Containing two slippery elements — sliced
tomatoes and mayonnaise — it is more of a sandwish. Take care
or you may end up with a piece on your lap.

The first rule in assembling a tomato sandwich is to spread
mayonnaise atop the bottom slice of bread. "Why?" No one
knows why. It is just one of those veils still to be removed. After
all, Einstein's theory of relativity hasn't been totally proved.
Every time there's a discovery in the heavens, scientists say that
while it does not prove relativity, it is consistent with it, whereupon all heave a sigh of relief. The main reason for accepting the
theory is that Einstein looks so smart with that luminous cloud
of hair as if his head were in the Milky Way and dark basset eyes
peering into the depths.

Putting mayonnaise upon the bottom slice is the theory of relativity in making a tomato sandwich. Do it and forge on. Just make sure that the mayo is spread evenly without slick patches. If it is a large tomato, cut a quarter-inch thick slice out of the middle. It will fill the face of the slice of bread without overlap and enhance a firm grip on the sandwich. To hijack the center slice runs counter to marriage vows; so if, as you complete the sandwich, your spouse enters the kitchen, thrust it into her hands and cry, "Dear heart, I just assembled this center-slice tomato sandwich for VOUS!"

With the center gone, resort to thin slices arranged evenly to avoid any upheaval in the surface. You are dealing with the fundamentals of tectonics in which plates of rock in the Earth's interior, forever on the move, thrust over each other and send shock waves that make the surface quiver. Don't let one tomato slice slice jut over the other. Keep them on an even keel or you'll have an earthquake on your hands. Or in them. Now to consume it, some people take a big bite in the center of one side. Do that at your peril. Removing a sizable bite from the center of the outer rim leaves two ends, to the right and left, projecting into the air. One or the other or both of the outthrust portions may dip and spill the filling on you. To avert that breakdown, take a bite from one side and then from the other, and then, quickly, from the center portion and thus proceed through the rest of the sandwich. What you must do, colleague Dave Addis observed, is preserve, as you eat, the sandwich's structural integrity.

How 'bout A Hayman?

Were it possible for me to confer on you a gift for Thanksgiving, it wouldn't be a half-dozen seaside oysters or a batch of apple butter from the Valley of Virginia or even a slice of long-cure salty-sweet country ham.

It would be a lowly sweet potato ...of a special variety. A Hayman. From Virginia's Eastern Shore or North Carolina's coastal farms. That is, if I had two Haymans, I would give you one.

It is amiss for me to call it "lowly." It only looks that way. It's a prince disguised as a pauper. Seen in a bin in the fall, it is grayish, smallish, misshapen, nearly as white as an Irish potato. Indeed, some old–timers call the Hayman a "white yam."

And you are apt to pass it by as a cull from a field of Idaho potatoes.

Don't. It is a viand of exquisite sweetness, packed with syrup.

Some advise you to grease Hayman's jacket lightly before putting it the oven to lessen the chance of its cracking open and spilling the juices.

When a Hayman is baking, the aroma permeates the house. The aroma escapes through the chimney, and you can see dogs running around outside trying to track it down. I have to go outside and sit in the car with the windows rolled up, and singing at the top of my lungs the "Battle Hymn of the Republic," else I'd go mad with hunger.

Some would say I already have.

Why, you ask, aren't Haymans on the market in abundance?

For one thing, they don't travel well — they can't abide being bounced about unduly — and their shelf life is not quite as long as that of a commonplace sweet potato. Then, too, Haymans, as Jerry Nottingham Jr. once explained to me, are like wine.

Some seasons the crops are vintage. Other years, they are not notable. The quality among Haymans may vary even from patch to patch, just as there are special vineyards in one region.

When peeled, ready for butter, Haymans are not prepossessing. The flesh, generally, has a greenish tint. But you forget all that upon encountering their aroma or flavor.

The flavor is a little as if the Hayman has been drenched in cane syrup. I bet you that with Hayman potato pancakes or biscuits, syrup would be redundant.

The crop this year is about average, says Dr. Herman Hohlt, horticulturist with the Eastern Shore Agricultural Research and Extension Center at Painter.

I would hate to have to reel all that off with a mouthful of Hayman. It is an offspring of Virginia Tech, and it is meet that we get it right.

It was a very dry year, Hohlt noted, and the rains, when they came, tended to be spotty, so that in some places, with lots of rain, the crop has been above average. That's how life goes with Haymans.

The scientists at Painter have been developing for 20 years a strain of Haymans that retains all the good qualities but has a higher yield per acre. The potato is smoother and it has a much higher percentage of marketable roots, Hohlt said.

"It is significantly better than the old strain that has been floating around for years."

The thought of an even better Heaven — pardon me, that slipped out, I meant to say Hayman — is almost more than can be borne.

Hooked on Okra

Word of an okra shortage will be received with mixed emo-

269

tions from gloom to glee. For okra is the oyster of the vegetable kingdom. A poll of okra consumers would show that more people flee from it than eat it. Okra is an acquired taste, best learned by children whose mothers keep poking it at them in various dishes. Let me tell you how one mother indoctrinated her son into becoming an okraphile.

Much as mothers introduce children to oysters in a stew, she fed her son gumbo, full of several vegetables, not to forget okra which is the defining element in gumbo. If the gumbo lacks okra, it doesn't make any difference what else it contains or how good it tastes, it isn't gumbo. Each time, she increased the amount of gumbo in the pot and reduced that of the other vegetables so that soon the okra was predominant, until one day, her son yelled, "HEY, THIS AIN'T GUMBO, THIS IS OKRA SOUP!"

But by that time, he was hooked on boiled okra. Another way to sidle up to okra is to cut the pod into little plugs, roll them in corn meal and fry 'em.

The prevailing impression of crisp, corn meal-coated fried okra is a toasted crunchiness with a kind of peppery flavor. Some advocates of fried okra put it right up there with black-eyed peas. And it does crisp up a vegetable plate.

Boiled okra also goes well, near the end of a serving, as a kind of pot likker in which other vegetables mingle, admirable for sopping with corn bread.

An editor, who has eaten okra in gumbo, asked if it were those little slices that look like wagon wheels. "Precisely!" I cried. "Serve steaming butter-flavored bowls of boiled okra to devotees, and it won't be long before the whole lot is singing "Wagon Wheels," the okra anthem, closing: 'Wagon wheels roll along, car-ry me home.' "

The okra shortage stems from a scarcity of labor to pick it, along with unfavorable weather. "Okra has little prickly spines that are itchy and scratchy. Nobody wants to pick it any more and if they do, it costs too much," said Jimmy Boudreaux at Louisiana State University's agricultural center in Baton Rouge. Okra is the only vegetable that is both prickly and sticky in its natural state. Farmer John Williams of Virginia Beach notes that there is an improved okra not nearly so fuzzy, but the problem is getting somebody to pick it. And if you don't gather it every day, okra grows too large and pithy.

Mary Williams sometimes stir fries the small, tender pods in butter. She doesn't remove the caps, lest the juices drain away. Makes one's mouth water to think of it. But then that comes from a guy who sings "Wagon Wheels."

Pease, Pease More Peas

Is it any wonder that after the rich foods of Christmas we turn on New Year's Day to the common black-eyed pea to bring us back to earth? For it is of the earth, earthy, bushlike vines hugging the ground. It can be the main dish with cornbread and a glass of cold buttermilk, and a side dish of tomatoes, fresh or from a can. People also add onions, bell peppers or vinegar from cut glass cruets holding little hot green peppers. On the second day, mash and fry the peas with corn cakes from the skillet.

Some bread the tomatoes into a stew or pudding. There are those who add sugar, although the devout debate whether to sweeten the pudding. Partisans on both sides can become quite rabid as if the decision touches on their ancestry, character or even patriotism. Three topics should never be discussed at a party: religion, politics and whether to sweeten tomatoes that go with black-eyed peas. I say, live and let live, eat and let eat as a body pleases with his or her peas. Just as long as we have ample peas.

Bring up sugaring tomato pudding, and revolution may break out. In 1775 in St. John's Church in Richmond, Patrick Henry argued for war, not peace, with the British. Just before he offered to the convention delegates his challenge of liberty or death, he shouted: "The gentlemen cry Pease! Pease!, but there is no pease!"

The whole place went into an uproar.

The black-eyed pea is easily fixed — or cooked, if you prefer. Submerge dried peas in water and let them soak overnight, absorbing moisture and plumping up. Or, to hasten the immersion, dump peas into a pot, bring the water to a boil, cut it off and let them sit a spell, meditating. Bring them again to a boil, then turn the heat to low and let them simmer an hour or so. For seasoning, nothing beats a piece of country ham. Or, if you like, open a can or two of black-eyed peas and warm them in a matter of minutes. Generally, they are flavored with salt pork.

Now comes time for a news bulletin, or, as Walter Winchell used to say: "Good evening, Mr. and Mrs. North America and all the ships at sea, let's go to press!" In Mechanicsville, the family firm that produces and cans the tried and true Mrs. Fearnow's Brunswick Stew began marketing recently Mrs. Fearnow's Black-eyed Peas and Stewed Tomatoes. Seasoned with country ham, it also contains chunks of bell peppers, onions and celery. George Fearnow recalled that his mother, Finnella, has always taken the broth left over from cooking country ham and used it in cooking black-eyed peas. "And I always thought it was wonderful," he said.

So he and his mother, who still works at 73 in the cannery's cook room, and his cousin Raymond and salesman Artie Cray be-

272

gan concocting a recipe in early spring, and finally achieved what pleased them. George said that three grocery chains — Lukhard's, Ukrop's and Mill's — helped with taste testing. Had I but known, I'd 'uve been there.

The family enterprise began in the late 1920s or early 1930s when George's grandmother, Lillie Pearl Fearnow, sold jars of Brunswick stew — 40 cents a pint, 80 cents a quart — in Richmond at the Womans Exchange on Franklin Street.

"She couldn't keep up with the demand so she asked her two daughters-in-law to help in their kitchens, too," George Fearnow said. "It stayed in the kitchen until 1946 when we built the factory."

So the Brunswick stew now is joined by black-eyed peas with tomatoes, seasoned with ham, and the Fearnows expect another run of more than half a century. The saying is that for every black-eyed pea you eat New Year's day, you'll get a dollar during the year, which is as good an excuse as any to ask for seconds.

I hope you get every dollar of it.

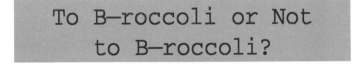

To B—roccoli or Not to B—roccoli?

Ladies and gentlemen, I give you broccoli. Take mine, too, while you're about it.

I'm in a quandary about broccoli. I don't either like it or dislike it. All the time I'm eating it, I am pondering, "Is this stuff good or isn't it?" One positive feature is that it's green. And it does have body to it.

273

So many of the greens — I'm talking now about fresh raw salad leaves, not turnip greens and its cousins — are just big piles of fodder, and one's jaw can grow tired trying to munch on a sufficient quantity of iceberg lettuce, say, to satiate one's hunger. Cows' mouths, come to think of it, work sideways, in a kind of grinding which must equip them to chew grasses and leaflike food. At least, that's the way their contemplative faces come to mind, their mouths wigwagging.

I just took five minutes off to check with a farmer about cows' mouths — there is no end to the trouble I'll take to keep you informed — and he tells me that not only do their jaws work sideways, but cows have three stomachs. They take in a great quantity of roughage in the pasture, swallow it and let it begin digesting in the mass, so to speak, and then, back in the barn, they bring it back up in a wad, chewing the cud as a man would chew tobacco.

Getting back to broccoli, it has been around a long time, came here from Italy and began appearing on American dinner tables in the mid-1920s. It took off, as they say, 15 or so years ago when nutritionists were looking for vegetables for salad bars. Of course, it doesn't do much good to eat like a cow when, having gone down the chow line, ignoring red meats and high-cholesterol milk products, one dumps gobs of salad dressings, most of them rich in cheese, atop the leaves. You never saw a cow pull a stunt like that.

This is not said in a negative way. If people choose to smother salads in heavy dressings to make them tasty, that's fine. This old world was a happier place when more stout persons were around. At a party, notice how other guests gravitate to the few well-padded people in the room to hear them laugh and tell jokes, like old times.

Remember Julius Caesar warning, "Yond Cassius has a lean and hungry look." Cassius was full of distemper, no doubt, because his wife had him on a diet of bean sprouts. He was out of sorts because, in truth, he was hungry, and, vexed, he sought peace of mind by prodding others into trouble just as he coaxed Brutus to join him in a conspiracy to slay Caesar. Had Cassius been eating slices of country ham and red-eye gravy next to a platter of hot biscuits with a heaping helping of Southern-style potato salad on the side while he listened to somebody turning the ice cream freezer on the back porch, mindful of the bowl to come, he wouldn't have been restive. He'd have left noble Brutus alone. "Let me have men about me that are fat; sleek-headed men, who don't diet and such as sleep o' nights," Caesar might have said. A shrewd observer, he.

If Cassius was bound to subsist on leaves and such, it would better have been a Caesar salad, chock full of goodies. Broccoli is best when cooked lightly to the point of tenderness and not beyond, else it becomes frazzled, limp, tasteless. Lemon juice and melted butter help broccoli. In fact, lemon juice and melted butter help anything. Be sure it's unsalted butter so that you are at least cutting down on sodium. More important, it tastes like country butter. Back there they made butter the old-fashioned way. They churned it.

The National Garden Bureau named broccoli the 1990 vegetable "with more vitamin C than an orange." It also honored the nasturtium as one of the easiest flowers to grow from seed and because its blooms and foliage are edible. I cannot imagine the circumstances, no matter what the dressing, under which I would eat a nasturtium.

Dig In, Muffy

A study from the National Institutes of Health asserts that after decades of dietary improvement, upscale white Americans are finally eating nearly as well as poor African Americans. It's not surprising that some of the poor have been eating better than some of the rich. The reason is the predominant place of soul food in the diets of many African Americans.

For a couple of decades nutritionists have been stressing the need of eating more vegetables, especially leafy ones: collards, turnip greens, spinach, mustard greens. All that came natural without benefit of dieticians to poor blacks and to a great many struggling whites, as well, throughout the South, especially in the 1930s during the Great Depression.

Too much is made of the use of fat back or streak-of-lean streak-of-fat bacon or salt pork in Southern diets. There wasn't enough meat to go around for everybody at many tables in those days, so it was used often for a little judicious seasoning in the bubbling pot of greens or string beans, butter beans, or black-eyed peas. The juices, the essence of the vegetables remaining in the pot, were called pot likker. A steaming bowl of pot likker, with cornbread crumbled in it to produce a dish just short of mush, would, as they used to say, "stick to your ribs." A glass of buttermilk on the side made it all the more delectable.

Over the generations as families made their way up the ladder of economic opportunity, their love of soul food persisted and children of the 1950s picked up the tastes of their Depression-conditioned parents. Had the nutrition study, instead of being of national scope, centered on the South the disparity of diets would not have been as marked.

276

The roots of soul food, of course, go back even further than Southern culture, all the way into the Old Testament. A grateful king offered Daniel and his young followers a place at his table of rich foods, but Daniel and his fellows declined politely and said, if he didn't mind, they'd just as soon continue to eat from the fields of greens. The king was dumbfounded at their hearty health.

Guidelines after World War II stressed high-protein meats and dairy products; but starting in the 1980s, nutritionists extolled vegetables. In a kind of closing of the circle, hamburger drive-ins installed salad bars although few had any field greens, save raw spinach. Even at those bars patrons neutralized the salads' benign effects by heaping them high with dollops of creamed sauces that Daniel and his men wouldn't have thought of touching. Soul food fortified Daniel in the lions den.

The Dairy Section

In a survey of American cities with overweight populations, a report from Chicago cited the wide-spread preference in the Windy City for high caloric soul food as one reason for its fatty citizenry. Among dishes supposedly loaded with calories, brought along with immigrants from the southland, it listed pork, collards, turnip greens and other greens cooked with greasy fat back — and buttermilk.

What in the world is wrong with those people? Haven't they lived?

Their black-listing buttermilk as inducing weight demonstrates how little they know of rural cooking. Don't they know that dieticians prescribe consumption of calory-free, non-fat buttermilk as a way to reduce weight? You might as well be drinking spring water as far as any fear of buttermilk's adding avoirdupois. Even as you swig buttermilk you can tell it doesn't convey a sense of filling you up as much as does the imbibing of plain sweet milk.

Buttermilk is a light liquid. The ratio of that filled-up feeling is two quarts of buttermilk to one of plain milk. In a milk-drinking contest at a county fair your average buttermilk addict drinks the plain-milk champ under the table. If the Norse god Thor, drinking from a vast horn attached surreptitiously to the sea, made his hosts stir uneasily when the ocean level dropped an inch or two, think what would have happened had it been connected with buttermilk. Thor would have had every farmer's wife in Scandinavia churning milk to keep up.

Home-made sugar cookies dusted with powdered sugar demand sweet milk. Who cares what pounds you may take on by washing down sugar cookies with a fruit-jar glass of cold sweet milk? But plain milk is not as compatible with corn bread, especially that which has sugar in the batter, making it more cake than corn bread. Sugar in cornbread is abominable.

Nor does plain milk have the sour stamina to stand up to boiled field greens of any variety. For that you need coarse corn bread, especially thick-crusted corn pone, to crumble into the greens' pot likker laced with a trace of vinegar. Why, even to think of pot likker and corn pone, with buttermilk on the side, makes my mouth water. It breeds fortitude in a body. And no beverage is more thirst quenching on a sweltering hot day than a glass of cold, tingling buttermilk.

I will grant you this. Buttermilk is not tasty on cereal.

A Simple Thing

An old-fashioned picnic being in order — the sort where somebody makes a jug of ice cold lemonade and somebody else leaves it on the kitchen sink, you discover when you're 20 miles way — they sent me to buy the pimento for the pimento cheese sandwiches. A simple thing, you say, referring, I trust, to the cheese, not me.

As it turned out the mission was not so simple because to build a top-flight pimento cheese sandwich you must, for the tastiest results, have whole pimentoes, the plural of which, I hope, is spelled the way it is there. You have seen them, of course — two or even three fiery red fellows, about the size of little plastic coin purses, nestling cheek by jowl in their own oily juice in a two-inch tall jar.

That was my recollection, but finding them was another matter, as always. The pimento has no settled place in the grand design. In one store you find it above the dairy case. In another it occupies a niche between pickles and vinegar. Once it even turned up with the Post Toasties. It is nearly as difficult to locate as anchovies.

So you wander around the store, feeling, if you're tired at the end of the week, increasingly cross and finally, ask a clerk, Where the doodlysquat are the pimentos? — the plural, I just checked in Webster's is spelled without an "e" in the last syllable — and he or she says, "Right there by your left elbow with the macaroni, you dolt!"

That is the usual course of events. Imagine my chagrin, having tottered around the store for 45 minutes looking for pimentos for the picnic, to find that in place of jars of whole pimentos there were little mite-sized jars of pimentos diced into tiny squares. Have consumers, I thought, become so effete that the manufacturer has to dice the pimentos for them?

A great satisfaction in preparing pimento cheese comes when Gin, having shredded the cheese on the colander, spooned three or four dollops of mayonnaise into the bowl and added a slug of vinegar, calls that the time has come to slice the pimentos. That's my task.

This, I tell her, is where you make or break pimento cheese. You do not cut the pimentos so fine as to render them into a spread; nor do you whack them into such large chunks that they fail to permeate the mix thoroughly. The pimento man, or rather, the pimento person, must be careful, using a sharp knife and fork, to cut them lightly and precisely into varied sizes, as if preparing a jigsaw puzzle of pimentos. Thus the person eating the sandwich feels a sense of suspense, not tasting a trace of pimento, then chancing upon a nugget, and once in a while, coming upon an squishy mother lode of it.

The mildly bitter pimento is essential, as, for that matter, is the cheese or the mayonnaise. It is not one of those concoctions in which you may insert substitutes. It is a team sandwich of equals.

"The only piquant irregularity occurs in the pieces of pimento," I told the clerk. "Diced the same size, they become homogenized into monotony."

"Yes, I know," she said, calmly.

Just that. She didn't add that a shipment was in transit and might arrive by Christmas or that a strike of pimento pickers had delayed the harvest or that half the town had been seized by a whim to mix pimento cheese. Just a mild acknowledgment that she knew there were no whole pimentos.

I can't say which dismayed me more, the disappearance of whole pimentos or the apathetic response of the clerk to their absence.

What, I ask you, is this world coming to.

Diced pimentos, that's what.

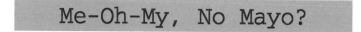

Me-Oh-My, No Mayo?

On a buffet the other day at one of those power lunches where a dozen or so people eat and confer around a long table, not one among an array of sandwiches had mayonnaise on it. Such is the power of the Center for Science in the Public Interest.

Mayo, as delis call it, emerged as the number one public enemy in a dietary study issued not long ago by the Center in Washington, D.C. Mayo has far too much fat, the center avers. In the Center's eyes, mayonnaise is the John Dillinger of dressings. Substitute the J. Edgar Hoover, which is mustard, the center says.

No fiat on earth could induce me to put mustard on a turkey sandwich. Or on sandwiches of chicken salad or tuna salad. Before I'd desecrate that trio, I'd eschew — instead of chew — them. Horseradish, searing to the tongue, goes well with turkey but never mustard. Turkey and mustard don't mix or match in my book. If they do in yours, I'm not one of those knee-jerk ideologues who is going to condemn you. Enjoy! Just don't offer me one.

Nor do I have any use for mustard on a tomato sandwich. Not unless the tomato sandwich also has crisp bacon. Conversely, I don't like mayonnaise on a bacon and tomato sandwich.

If tomatoes were in season — Oh Lord, if only they were in

season — I would set up a taste testing counter for brands of mayonnaise right here with thick slices of crusty white bread and a tall glass of cold milk on the side. I wouldn't mind if it were buttermilk. My favorite mayonnaises are Duke's, Sauers and Hellmans. Mrs. Filbert's gets a lot of votes, too. One suggestion is that we use light — or lite, as they spell it — mayonnaise on sandwiches. I tried a lite Hellmann's last year, and it was well nigh tasteless.

My theory, yet unproven, is that if you eat a lite variety under stress, it produces even more cholesterol than does the undiluted original.

Up to the time of the center's decree, I'd been able to quell any thought of tomato sandwiches, just shove it to the back of the lowest shelf of my refrigerator mind. Now the lure of tomatoes is out in the open, thanks to the center, and at least once a week I'll remember with regret that the red orbs ripening in the fields are three months away.

Any day now, I expect to hear somebody accuse the Center of the Public Interest in Science of having a liberal bias for daring to tell us what to think of what we eat. But I'd rather know the consequences and suffer than remain in the dark.

Break-Fast

On TV the other morning as I was leaving for what is laughingly called work, a George Washington University professor, Arthur Frank, was telling viewers not to bother to eat a big breakfast. Don't eat one at all, if you choose.

The Produce Aisle

So saying, he flew in the faces of MOA, Moms of America, whose motto is Eat Your Breakfast. It is, they have said for eons, "the foundation for the day."

Dr. Frank caught my ear as I'd just thrust in my coat pocket a three-day-old corn pone. To eat one in that ancient state is like munching on a boulder out of a creek bed; but it stays with you. Corn pone is mostly stone-ground meal and water, which sustained Lee's Miserables during long marches.

Do you find the topic of corn pone risible? Not nearly so much to my taste as the fare that has taken hold of our younger baby boomers, namely, bagels. They spread a decade or so ago from New York, Philly and the like.

Dr. Frank, who probably hasn't eaten corn pone or bagel, said there really was no biological need for three meals a day, which MOM would regard as heresy.

My advice to youths is simple: Eat something, ANYTHING, for breakfast. Otherwise, I warn, your innards are left with no vittles on which to work and so they grind on each other, a cement mixer turning with nothing to mix. That shocks you? I have no idea whether it's true, but it sounds logical, and, invariably, the youth stops in his tracks and grabs a bite to eat.

One item quickly prepared, tasty and nourishing is oatmeal. Not the instant or even the three-minute kind. I mean the regular variety. Dump into boiling water enough oats to fill the family, stir it a while, maybe three minutes, long enough to show the oatmeal who's master; then cut the heat down to warm — or almost off — and leave the confounded oatmeal to ruminate and cook itself while you dress.

You may wish to add a little salt and a chunk of butter. If you are going to eat anything as wholesome and virtuous as oatmeal, essentially fodder for dray horses, you may reward yourself with

283

an extra helping of calories. A person ought to be saluted for consuming oatmeal. Further, you start the day feeling you have accomplished something.

I hear you saying your children would never eat anything as basically dull as oatmeal. Nonsense! Let me tell you a secret. All you need do is top it with brown sugar, either the light tan kind, which is probably mild enough for children, or the dark brown. As a final lure, let them sprinkle it, as if preparing a dessert.

Your friends will be impressed when you mention you had oatmeal, the regular sort, for breakfast. You will be regarded as a person of substance ever after. Full of oatmeal.

Einstein, Newton and Friddell

Devoted readers of this column, all two of you, will recall the breakthrough, about a decade ago, that stunned the scientific community when I discovered fissionable Grape-Nuts.

I made no great fuss over it. I simply reported the finding to you and my wife, who frankly was incredulous, and let it go at that. After all, it was just one of those intuitive leaps that individuals make now and then. I'm not looking for the Nobel Prize. If the theory advances the lot of mankind an inch or two, then I'm pleased, in a wan sort of way. I only mention it now because an equally significant corollary to fissionable Grape-Nuts has flooded my consciousness.

The first discovery came about one morning, when — eating in the trancelike state that overtakes one at breakfast occasionally, thinking of nothing, merely munching away like a cow on a cud, preparing for the day subconsciously by not preparing, clearing the mind of everything as if erasing a slate — I suddenly became aware that although I had been chewing a spoonful of Grape-Nuts steadily for half an hour, I had more Grape-Nuts in my mouth than when I had begun.

Looking at it one way, I simply was not making any headway in devouring the bowl of Grape-Nuts. In fact, the Grape-Nuts were gaining. Looking at it on an entirely another level, I had hit upon a Great Truth. Or rather, a Great Truth had hit me.

"Gin, I said. " I do believe that I have discovered fission."

"Where?" she asked, looking around wildly.

"Right here in this very kitchen, in the Grape-Nuts."

"Don't tell anybody," she said.

Some of the world's greatest discoveries have come about in such a desultory fashion. If Necessity is the mother of invention, Serendipity is the father. Mankind tends to stumble forward. Sir Isaac Newton, sitting in an orchard thinking of nothing, was hit on the noggin by a falling apple that drove the idea of gravity into his thinking. Those who saw Newton's face when the apple landed on his head contend that gravity should have been named hilarity, but you always find people like that ready to jeer at the serious ones of this world.

Or Einstein, informed one day that his wife's parents were coming to dinner, remarked, off-handedly, how much more slowly time passed with one's in-laws than it did with one's own relatives, and, having said it, sat down and propounded the theory of relativity.

Or Archimedes, assigned to determine if the king's crown was made of pure gold was lowering himself in his tub with his ships and toy ducks — they were celluloid, mind you, none of this flashy plastic — when, noticing the water rising under his weight, he realized he'd found a way to determine the specific gravity of the crown. Overjoyed, he leaped from the water, grabbed a towel and ran through the town shouting "Eureka! Eureka!" It is such antic behavior that makes all of us searchers for the truth regarded as eccentric.

All science, when you get down to it, is mere play, dress it up though they may with complex terms. The high multiple factor of Grape-Nuts — wherein the more you chew, the more there are, splitting smaller and smaller components of Grape-Nuts in a sort of explosive chain reaction — may seem difficult to have constructed, but once laid out, one realizes that anybody could have thought of it. Think of a Grape-Nut as an atom, and there's nothing to it.

Having loosed the theory of fission through Grape-Nuts on the world, I'd paid no attention to the uses to which it was put. Pure science is my concern. Let others look to the application in everyday life and make a million dollars. Run cars on Grape-Nuts, for all I care. Light the city with the energy derived from their incessant multiplication. I'd more or less put them out of mind, and my wife had taken them off the menu. Then the other morning she placed something new in the cereal bowl. Grape-Nuts with Raisins. As I chewed on this new fare, my first thought was that the Grape-Nuts were not nearly as close to being gravel as they had been of yore.

I happen to like their flavor, a sort of grapey, nutty taste, and now, the chunks of grain being somehow puffier and crunchier, it was possible to savor them without worry about collapsing one's jawbone. Definitely a gain. Even more significant, the addition of raisins had been a boon, consonant with the Grape-Nuts because raisins, I've been told reliably, are nothing but dried grapes, anyway. So the cereal company was developing along the right consistent line.

But, more important, as I chomped the Grape-Nuts, they adhered to the raisin nicely in a natural grouping process, making it possible to chew and swallow them easily. That process, the reverse of splitting the Grape-Nuts, simply fused two or more into a larger entity. Suddenly, the corollary came in a flash.

"Gin," I said, "I just made a discovery with Grape-Nuts with Raisins, one to rival the splitting by fission!"

"Oh-h-h-h NO," she wailed. "What is it this time?"

"Fusion", I said.

There it is, make of it what you will.

Chapter Fourteen

War and Peace

Supreme Daring

The snow was hip deep.

In the woods up a slope were German machine guns and a Royal Tiger tank shielding foot troops. Staff Sgt. Archer T. Gammon charged them, giving his life on Jan. 11, 1945, to save his platoon near Bastogne in the Battle of the Bulge. Gammon was awarded the Congressional Medal of Honor for his "intrepidity and extreme devotion to the task of driving the enemy back, no matter what the odds." A bridge at Danville will be named for him Thursday. In the crowd will be eight of his 10 living siblings, five from Hampton Roads.

Archer grew up in Pittsylvania County in a hard-working sharecropper family of 15 children. As tenth in line, Archer "always took care of the younger children while our mother cooked and washed and cleaned," the youngest sister, Elsie Stovall, recalled at her home in Virginia Beach.

In a letter to the Chatham Star Tribune newspaper, a classmate remembered that Archer, a gifted athlete a head taller than other boys in the fourth grade, "would take up for the smaller youngsters being mistreated by older boys." He was smart "and kept up with the rest of the class with little or no noticeable exertion." He was called upon often to read aloud.

"We were hard workers," Elsie said. "Except for feeding us, all the farmers loved to have us harvest tobacco. They cut watermelons first, to fill us up, but we learned to wait until we had eaten fried chicken."

They went to the fields together, the older ones walking the dirt roads, the younger ones riding the wood sleds behind the mules. Sunday, they lined up chairs in rows, as if they were pews, in front of the radio and listened to the church service. "Archer was happy but more reserved than the others. He thought a lot before he did anything. He wasn't one to jump right in. He weighed pros and cons. One night we went bowling and had as much fun as at any time we were young."

The dedication of the Archer T. Gammon Bridge will be at the entrance of Dan Daniel Memorial Park. Kin from hereabouts are Elsie, Virginia Beach; James Gammon, Norfolk; Ethel Carl, Hampton; Ruby Lerner, Phoebus; Gertrude Burns, Yorktown. Guests will hear how, when enemy fire pinned his platoon, Archer charged 30 yards and silenced with grenades a machine gun crew of three. "Disregarding all thoughts of personal safety," he crossed the width of his platoon's line and wiped out a second crew of four.

"With supreme daring," he moved within 25 yards of the tank, shot two infantrymen. The tank withdrawing, stopped to fire, began backing again, then stopped to fire from its heavy gun the last round that killed him instantly. He was 27.

"That day he had little time to ponder," Elsie said. "God must have been with him."

This Here, That There

When the Army decided to place carbines in our hands, Sergeant Bull Maypop said he was going to take them right out again and lock them up. To arm our outfit was, in his eyes, a mistake that compounded the risk in the Army's daring experiment in recruiting 4-Fs. We were all deemed limited service except the Sergeant and a cadre of other regular Army noncoms and, of course, our Officers.

In time, my comrades did wonders in setting up and running a hospital on the Big Island of Hawaii and then on Okinawa, but of our basic training, he said: "I hope one day yers will do something to make Maypop and yers mothers proud of yers."

He did let an ordinance officer come before us in the long rectangular mess hall. The officer named the parts of the carbine all the way down to the "sear," a tiny catch, scarcely larger than an eyelash, in the trigger assembly. The officer was at the far end of the dim hall, talking suddenly about the sear, holding up nothing as far as I could see, and every time he said "the sear" I thought he was saying "this here."

That's just like the Army, I thought. Send a supposed expert to tell us about the carbine and for all the expert knows he can only say "this here" and "that there." What a way to run a war!

When the ordinance officer had finished, Sergeant Maypop, standing with hands clasped behind his back like Napoleon brooding at Elba, said he would ask a few questions in review. "Friddell!" Maypop called. "What is the sear?"

He caught me flat-footed. I thought Sergeant Maypop, in a commendable effort to lighten what had been a dull demonstration, was hiding something behind his back, as children do, and wanted me to guess what this here was. The old brain, clicking all the time, told me he was probably holding a vegetable from the kitchen back of him. If he wants to play games, I thought, Sherlock Friddell is ready.

"FRIDDELL!" roared Maypop. "I see yers lurking back there in the darkness. What is the sear?"

"AN IRISH POTATO!" I yelled back, with conviction.

There was silence, then a crash of wild applause from my

comrades. Guessed right, by George, the first time, I thought; but no, the Sergeant was bellowing to me above the tumult.

"Friddell, yers mad fool, before it's too late: WHAT IS THE SEAR?"

"A SWEET potato," I called, determined to set things aright.

"I'll give yers one last chance before you go on KP," roared Maypop. "NOW...WHAT...IS...THE-SEAR?"

"A RUTABAGA!" I yelled, in a moment of divination.

But that was wrong, too. Later, after the ordinance officer departed, shaken, Sergeant Maypop called me to the headquarters tent. To my surprise, he was benign."I will hand it to yers," he said. "Yers convinced one member of the brass that this outfit wasn't ready for firearms."

"You mean they're going to take away our guns?" I asked.

"We can keep the guns," he said, "but they're NOT going to give us any ammunition."

"Sergeant Maypop," I asked, "what WERE you holding behind your back?"

Home to Heal

That the Navy knows the worth of ritual was evident in the two-day healing and binding that began Sunday when the faint spire of the incoming Iowa thrust above the bristling skyline of booms, derricks and cranes of the Norfolk Naval Station.

As the damaged battleship rounded the bend, the misty, wavering image of its superstructure hung against the sky. It was just there, suddenly, and from among reporters huddled like sea birds at the river end of Pier 5 came a cry: "There it is!"

292

In the distance, the slinking hull, low-slung to hide it from the foe, wasn't visible, and the huge mass of the dreadnought seemed planted, a proud castle, in the water. Then, moving nearer slowly, the mythical castle began to take on an iron substance. From the chorus came another shout: "The men are on the deck!"

The first sighting of the sailors, lining the rail, was of soft, thick bristles, ice tusks, rimming the hull, and, later, elaborate macrame embroidery. As the ship started turning toward the pier, the sun shone on the sailors' spotless uniforms, popcorn white, and someone in the press called, "They're wearing black armbands!"

Now apparent, too, were the three huge guns — two pointing skyward, one nearly horizontal — wrenched out of alignment and locked awry by the explosion that had rocked the ship and took 47 lives in the No. 2 turret where men had been practicing gunnery in the Atlantic.

As the Iowa swung toward the naval station, its prow inched into view of the thousands of spectators behind fences at the far end of the two-block-long, six-lane-wide Pier 5. At the sight of the great ship, a high-pitched, almost keening cry came from the women waiting, a thin ribbon of sound. Men's deep voices, trying to call, caught in a sob. Silently, the ship moved into its berth along the pier, becoming, close up, a massive gray mountain, white uniforms lining its many-layered ledges and sifting like snow into its cracks and fissures.

Engines muted, the Iowa swept by soundlessly, disclosing the full sweep of the long, lovely shallow bow line of the hull, three-quarters of it seeming to be nearly flat against the water, just another flattening wave, rising at the prow into a subtle breast curve against which played sun-scalloped reflections of shining water. You could read the men's faces now, as if they were passing in a slow, steady review. No longer toy sailors against the gray mound, they were human, most of them serious, impassive, quite different from radiant expressions they show in returning from a normal tour.

The decks were not as crowded then as men huddled near the gangplanks. This time those who weren't on other duty were at their places along the rail, making a statement en masse for the comrades lost and the hurt ship. And, normally, when the ship is secured and sailors are released from formal stance, they search out faces of loved ones on shore, pointing, laughing, shouting, waving their arms, throwing their white caps into the sea of faces. Ordinarily. the milling crowd below would be waving placards, screaming, loosening balloons, raising high the babies, fruit of an earlier homecoming, for their fathers to see, while the band played.

There were no bands Sunday, and the men, released from orders, continued to stand, not stiffly but still, like the ship itself, which had become, at last, a gray, slab-sided, monolithic monument. The gates opened and the crowd streamed aboard. From within the iron shell was heard the welcoming, a lilting birdlike chorus. The Iowa was home.

Yesterday morning, President Bush came to honor and try to console the sailors and their families. First they heard from the ship's commanding officer, Capt. Fred P. Moosally, who told them: "We came together in times of trouble. We shared the good and the bad. The grief we share with you and their families is deep. But we must go on. For we are the crew of the Iowa.

"Permanently fused, like the steel of the ship we sail, our sides are strong, our towers high and our course is set. We are the Iowa, a part of every rivet, every plank and every line. We are the ship.... As long as she sails the seas, we will be a part of her, a part of the Iowa spirit. That spirit lives and the men of turret two will forever be a part of that living spirit."

Promises to remember ran, too, through Bush's remarks, and he concluded, "Your men are under a different command now, one that knows no rank, only love; knows no danger, only peace." Then, to the swelling, oceanlike strains of the Navy hymn, "Eternal Father, Strong to Save," he and first lady Barbara Bush moved among the families. On the far side of the hangar, the men, hands folded before them, peered and bent to 65-degree angles trying, childlike, to catch a glimpse of their commander in chief.

And at Pier 5, three fingers raised against the sky warned that in war or in practice at peace, the proud castle that dreads naught also is vulnerable, even by its very might, from within, and the nation's guardians always are at risk, in harm's way.

Her Ship Came In

Standing in the rain on the pier at the Norfolk Naval Station and holding 2-year-old Brittany, Debbie Adams looked up to her husband, Harry, at the railing of the combat stores ship Sylvania and shouted, "GET OFF THE DAMN SHIP! And he, looking down four stories and across a gulf of seven months at her tousled russet curls and brown eyes, called back, "I CAN'T! YOU'VE GOT TO COME ON BOARD!"

He looks as if he's about to cry, she thought. Harry pointed at the wedding band on his finger and mouthed three words, and she read his lips: "This means everything."

She nodded, smiled, and held Brittany up to see him.

Behind her, somebody offered to hold the child until families got the signal to climb the gangplank to an open house aboard the ship, the first vessel to return to Norfolk from war in the Persian Gulf.

No need, she said: "I saw my husband. It strengthened me."

Hundreds had endured two hours or more in a downpour. They began gathering shortly after 8 a.m., so intent for sight of the Sylvania that they scarcely noticed the rain. On the dock, band music swelled from a school bus where 22 instrumentalists from Portsmouth's Churchland High School played "Wind Beneath My Wings," this year's song of reunion.

The deluge would have ruined the woodwinds and turned the sheet music to sop, so band director Mary Gugler had her musicians open bus windows, aim at the crowd and play loudly, as if a giant jukebox were blasting away. The tenor sax sat sideways to avoid the slide trombone, cymbal and snare and bass drums jammed at the door, and the piccolo noodled near the back of the bus.

The crowd was mainly a young one, bright with toddlers bundled in Easter egg pastels of yellow, blue and pink, and young mothers — a reminder that war devours the freshest flowers. Here and there was a watchful grandparent.

All huddled under massed umbrellas, a protective carapace of whirligig colors while the rain beat down on them. Suddenly came many cries as one, a feminine sighing in the wind, "THERE IT IS!" as the swan-neck arc of the ship's bow slid into view on the Elizabeth River, knifing the gray water, attended by two tugs. Its men, standing at attention along the rail, outlined the ship's contour in a living fringe. On the shore, smiles and tears of joy mingled with raindrops. Signs, poking high and scrawled in crayon or finger paint, hailed loved ones. The ship parked at the pier, and sailors aboard and families ashore — so near, so far — brooded on the faces of their kin, mighty tides of love flowing between them.

Now the families were scrambling up the gangplank. Debbie Adams came to the spot where Harry had stood. "He's not here," she said. She moved inside where couples were embracing, children dancing, leaping, and she looked around, dismayed. Then, abruptly, she was darting through the crowd, nimble as a minnow, still carrying Brittany. A moment later, a tall youth engulfed them in his arms. Her hand smoothed the hair at the back of his head, as if to prove he was there. They stood apart, to look at each other again, and Harry Adams said to a bystander, "She defines the Navy wife."

And then he said, "If you ask me, the heroes were the ones standing on that pier in the rain when the ship pulled in. There wouldn't have been a war front if there hadn't been a home front."

Along the Sylvania's corridors, Harry stopped to introduce his wife to shipmates. He carried Brittany and held Debbie's arm down the gangplank. As they walked along the pier toward home, holding hands, the sun came out. But they scarcely noticed.

Stormin' Norman

To protect our troops invading Kuwait and Iraq, there would be a lid on news, Defense Secretary Dick Cheney warned Saturday.

But Sunday, if you had your television on at 8:45 a.m., there was Gen. H. Norman Schwarzkopf, primed to talk. His bulky self filled the screen, a cross in girth and gusto of Santa Claus and Falstaff. He need not have said a word. His beaming presence communicated all was well.

He tried to hide his zest under brusque bursts through his inch-wide slit of a mouth, narrow as a jukebox coin slot, but confidence — no, joyous pride in his troops — kept breaking out as the thin lips turned up at the corners.

He read a statement and said he'd take a few questions before he had to return to the war room, as if everything might get out of hand if he weren't there. But the demands of time gave him the license, if he didn't like a question, to swing his ham arm and point to another reporter. They were as eager with questions as dogs jumping around a butcher carrying a sack of scraps.

He has a broad mountain slope of a chest, so broad that the curlicues and splotches of his camouflage shirt seem delicate in contrast. On the right breast of that shirt is printed, in bold, black letters: SCHWARZKOPF — a blunt cough or bark commanding attention. On the left is, stark, simple U.S. ARMY, as if this battle tank of a man defined it.

His open collar, embracing a fleshy neck the size of a depot stovepipe, was ample enough to bear in full view on each side four stitched, spider-black stars. (My editor said he could almost see the fifth star, which should be joining the other four any day now.)

Schwarzkopf dropped word (a bone for the dogs) of more than 5,500 prisoners, with hundreds of others seen northward waving white flags; that allied casualties were remarkably light; that resistance had been slight; that the offensive had been progressing with "dramatic" success; that "the troops are doing a great job" — then, suddenly realizing he might become euphoric: "But the war is not over yet."

A reporter wanted to know how the foe was fleeing, listing four possible ways. Schwarzkopf shot back: "All of the above!" Asked if our troops were circling around Iraqi fortifications, he snapped, "Around, over, through, on top of, underneath and any other way we can!"

He had said before the start that the Iraqi army was near collapse, and the first pictures confirmed it: men exhausted, hangdog, glad to be alive. There had been no barbed wire, no flaming pits, no gas. The pitiful bunkers from which they emerged were as slight as burrows built by boys at play, throwing a few shovels of dirt atop boards slung across a gully. They didn't seem capable of rebuffing a BB.

Schwarzkopf and President Bush and Gen. Colin Powell — also to be star-struck the fifth time soon, no doubt   had taken a bold gamble, and in the first 10 hours the troops achieved a full day's objectives with only 11 U.S casualties.

Signaling the start, Bush, his eyes tired and worried behind his glasses, spoke at his best, softly, without rhetoric or gestures, of a "swift and sure" victory. He suggested that Americans take time for a prayer for their young men and women.

One young soldier, waiting for the fighting to start, discovered, as many had before him: "There isn't anything to do in the desert but think. You try to depict in your mind what is going to happen and how you're going to meet it."

At day's end, Saud Nasir Al-Sabah, Kuwait's ambassador to the United States, was asked why there couldn't have been a delay of a day or so. Torn between anger at Saddam Hussein and anguish for what his people had suffered — the torturing, the burning, the murdering, the kidnapping — he replied, "It had to be done now in justice to them and for the safety of the troops."

He paused and said, "He asked for it, and he got it."

Saddam had vowed the mother of all battles. "Evidently," the ambassador said, "it's going to be the mother of defeat, the mother of shame for Hussein and his army."

Gentle Bear

When Gen. Norman Schwarzkopf came home from the Persian Gulf to Tampa, Fla., he stepped from the plane's doorway and, from that high perch, surveying the applauding crowd of 2,000, he gave it a crisp salute.

Then Schwarzkopf, nicknamed Bear, came down the steps and was greeted by a huge black Labrador retriever, also called Bear. So Bear met Bear. (Odds are 20 to 1 that any black Labrador, and even some yellow ones, weighing 125 pounds or more will be named Bear. Schwarzkopf weighs 240 pounds.)

As he descended the steps, wearing a desert uniform of blobs of beige, gray, light yellow, green, he came straight toward the viewer. In camouflage, the general seemed to be an advancing landscape, what with the energetic vibrations of his vast girth that set the color patterns shifting, as from a breeze.

Just then Bear, the family dog, burst on the scene to welcome his master. He was bounding, tossing his head in a frenzy of adoration, but no sooner had the cameras given us that enticing glimpse of the joyous retriever than they pulled away. But it is hard to contain a Labrador. Every so often, a wagging tail, an ear, a nose intruded on screen. You could tell he was having his say, off-camera. The dog has emotion to match his master's.

Why are TV directors reluctant to give watchers what they wish to see? Many of us would have enjoyed a long look at that capering dog. There is a mercenary reason not to let our eye dwell on dogs more than an instant during commercials. Anything more than flash of the dog distracts the audience from the product for sale. We catch only a fraction of a second with the dog, just enough to fix our attention to the ad, and then he is gone.

War and Peace

Gen. Schwarzkopf blends toughness and sentiment. On the platform, he came to attention for the Star-Spangled Banner, motionless throughout, with the exception of his chin, which could be seen trembling at almost the rate of a hummingbird's wings. Hearing the anthem, many people feel gusts of emotion, which they suppress. Schwarzkopf expresses them openly. With the model of manliness willing to show his feelings, given time, we all may be blubbering buckets.

Sheik Saud Nasir Sabah of Kuwaiti said it was "'a great day for the soldier who saved my country." And Schwarzkopf, bringing Bear back into the picture, verbally, anyway, said: "It's a great day to be a husband, a father, a brother. It's a great day to be the master of a great old dog. It's a great day to be a soldier and a great day to be an American."

In pronouncing the word "soldier," he gives it a lighter, softer inflection, as if in tribute. He was departing with his family when the band struck up "God Bless the U.S.A.," which has become the celebratory theme song of the allied victory. Schwarzkopf came back on the platform and stood at attention. Should he, as many wish, run for a major political office, the campaign will make George Bush's posturing in a flag factory seem lacking in patriotism.

The homecoming with the great old dog brought to mind another meeting of a war hero with his dog. Homer, in "The Odyssey," depicts Odysseus who through deception, brought about the downfall of the Trojans, reaching Ithaca after a trying 10-year journey from Troy.

His house is beset by voracious suitors seeking his wife's hand so the goddess Athene disguises him as an aged beggar to spy on them. When the homecoming warrior approaches his house, his old dog, lying in the sun, recognizes his master's footstep and struggles to his feet to lick his hand. Then he lies down again to die.

I think Homer might have left out that last bit.

A Potent Symbol

Soon the U.S. Senate will be debating whether to adopt a Constitutional amendment prohibiting the burning of the Stars and Stripes. The flag — any long-standing flag — is a potent symbol. Southerners can attest to that. An elderly relative, who heard from my grandmother's lips of Sherman's incendiary march through Georgia, was unable ever after to stand under the flag of the United States.

When many of her generation mentioned "The War," it was not of World War I but of what they called the War Between the States. For some it is with us yet. Maynard Jackson, former Atlanta mayor, now head of the Olympic Committee, is trying to have any vestige of the Confederate battle flag removed from the state flag flying over Georgia's Capitol lest it embarrass athletes coming from all over the world. The Lost Cause was stained irredeemably by slavery, but being a stout states righter, I leave the issue to Georgians, some of whom tend to be a wild, unruly lot, as I know from my own outbursts.

On flag burning, I side with the protesters. Before you throw down the paper and yell, "Irma, he's at it AGAIN," give me your ear. To thousands, the flag is the symbol, well nigh the soul, of this country for which loved ones died. They can't bear anyone slurring it in any way.

When at my father's funeral, someone handed me, tightly folded, the flag that had covered his casket, I held, for a moment, the laughing sailor boy. So my heart is with those who revere the flag. But I differ with them on flag burners. Some flag burners are on ego trips. But then, so are many congressmen. And others of us. Some dissidents, out of love of country, seeking to redress a wrong, would awaken the majority by striking at what is most dear. So they burn the flag.

America's founders understood how difficult it is to parcel out dissenting groups, or at least without hearing them all out. Dissidents themselves, the founders devised the First Amendment to protect us all, even the measliest.

Dissent erupts at critical junctures. If at times it comes from a seeming scruffy lot, that should not deter us from weighing their ideas. The words from plain Tom Paine, oft deemed extremist by his peers, still come to us loud and clear. What troubles me more than flag burners are self-serving politicians who wrap themselves in the flag. Looking back from a short lapse in time, we sometimes wonder how we in the majority failed to see what the dissidents sought to point out.

In the 1988 Republican convention in Dallas, hell bent on an assignment, I rushed by a flag burner, meaning to return; and didn't. We had best pause to examine what has seized some dissenters that, out of love, they dare to appear fools amid the swarming majority. And in the mounting national debate, we should not disregard out of hand those who have the nerve to defend the right of dissent.

Make Room

Virginia without the Virginia Military Institute is unthinkable. If VMI had done no more than produce George Marshall, citizen soldier, it would lock our affections.

The four-story barracks, framing the parade ground, makes the little plateau a stage with mountains as a backdrop. In the rising sun, the fortlike stucco walls are white. As the day wanes, hues on the battlements shift from light beige after noon to a shade close to English mustard near sunset on its towers.

To parade, more than 1,000 cadets form, unseen, in the anthill-busy courtyard. At a bugle call, the regimental band appears under Jackson Arch in the clifflike face. One second the building is still, the arch, tall enough to swallow an 18-wheeler, is empty. As bugle notes fade, the arch fills with marching men, sun glinting on silver swords and brass instruments as if a box of toy soldiers has been emptied under the door of a play fort. Six companies emerge from Jackson Arch, three more from Marshall Arch. They march as one. Even creases in the uniforms occur in the same places at the same time in the gray-clad ranks, a sculptured frieze of moving men.

On Founders Day, the band plays the Doxology with which churches close services, beginning, "Praise God from whom all blessings flow...." At VMI they sing it: "Red, white, and yellow float on high/ The Institute shall never die/Lo now, keydets, with one voice cry/ God bless our team and VMI." As the band plays "The Spirit of VMI," the Corps disappears under the arches. The barracks face is a shut toy chest. Such a scene moved cadet Marshall to become a soldier.

Now under Supreme Court orders, VMI, summoning creative energies, will make room for women and make it an even finer place. No fret! Build quarters for 'em. Bob their hair to fit under a hat. Set up rigorous exercises. Drill the lot with men. Let 'em compete in classes. What is so fearsome about the prospect of VMI rat-dom, anyway — child's play to women who face the pangs, one day, of birthing men.

When the University of Virginia desegregated and then admitted women, some wahoos bewailed the loss of a "Way of Life" consisting mainly of getting drunk and rolling around to women's colleges on weekends. Women in classes raised the intellectual level nearer that envisioned by Jefferson in founding his university.

Women are enlivening every phase of society, including management. In clinging to monastic seclusion, VMI would drop out of step with a changing universe. Noticing VMI men around him before the battle of Chancellorsville, Stonewall Jackson said: "The Institute will be heard from today."

To continue to be heard from today, let its cadets join the swelling national chorus of men and women.

Chapter Fifteen

The Final Frontier

We Need Heroes

Report on the moon voyage to three teen-agers camping, minus TV, on the Maury River:

For a week we on earth Earth hovered around the tubes watching the journey to the moon that ended on the deck of the carrier Hornet with the three astronauts cooped in a glass-fronted box that looked for all the world like a console television set. Behind the box bulged a silver van in which the astronauts will live a while, Jonahs in the belly of whale.

Peering out of their windowed whale, they saw, astonishingly, President Nixon telling them of our pride in their conduct, inviting them to dinner three weeks hence. In his earnestness, raising and lowering his hands and his voice, his debating gestures — all speeded up, President Nixon looked like someone caricaturing President Nixon. The past week, a long, eight-day week, had been the greatest since the creation of the world, he said, which was a stretcher, but never mind, all the adjectives, as he noted, had been used. And these are bold times.

The country is jubilant, but most of the rejoicing, I believed, is for the sake of the human race, not simply for the United States, just as we think of Columbus as a man, not a national. Americans in fact, tend to take their successes for granted. Our patriotism rose highest when the Russians orbited Sputnik in 1957. The youngest of you three was only one then.

The faint, mindless beep-beep of the circling satellite, like a bird on a stick, and the fizzling sound of Spootnik, a name that seemed to smack of a dialect joke, only heightened the note of danger in the Russian dare and the unknown.

The launching for the moon journey drew attention to match the early blastoffs when we tensed, not knowing if the rocket would go up or over. Now there again were the white clouds billowing at the base of the craft, and slowly, the liftoff, so slowly that the rocket seemed to hover, straining a moment, and then soaring free, made a wake through the sky.

The night of the moon-landing we visited friends who had color television: The moon was photographed in black and white; we did see Walter Cronkite in color. His pursed features have become almost a familiar as those of the man in the moon. Eagle, the lunar vehicular module, looked like something you might have put together with an Erector set and Tinkertoys, or hammered, wind-blown, into a tree with worn boards, rusty soft drink signs, and old stove pieces.

The hatch opened and a foot appeared, feeling its way cautiously, then withdrew, and then stepped on the first rung of ladder. As the lower half of the astronaut Armstrong backed into view, your mother exclaimed that it was exactly the way she taught the three of you to come down stairs.

"What do you mean?" I asked.

"When they were babies, I just kept turning them around until they learned to come down backwards. That way, you've got all fours to use."

So the astronauts exited onto the moon. There'd been much discussion of what their first words should be, and Armstrong said, hurriedly, like a boy reciting his lines by rote on a stage, something about man's first step and mankind's great leap. More likely he was thinking, well, we made it.

The moon's surface around the craft was pitted and broken like a stretch of old macadam road that has been left to go to pieces near the new interstate. An astronaut bounded about the pocked surface like a boy frolicking in snow, except that weightlessness turned his kangaroo leaps into gorgeous slow motion.

They put up the Stars and Stripes and gathered rocks, including a prized purple one, the sort indeed a boy would cherish here on earth. Then President Nixon called from the White House (how telephonic Lyndon Johnson would have relished making that call!) while they leaned to attention.

As the astronauts cavorted, I noticed they had long back packs similar to those Buck Rogers wore and the ones we drew on our tablets in school, imagining our own moon landings. Consciousness that they were really there came and went, like the flickering spectral images now black, now white on the screen. Once they were out of sight, with just the Tranquillity Base showing, and then, on the edge of the screen, rough-shaped, goggle-headed forms appeared suddenly, and you knew men were, truly, on the moon.

Then they were coming home and the luminous blue earth Earth shining outside the Columbia's porthole was no larger than a volleyball, lolling in space. They were fished out of the sea and sealed in a box, like Gulliver, and then Mr. Nixon came across the Hornet's deck to the strains of "Hail to To the Chief."

"When you hear that song , what do you think of first?" she asked.

"Kennedy, I guess."

"He was so young, the handsomest president we ever had," she said. "He started the trip."

Mr. Nixon did well, expressing our awe at them, and they, huddled triplets in an embryo, still maintained their wonderful naturalness. It was as if he, and we, were in the awkward position.

"We need heroes," she said, "and they, rugged and unassuming, make the heroic seem within reach of anybody. When they overshot the landing area, and had only 20 seconds of fuel, no wonder Armstrong's heart beat quickened, but they gave no outward sign of stress.

"It shows man can do anything he sets his mind to do."

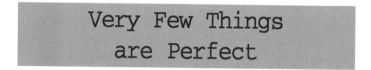

Very Few Things are Perfect

The teacher had answered questions on Monday when the Challenger exploded and now expected new ones when she met her class of fifth-graders, so she was not of a mind Tuesday to talk with a reporter. Being a teacher, she did.

A portrait of Christa McAuliffe was in her classroom. Her pupils had studied pamphlets from NASA, and she had almost a weekly correspondence with its experts. "They've tried to do everything they could for education," she said.

Right to the end, she said, McAuliffe "had done what should have been done. She was going to keep a diary. For her classes in space, she had prepared two lessons, not overly complicated, so all the students could grasp the wonder of the universe. We were all ready to go with her."

The teacher and her fifth-graders had felt that "when you have 24 missions and they all come home, you begin to think NASA can handle any trouble." Then, on the screen, the spacecraft became a torch.

"Some persons would have cut off the set and maybe that's the best way," she said, "but children keep thinking about it, and they wanted to ask questions, as they do about everything, so I just answered them straight.

"One even asked how many chambers were in the shuttle and whether the astronauts could get on the inside of one that wasn't burning. Another, who had seen frogmen pull astronauts from the water, wanted to know why the seven couldn't be saved. And another — and this one just about put me in tears — demanded to know why, if there were so many buttons, they couldn't push one that would eject them from the shuttle.

"The explosion was so immense,' I said, 'that I think everything is over for them. I don't think they even knew what happened.'

"One little boy just refused to believe that they had all died. He declined to think that it couldn't be fixed. I left the television running until finally it had no more to say, for the moment. I told them that the astronauts were risk takers, as is true with most worthwhile jobs. I reminded them that hundreds of people connected with the launching didn't get publicity, and when you looked at the thousands of parts in the spacecraft, you couldn't pin success or failure on any one person.

"We talked about how important every little part is, how each must work. First, the door wasn't set right; next, the electric screwdriver needed batteries; then the needle itself wouldn't work — and all such imperfections have to be corrected.

" Everybody has to do his or her part. If one person pushes someone on the stairway, 10 go down on their heads. I have some bright little boys, and they kept probing. I said we all have to go about our work, and that it takes many brave persons even to get the spacecraft into the air, and that when we get into such a venture, we know of the dangers. The settlers were like that, coming across the ocean in tiny ships, which is the way people do when they wish to achieve something good. I was just telling them anything in my mind so they could get their minds off the tragic part of it.

"Gradually, I tried to ease them into work. I gave them problems that required close concentration. Afterwards, they were quiet all day. There wasn't one piece of misbehavior, not even any of the little funny, mischievous things. Everybody simply went along. They were disappointed, disillusioned, depressed. They were just crushed, that's all.

"The children had all these visions, like: 'I'm going to be an astronaut and make a store up there,' and 'They're going to have a football field in space.' There's no end to their futuristic outlook — ever.

"And then something like this happens, and the optimism is knocked in the head. They were left, for the time anyway, with a feeling of disbelief, lingering doubt, not realizing that very few things in this world are perfect.

Get Back Inside, Pleez!

The instant the car radio reported last week that the astronauts couldn't open the door of the space whoosemajoosis, I yelled to them: "DON'T TOUCH THE CONFOUNDED DOOR!"

Actually, what I said was "damn door," but this is a family newspaper which you do not profane with cuss words. This present reference gets by only because I am not uttering the word as an imprecation but merely informing what was said within the privacy of my car, heard by no one but the Labrador retriever who leaped to his feet in the back seat and licked the back of my neck to calm me.

It is really touching and a kind of tribute to newspapers that while people accept all kind of TV trash pouring into their living rooms, they are shocked by the slightest indiscretion in their newspapers. It is as if, still, bless their hearts, they sense that newspapers are for real and much of TV is fantasy.

Had I been at the Cape, I'd have grabbed a bullhorn, run outside, pointed it at the sky, and bellowed: "All right, fellows, come on down NOW! This instant! Don't open the door, even if you can, because through a glitch somebody forgot to assure there was a way to get in and out of the door up there, once it's closed on the launch pad — a minor oversight, to be sure, but not one to be trifled with lest you spend eternity floating about like a clueless kite.

"JUST COME DOWN! I ADJURE YOU!. YOU ARE NOT SCRUBBING THE MISSION. YOUR JOB IS DONE! JUST GET THE HECK DOWN HERE, YOU HEAH ME? OR I'LL TELL YOUR MOTHERS! BRING THAT BLITHERING WHATEVER IT IS TO SWEET MOTHER EARTH.

"MAKES NO DIFFERENCE WHERE YOU LAND. ALL THE OLD SEABEES OF WORLD WAR TWO HAVE TURNED OUT TO THROW IN A TARMAC WHEREVER YOU TOUCH DOWN!

"OH, AND ONE MORE THING! DON'T BOTHER ABOUT THAT EXPERIMENT BREEDING TADPOLES IN SPACE. NEITHER WE NOR THEY CARE HOW FAST THEY PROCREATE. FORGET IT!

"The president is on his way here with medals to pin on your chests after the mother of all can openers has been wheeled out to peel away the sides of that space whichamadoodle and spring you free!

"Once that's done, I'm going to advise him to end the madness of spending billions to fetch a stone, a leaf, not to forget that misbegotten door, to this good earth. Let us just tend to our gardens."

About then, they'd have thrown a net over me and slapped me in a room with no windows and no knobs on the confounded door. That's what gets you in the end, those doors.

A Wondrous Place of Childhood Fantasy

Imagine my surprise to find James Cogsdale of Newsoms on my side in questioning the wisdom of spending time and money on Mars when so much goes undone on earth. He concluded a recent letter to the editor: "I doubt there are any aliens out there, but if there are, please do not disturb them. We have enough problems to contend with now."

And how ironic that I, pioneer in space with Buck Rogers and his significant other, Wilma Deering, not to forget inventive Dr. Huer, have become aligned with the skeptics — if there are any others.

In 1929, Buck arrived in a comic strip. In 1934, I joined Flash Gordon, Dale Arden and scientist Dr. Zarkov battling Ming the Merciless of Mongo. I spent hours in the third grade, ducked behind an arithmetic book, drawing space ships. Now scientists go gaga naming rocks. Where are Huer and Zarkov?

Gazing at the sky the night our astronauts landed on the moon, I seemed to see them walking ant-like across its golden face. I yet feel the lure of learning , at the end of the quest , the beginning of creation. But so many steppingstones, planet to planet, lie ahead. One night pacing a hospital corridor blots out all else. And there are so many vigils for kin and friends. So many for young and old.

This country should pour resources without stint in warring on disease — the major ones, such as cancer and stroke, and the minor ones, the likes of lupus and Lou Gehrig's disease, which are major to those afflicted. Do you recall the fear everywhere at the polio epidemic in the 1950s?

Yes, as one writer noted, this writer is "stupid." But in 1958 at Washington and Lee University I talked with historian Arnold Toynbee who traced in 10 volumes the ebb and flow of civilizations from the dawn of history. His view of space exploration startled me. The space race, he said, had about as much importance as the Harvard-Yale football game, "especially since it isn't going to find a new place of habitation.

"It's a nice thing to do on the margin if you have the time and the money, but other things are more urgent." He found it premature "to think of outer space before we have learned to keep peace with each other on this planet."

He characterized the enthusiasm for space as "a form of escapism because we've got difficult problems on Earth which we have been singularly unsuccessful in solving so far."

Yes, it would be nice, but the margin, just now, seems thinner than ever.

Chapter Sixteen

Fur and Feathers

Whuff, Whuff, Wolf!

Scientists, running DNA tests on several breeds, conclude that the dog is man's oldest as well as his best friend — which doesn't surprise me one bit.

What does surprise me is that scientists, rather than spending eons and tons of cash on research, don't just call me for answers.

With the wolf as its ancestor, the dog wagged on the scene 130,000 years ago, DNA tests show, instead of the 13,000 indicated by fossils.

Had they asked me, I'd have advised that dogs and humans are practically coeval, neither finding it possible to get along comfortably without the other, both yearning for loyalty from a creature with whom they feel at home. In biblical terms, the Lord realized Adam and Eve needed some droll object of affection, along with each other, and, populating the Garden with animals, the Almighty thought first of the dog.

One of the scientists, Dr. Keith Crandall of Brigham Young University, said he doesn't find it unlikely that a human being would try to exploit the wolf's acute senses of smell and hearing. "You can see how a hunter-gatherer would be interested in the domestication of a dog if he picked any (animal) to use for hunting."

Pardon me, but that is not the way to see it. Why is it that science always has to think of man first at initiating change? More likely, the bonding between human being and wolf-dog came about this way — in fact, this is my imperative vision. The cave family, gathering around a fire, became aware of would-be dog creeping on its belly, ears lowered, into the warm circle of light, supplicating with a whine or two. Some youths picked up stones to throw at the wolf that was bent on breaking new ground as a dog; but the family head, a wise old man, raised his hand and said, "Oh, knick knack paddy whack give the dog a bone."

Which they did, and in no time, the children were playing with the dog-wolf. They had gained a friend who has hung around down the centuries offering adoration to human kind. To make the advance into the circle was natural for the wolf, a social animal that lives in a pack. Indeed, in some instances, the wolves' society is less acrimonious, more civil among its members than is the human counterpart.

No doubt, the wolf's habit of looking to an alpha leader in the pack eased his entry into the human den with its master. But in households today the dog is apt to prevail as often as its so-called master. Boomer the Lab has become so acute that, at my lowering the newspaper of a morning, he commands we go outdoors and test the air as sensible dogs should.

Aristocats

As befits those whose ancestors were revered as gods, America's cats disdained findings last week that dogs have been man's best friend for 135,000 years.

"So what have dogs done in that time," an elegant Persian sniffed, "except pant and slobber and track mud on the Aubusson."

"How do you spell that?" I asked that haughty cat.

"If you have to ask, you needn't know," she said.

The cat, she said, is the aristocrat, kin to lions. So it is. In Egypt, cats kept rats out of grain bins. Sun goddess Bubastis had the head of a cat. Phoenician traders brought Egyptian cats to Europe. Mating with wild cats, they bred domestic cats that traveled with colonists to the New World. They became ancestors of most cats in America.

That they are much beloved is evident in statistics from the American Pet Products Manufacturers. Some 54.6 million dogs are pets, compared to 66 million cats. Among 68 million pet-owning households, 36.4 million have dogs and 31.5 million have cats. Those figures break down to 1.5 dogs per household and 2.1 cats.

A friend who harbors three cats explains that dogs need endless attention. Cats consider them big babies. Dogs demand more hours than many Americans can spare from their jobs. It is easier, she said, to mind three cats than one dog. The lordly cat can be left alone for hours without sniveling. It is confident its provider will return and it has the wit to wait and amuse itself.

Independent-minded cats won't deign to do silly tricks, but they can open refrigerator doors. You don't have to bathe a cat. It grooms itself with loving care. To the blueblood cat, every day is an Easter parade. The graceful cat walks as if it is picking its way through glass.

My friend had two cats — Shadow, a smoke-gray male, and Maeve, a long-haired patchwork cat — when a tabby showed up in the garden. Wary, stand-offish, the stray valued her selfhood. Though famished, Garden Cat declined to let anyone touch her, and she refused to accept food. What kept Garden Cat around was her fascination with Shadow. They became pals, she shared his food, and, finally, friendship with their provider. "To bring Garden Cat into the circle," her provider said, "took another cat."

But the emerging triangle displeased Maeve. She hissed, cuffed at the other two cats, and became out of sorts, frowsy. One day as I sat on the front steps, cowering, the cat's owner stood, arms folded, blessing me out for some miscue or other. In the midst of her scolding, I felt something fan the back of my neck, and then a push beneath my elbow as Maeve came under the crook of my arm and wound around, settling in my lap, insinuating her head to rub it under my chin, fond as any dog.

She had found a stray of her own.

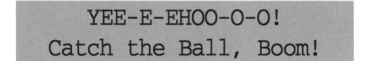

YEE-E-EHOO-O-O!
Catch the Ball, Boom!

The Labrador retriever has rules.

One is, when he sets his mind to fetch a ball, nothing can deter him, if it goes astray, from finding it. That is his mission. Would we all were as constant. Oh, once in a while, he won't commit himself fully. If something else crosses his horizon which he must investigate, he will, if you throw the ball, trot after it, to humor you; but his heart is not in it, and after a toss or two he will drop the ball somewhere in an offhand way.

Which explains how, out walking, every so often he will thrust his head into a hedge and emerge with a tennis ball to drop at his companion's feet. He has tennis balls stashed everywhere. The nearby field is a vast playroom. If he spies a newcomer, a promising recruit, he can come up with a ball to snare him. But once engaged, the Lab won't quit. If the ball goes astray, on an errant throw, he will run untiring, circling, criss-crossing, nose down, covering the area, returning, off and on, to where he thinks it ought to be.

Sometimes, while he is coursing, I come across another, identical looking tennis ball. When he fetches the first, I throw the second one instead. He bounds after it, but, nearing it, he dismisses it, and rushes back, head high, for the original.

On a hot, muggy day, as we started for the beach, the Lab grabbed from nowhere a battered tennis ball, which was fine; it's hard to discover a stick on the sand. Most times, the bay off Norfolk's Ocean View Beach is as placid as a lake, but it was kicking up two-foot waves. Plunging after the ball, the Lab played the waves with ease. Pursuing the ball, he raised his head to clear the breaking surf. Swimming back, when a wave caught up with him, he rode it, his dark, bronze head and sinewy shoulders a brown horse amid tossing white manes. Ashore, he dropped the ball and dug under it, throwing it, with a plume of sand beneath his legs, into the water. He turned and pounced on it, as if it were alive, elusive. Once, gnawing, shaking it, he broke a seam and rent it nearly in two. I managed to throw it beyond the fourth oncoming wave toward which he was swimming; but when the ball touched down, it shipped water and sank, unseen by him.

Paddling where it should have been, he reared, looked around, swam in a tight circle, widening it steadily, maneuvering as he would have done in trying to track a ball in the field, venturing farther out, but returning each time to where the ball had disappeared, ignoring my shouts for him to come in.

I cast about for a stick to distract him. He kept circling. I ran up the beach, climbed the dune. On the bay, the Lab, as if making up his mind on a drastic course, set off in a straight line, outward bound. How far could that fool Lab swim? Atop the dune, I ran to the car to look for anything to throw. Opened the trunk, cast things aside. Nothing there. Explored the back seat. No help. Looked under the driver's seat. AHA! A TENNIS BALL!

Tore back toward the water, shucking my shoes. Waded and dog-paddled to where the ball had sunk. "LOOK, BOOMER!" I hollered. "I FOUND THE BALL." Tossed it in the air for him to see. "YEE-E-EHOO-O-O! CATCH THE BALL, BOOM!" He turned back, a dark arrow thrusting the waves. I clambered ashore, dog-trotted up the beach, a headline forming in my mind:

COLUMNIST
KEELS OVER
CHASING LAB

I sat by the dune. He charged from the water, up the beach. Did he never tire? Six feet away, I threw him the ball. He leapt, caught it, dropped it, sniffed it — and turned and headed back to the bay.

Wrong ball.

Stubborn as a ... Basset

What drew me to the recent circus was word that it presented a basset hound in a dog act. Which was surprising inasmuch as bassets are untrainable. Intractable, even. Bassets are not, as some cynics would have you believe, dumb. Indeed, many a basset would like to fake you into underestimating his superior intelligence, the better to catch you off-guard and get his way. Rather they are the masters of their own fate and don't need meddling from humankind.

Fur and Feathers

If on this globe there is an obedient basset, it isn't a bassett, it is an imposter. A basset is the most willful animal the Lord ever put together, not excluding the mule. You know how the Bible records in Genesis that the Lord, working six days under heavy pressure, created this and that, the narration concluding each time, "And it was good."

Then the Lord rested.

On the eighth day, with a little mud left over, just as a cook will take a surplus dab of biscuit dough and shape a doodad, the Lord, not wishing to waste volatile matter, picked it up and worked it around and made a basset hound.

And it was bad.

Went its own way, sort of a predecessor to Adam. I expect that when Adam and Eve left Eden, under a curse, the basset went with them, ears flapping, tail wagging.

The basset in the circus act was rather like a happy child at a birthday party, just having a good time, running hither and thither, unhindered, on its own amongst more dutiful performing dogs. The basset's big moment was to run around atop the ring apron at one point, guided by a young woman. Which, with her help, it did. Then it was supposed to run around the apron by itself. That would have been a breakthrough for the breed.

It ran around outside the apron.

Afterward, I talked with the troupe's trainer, Johnny Peers. He noted that he picks up the dogs from pounds, except for two greyhounds, retirees from a race track. The 6-year-old brown and white basset, Daphne — or Daff, as he calls her — is from a shelter in Arkansas. When we met, near the pie wagon (the circus fast-food truck backstage), Peers patted a chair, and Daphne jumped up on it and sat down.

AHA, A TRICK!

323

Then she jumped down and made for the pie wagon. That was the way, up and down, as we talked, until at last he held her collar. Dogs from pounds, he said, are inclined to adapt more readily than thoroughbreds from mama's lap. Except for bassets, he should've added.

He set off briskly, and, not looking back, whistled for Daphne.

Who went the other way.

Thundering Applause

The circus comes to town next week–The Big One–and I'll be looking for Ivan Vladimirov, who makes a specialty of scaring audiences out of their seats.

Standing on the back of a galloping horse, he launches himself backward from that moving platform, turns heels over head onto the back of a second horse, and flips into another midair somersault. But when he lands on the back of the third and final galloping horse, he overthrows, as if losing his balance.

His chest goes backward, his arms flail, his feet go over his head, but as he is plummeting headfirst in his fake fall toward the ground, his feet lightly touch the horse on the flank, and he twists his body, landing with his right shoulder on the ring curb's flat surface, not the curb's cruel edge.

Other acrobats rush to the side of the crumpled figure. After a moment he gets up, left hand pressed to his back, and, limping, motions with his right hand for another try. This time, teetering wildly on the third horse's back, he manages to straighten at last, to the spectators' thundering ovation.

Fur and Feathers

As Ringling Bros. and Barnum & Bailey Circus moves from town to town, newspaper critics mention the plucky lad who, despite his bruises, gets up from the sawdust to try again. It is a masterpeice of deception. Sometimes even the old circus hands come to him after the show and say, "Ivan, you really hurt yourself that time, didn't you?"

The question, though, is who's fooling whom. "You really fall," I said to Ivan when he was in town two years ago. All that saves you is that slight touch of the feet to the horse's flank–merely a point of reference - and then the roll in midair to land on your back atop the flat curb. It is a fall in truth at every performance.

"Every day I'm falling," he agreed,"and if I don't know how I'm falling, I'm going to kill myself."

One thing–risking his neck twice or thrice daily keeps him looking young. Stocky, blond, blue-eyed Ivan, who is 32, seems to be in his early 20s. He doesn't smoke or drink. He stays in shape because if he ever let himself go, he would require a year to work into condition. Everywhere he goes, he bounds as if he has springs in his shoes.

The trick began by accident. That day four years ago when he overturned from the last horse, he was frightened, but when he tried again and the crowd roared, he said to himself, "Here is a thing I can use!" Bit by bit he developed the art of falling accidentally on purpose.

For a while an epidemic of falling threatened to hit the acts under the Big Top, but circus producers Irvin and Kenny Feld decreed: "Nobody falls but Ivan. He falls the best."

Vladimirov was 14, a pupil in a gymnastic school in Sofia, Bulgaria, when he went to see the bareback troupe headed by the great acrobat Peter Romanov. "I had never touched a horse. I was short, a little guy. I was scared. 'Is this horse kicking?' I asked."

Under Romanov's coaching, Ivan became the first performer in 45 years to take off from the locked arms of two acrobats riding side by side on a pair of horses, somersault high above a second pair of running horses, and land on the backs of a third pair. When I last saw him, he was working with the launching team to perfect a midair somersault from the first pair of horses to a fourth pair–a tiny figure hurtling through the air, a distance about the length of a basketball court. A month later came a scrawled postcard from New York's Madison Square Garden. Ivan had bridged the gap from one to four.

He emphasizes that it is the Romanovs, working as a team, who perform the stunts. He is just another link in steps as logical as a geometric theorem. All the interdependent members of the family look up to Romanov, a stocky, gray-haired, smiling man. "When something goes wrong," Ivan said, "he is the first to see."

In Poland in 1958, Romanov raced across the ring and placed his broad back to catch a girl falling from a trapeze. He saved her, and, after a year in the hospital, returned to the circus as a teacher.

"I plan to ride a horse until I'm 50 or 55 years," Ivan said. "That's for sure. Then I teach somebody."

Three weeks ago, Ringling Bros. presented on television an hour-long preview of this season's show. Midway there was a shot of horses galloping, and two men riding bareback and launching a third high into the air–and at that point the camera flicked to another stupendous spectacle.

Never mind, I could see, as though branded on the eye's retina, the soaring figure, its light landing, deft as a butterfly's, and the arms outspread to bask in the sunshine of the applause.

Elephants in the Night

An elephant yelps.

A throng of 200 heard that incongruous sound Tuesday night when the Greatest Show on Earth pulled in 10 hours late at the Norfolk & Western Railway station in Norfolk's West Ghent.

The gleaming, silver train, stretching four city blocks, pulled alongside the N & W station at 6:30. Five cars containing the circus stock were detached, and the remainder of the train with its human cargo traveled farther down the track. The crowd stuck with the stock.

For half an hour they patiently eyed the closed doors. Then a vast door in the silver side slid open about three feet and the fragrant whiff of the elephants spread in a wave across the spectators. An excited murmur arose from the crowd and suddenly it was answered from within the vast car by a high-pitched yelp. Then a long dun-gray snout extended cautiously into the open air.

The crowd applauded. The elephant inside answered, squealing as excitedly as the children on the outside. The first snout was joined by another, and the two, like a couple of waving jug handles, kept extending into the open and then withdrawing into the dark, odorous gloom of the huge car.

A handler opened the door a little wider, and the spectators could glimpse huge, shifting shadows. An elephant thrust its head close to the partly open door, and a long ah-h-h-h went up from the spectators as they saw in a flash the droll, pendulous lower lip, the snaking snout, the huge double-domed forehead and the large, sad, wise eyes fringed with inch-long lashes.

Not until 10:45 did two elephants begin to move their great ponderous bulks out of the cars, like animals coming out of

Noah's ark, and march through the night, followed by the other wondrous creatures into Scope where tonight the circus will bloom like a magic fairyland.

And as the spectators made their way through the cold to the cars in the station's parking lot a child said, "I saw the elephant's snout."

Finally, a Befitting Lifestyle

Two sister Siberian tigresses ventured Wednesday morning into a brave new world and, satisfied after a thorough exploration, rolled in lush green grass and waved and kicked their huge paws. Shere and Shaka Khan were home. At last.

They had waited three years in make-shift quarters in the Virginia Zoo in Norfolk while the Tidewater community raised $500,000 to fund the shaping of the 8,000-square-foot habitat, a virtual garden, God wot. A waterway winds by trees and vines and dumps into a pool where tigers may play on a hot, humid day. At the back, a waterfall spills down a monumental rock cliff.

In 1992, U.S. Fish & Wildlife agents confiscated the two cubs from illegal dealers and sent them over to the Virginia Zoo for temporary care. Bob Young Jr., a zoo board member, enlisted his fellow Hampton Roads Exxon retailers to spearhead the drive for $250,000 to keep the pair in Hampton Roads. The Exxon company gave $27,000 to top the goal. The Norfolk City Council matched the total.

Tuesday the big cats were tranquilized and moved on litters into the rock-faced den, off exhibit, where they can be separated from each other and from keepers by doors with remote controls. The dens are antiseptic clean. Wednesday morning, animal Supervisor Louise Hill and keepers Betty Schmitt and Vicki Hulett studied their charges, who seemed relaxed but alert.

When the door slid open between the two sisters, each went to examine the other's quarters, as if to see who had the better. Then Shere returned to butt her huge head against Shaka's in a tigerish caress. All seemed well. The three women chatted with the two tigresses as if they were in a sewing circle.

A door slid open to the green and gold outside world, where three dozen employees awaited the tigers' entry into the sun. Expectation was that Shaka, braver of the two in encountering something new, would come out first. But Shere tends to be the more curious one.

A half hour passed. Shere's fierce face appeared at the hole in a crevice of the rock wall. Shouts encouraged her to come out. She did, in cautious steps, so dainty, so slow motion that the very tip of the pad of each clawed paw seemed to curl like a ballerina's toe as she placed it carefully on the ground.

From within, Shaka watched Shere proceed to inspect the outdoors with the intensity of a tabby checking out a strange house. She studied the waterway, put a paw toward it, and suddenly, gathering her sinews, the great cat leaped, quick as a snapping rat trap, across the stream. Behind barriers, human watchers gasped. A vast viewing window had been laced with shaving cream to alert the cats that it was a shield, not open space. Yellow bows were tied to nearly invisible, tightly strung stainless steel wires that enable feline and human kind to come within inches of each other.

Shere rolled on her back, displaying snow white, black-striped underparts. She reared head high, and then, sensing that her sister was leaving the lair, she craned her neck around in a great arc to greet her with a chuffing purr.

Coming in measured stride, her long length, tail-tip to nose, in profile framed in space, Shaka seemed larger than ever, an immense black and orange striped moving wall. Observing her majesty, Zoo Superintendent Gary Ochsenbeing murmured, "There are only 300 Siberian tigers remaining in the wild and only 357 in zoos and wildlife preserves worldwide."

Bob Young was all agrin. Pat McGlynn, Exxon's Tidewater manager, was handing out decals bearing the big cat's happy face and in bold black letters: "I SAW THE TIGERS." They are among novelties to be distributed free to Saturday's crowd.

He better order more.

Dumb Dove

No one remembers who spotted the bird, but there it was, a beige and gray mourning dove sitting on a nest on a limb within full view of the second-story classroom. The limb stretched toward the windows, only a broomstick's length away, although no one — thank goodness, the teacher said — thought to test the distance.

If there's a dumber bird than a dove, who can name it? The dove's nest is, to put it bluntly, a disgrace. A few sticks scrabbled together as if the dove had done it absentmindedly with its feet. The dumb dove made its perch even more precarious by laying three eggs instead of the usual two, enhancing the odds that one would roll out. But peril was even closer than that.

A truck rolled into the schoolyard and stopped by the tree. A man in a cherry-picker basket zoomed skyward from the back of the truck. He was carrying a chain saw, gasoline-powered. The saw zipped through branches thick as a man's arm. As it ate the wood it made a banshee's high-pitched keening.

The children craned their necks to peer out the window. The dove, single-minded, feeble-brained, just sat there seemingly more wooden than ever as the saw neared. Noting one child's horrified face, the teacher dispatched him to the library for a book, Dr. Seuss' "Horton," the tale of a soft-hearted elephant who sat on an abandoned nest and hatched a winged elephant.

The man with the saw was directed from below by the driver who kept motioning him to go higher. "Get 'em ALL!" he called. The teacher in the window appealed to the man with the saw, pointing to the children, the nest, the bird, folding her hands prayerfully. The man with the saw nodded, grinned. "Gotcha!" he called softly. To watch the man with the saw was wondrous. He whirled it in great gyrations, cutting branches here, crashing limbs there, but, always, as the blade approached the nest, shying away.

The driver kept motioning toward the limb, now shorn of its companions, as gaunt as a skeletal finger with a nest on the knuckle; but the man with the saw, a figure furious with motion, obviously couldn't hear. Once the quivering blade came within a foot of the dove. It sat, round-eyed, still, knowing only one thing to do — sit it out, beneath the knife.

The driver gave in first. He got in the cab and slammed the door. The man with the saw winked at the faces in the window and floated to the ground. The dove sat on the limb, naked now with nothing around it but God's air.

The next four days rain pelted the dove and the wind tried it and between times the sun sought enthusiastically to bake its silly head. Then one morning a boy — it was Hugh Nunn, Gin said — found fragments of shells on the ground beneath the nest. He and the others raced upstairs, caught the teacher in their wake, hurried her to the window, looked out.

The dove, Horton, was still there. It had company. Seen between the skimpy network of sticks ... one ... two ... THREE fledglings. The children, bright faces lining the window sills, cheered. The dove, motionless, eyes shining, just sat there.

Dumb dove.

Beak Beat

The merriest sound of spring around our house is not a song but the rapid tattoo of a woodpecker that thinks he is Buddy Rich. And Rich, if you never heard him, was a jazz drummer who moved the sticks with the blurred swiftness of a woodpecker's head drilling a dead branch.

Any of a dozen kinds of woodpeckers — from the tiny downy not much bigger than your thumb, with a touch of red on its head, to the giant, scarlet-crested pileated, larger than a crow — can raise a hellish racket, especially pounding on a gutter at 6 a.m. to make a statement to the waking world.

When a woodpecker gets on a roll on a galvanized gutter, it brings to mind comedian Jimmy Durante. For young ones among us, Durante was a big-nosed bald comedian who sang like a honking seal and played with such manic zeal that he dismantled the piano long before Jerry Lee Lewis took one apart. Once, while Durante was performing at a resort in the Poconos, a drum-rolling woodpecker roused him early every morning. At last, chancing to wake up before the woodpecker, Durante hurried outside and, beating with a stick on bushes and trees, shouted, "WHEN DURANTE'S AWAKE, NO BOID SLEEPS!"

With all its noise, the Buddy Rich woodpecker is so sly and quick you cannot easily lay an eye on him. No matter how you circle and peer, he is always hid on the other side of the limb. Neighbors identified him as a yellow-bellied sapsucker. It sounds, when said loudly — WHY, YOU YELLOW-BELLIED SAPSUCKER! — as if one is cussing. It is well-named. Instead of the long, barbed-tipped tongues with which most woodpeckers reach into holes to spear insects, the sapsucker's tongue is coated with fine hairs that allow it to sop up sap. Sap accounts for a fifth of its diet. Berries and insects make up the rest. A bank of four or so foot-long rows of holes pockmarking the bark, mystic hieroglyphics, tell you the sapsucker has been at work. Other woodpeckers, hummingbirds and squirrels drink from the holes. A favorite perch of the Buddy Rich woodpecker is an ailing cypress. He likes it as much for the whacking sound he draws from it, as if clattering sticks on the rims of the drums, as for the bugs he finds.

Trees are clustered so he can shift, without missing a beat, from tree to tree summoning a deep roll from an oak; a cascade of hard, high notes from a hickory; a rapid run from a gum; brief spurts of soft, almost tentative notes from a gingko, improvisational riff with a Woodpecker.

Sardonic, sharp-spoken, with long, bony face and dark glit-

333

tering eye, Rich was ready with a riff. When he was being wheeled on a gurney into the operating room, a friend said, "It's bad, isn't it, Buddy?".

"Yeah," Rich said, "it's bad. But not as bad as country-western."

A Mere Speck of a Bird

Astonishing how an addition to a household can change its routine.

Bidding friends goodbye in the dirt driveway, shaded by the Norwegian maple so that the side yard is like a room in deep green gloom, I noticed, looking back toward the house, some straw and leaves, apparently windblown, jammed through a piece of torn screening in the bottom left corner of the window by the door.

On the way back, I stooped to remove the debris, but, seeing two small eggs cupped in the center, stayed my hand just in time. Two days earlier a Carolina wren had darted from the windowsill, and now here was its handiwork, I figured. Showing the nest to Gin, I thought the eggs had disappeared — all was brown in its interior — but as I bent to look closer, the tiny bird shot from the leaves like a rocket, almost into my face. Camouflaged on the nest, it had shielded the tell-tale eggs from view.

"Now look what you have done!" Gin cried. "If it had been a turkey buzzard, it would have hit you. And deservedly so."

"If it had been an ostrich, it would have hit me, too, but I think that quite likely I would have seen it on the nest," I retorted.

"Don't count on it," she said.

"The wren," I said, "is but a mere speck of a bird. The ostriches I have seen at the zoo would fill that entire window. Easily. I doubt seriously that I would overlook an ostrich nesting in the window. The egg itself is as big as a football."

"Then how is it," she how-is-it-ed, "that even after you park your car, you can't find it in plain view?"

(Don't tell me women are not smarter than men.)

Anyway, we don't want to discommode so rare a guest, both shy and brave at once. We agree on that. Obviously, we had to stop using the side-front door beside which the "wren's window" is located, and use the front-front door or the back-back door or the the side-back door, or, I suggested, we could exit the house on the flat roof above the front-front door and shinny down a nearby hickory. "It would be but a short hop from roof to tree," I said, " and we could whistle and wave our arms as we descend. I am game for it."

That evening, in the gloaming, I dropped to my knees at the driveway's entrance and crept on all fours to retrieve the newspaper on the side-front step. I was reaching out with my right hand to snatch the paper, being careful not to look toward the wren, on the pitiful notion that if I can't see the bird, the bird is less likely to see me, when suddenly the side-front door flung open and there was Gin staring wildly at me.

"HAVE YOU LOST YOUR MIND?" she cried, "CREEPING ALONG THE DRIVEWAY LIKE A COYOTE?"

"It is pronounced ky-yo-tey, I believe," I countered. (It is a good thing, in debate, to question, when possible, your opponent's pronunciation, as it gives you time to think of an answer and puts your opponent into a frenzy.) "And, no, dear girl, I have not lost my mind. At the very least, approaching the side-front door on all fours will persuade the wren of my friendly intentions and bring me, so to speak, to its own level."

"GO AROUND TO THE FRONT-FRONT DOOR," she said, as she shut the side-front door. I had to creep on all fours — the paper in my mouth — around to the front-front door, whereupon the doctor from up the street called to ask me if Boomer had taught me to retrieve the paper, Boomer being our chocolate Labrador retriever. I did not deign to answer.

To do so, I would have had to drop the paper.

The Wrens Depart

Gin called the office one morning last week to report, "The wrens are gone!"

"GONE!" I shouted, envisioning cats, crows and a great horned owl assaulting their nest. It was certainly within easy reach, just a handful of pine straw and leaves tucked through a torn screen into a corner of the window next to the side-front door.

"You don't need to shout at me, for heaven's sakes," she said.

"Why are they gone!" I asked, nerves jangling.

"First, apologize for yelling over the phone," she said. "It was quite unnecessary."

That, bless them, is the way with women, or at least those in my family. They put you on a rack of suspense — and ratchet it tighter, notch by notch. When my mother started to tell a story, I would beg her, "Just tell me how it turns out. Is it going to be good or bad?"

Which is what I asked Gin.

"Good!" she said. "They flew away. Isn't that wonderful?" She had watched the two fledglings flutter to the ground. Then, she said, the mother wren (or maybe father, though probably not) hustled them to the ivy-covered back yard, where the two grew at a prodigious rate from ceaseless feeding.

Gin kept filing bulletins by phone. The "darling" adult wrens, she said, would perch on a huge, wrist-thick vine that swings within three feet of the ground, and from that perch tend their offspring. "You can start using the side-front door again," she said.

After I had spotted the wisps cupping the two tiny eggs, she had commanded me and the brown Labrador retriever to use the front door. But she continued to flit like a shadow by the wren's nest, such was her finesse, turning her head for one swift, keen glance at the nest on the window sill. The wren, she told me, sat with her bill straight up. There was a communion between the mothers: Gin's piercing look asking, "Is everything all right?" and the watchful wren replying, "Don't fret. Everything is copasetic. Just don't let that big oaf stumble out the side-front door again."

The wren was right about that. I exited, generally, as if from a closet full of coat hangers. The Lab wasn't so easily reconciled to exile to the front-front door. Soon as he doped out he was forbidden to use the side-front door, which he had been doing all of his three years on earth, he determined to find out why it was banned. One evening, he took off in a dead run for the side-front door, and I, yelling "BOOMER!" launched into a dive parallel to the ground and just caught his right hind paw. If the Olympic committee had seen it, they'd have introduced a competition: the headlong lunge.

As we lay panting in dust, the side-front door was flung open and a wild-eyed, petite figure cried: "MUST YOU TWO ROLL AROUND IN THE DIRT SO NEAR THE WREN'S NEST?"

"I was heading him off."

"That's right," she said, "blame it on Boomer, a dumb animal."

"He's smarter than I am."

"Both of you go to the front-front door, and don't let me see you playing again near the side-front door." she said.

So with relief last week I heard that the wrens were gone, though it was deucedly hard coaxing Boomer to resume using the side-front door.

A half hour ago the phone rang at my desk.

"I hate to tell you this," Gin said.

"Give me the worst first."

"The wrens are rebuilding," she said.

Chapter Seventeen

Celebrations

Henry Delivers the Mail

Two weeks before Valentine's Day, my friend Henry gave up working on the tree hut and began doing such unheard of things as hauling ashes out of neighbors' basements for a dime.

He saved 75 cents and on the way to school Valentine's Day he bought a valentine for the prettiest girl in the sixth grade or the world. A three-dimensional scene, it unfolded to show a boy and girl in a boat pulled by two swans. It was so big he could barely hide it in his blue-lined tablet with the horse head on the front cover.

First thing, he asked Miss Eubanks if he could be postman. Surprised at Henry's volunteering to do anything, she said yes. The girls, giggling, placed on the teacher's desk a huge cardboard carton covered with snow white tissue paper spattered with red hearts.

Everybody but Henry had dropped in valentines through a slot in the top of the box. He walked up and down the aisles calling names on the envelopes.

"Henry," Miss Eubanks said, "you can put down that tablet while you deliver the mail."

He kept it under his arm, taking no chances, waiting for time to hand it to the prettiest girl in the sixth grade, making sure the 75 cent valentine didn't go astray. I hoped he'd have the sense to sign his name and not put "Guess Who?"

Everybody liked the prettiest girl in the sixth grade. Blonde, blue-eyed, she seemed to be always smiling. She had dimples and when she walked toward you, laughing, she seemed to be dimpling all over.

As the stack on her desk grew, it became noticeable that one

girl in the class wasn't getting any. Not even a comic. She was out
of school more than she was in and had returned that day after a
month's absence which was why she had been forgotten. I knew
Miss Eubanks must be mortified that she hadn't remembered to
give her a valentine among those she distributed to the rest of us.

When present the girl was sullen, withdrawn, a regular briar
patch, hair snarled, clothes soiled often. Now she sat stiffly, looking dead ahead, her desk bare of a single envelope. I could almost
feel the tears in her eyes in mine. Henry went right on through all
the growing embarrassment, calling names, delivering the mail.
Nothing ever threw Henry. I knew him.

He stopped at his desk and, his back to the class, scribbled in
the big valentine and stuck it back in the envelope.

Now comes the big one, I thought.

Henry marched down the aisle, his valentine in his hand, right
toward the prettiest girl in the sixth grade — and passed her, still
walking until he stood before the Briar Patch. He extended the
envelope to her. "Here," he said, "take it."

The Briar Patch looked, unbelieving, at the huge envelope he
was holding out to her. She took it, her hand trembling.

"Open it," Henry said, as if he'd like to punch her in the nose.
Boy, I thought. Good ol' Henry! My pal! But what a terrible raz-
zing he's going to take when the class finds out he sent it.

"Who's it from? Who's it from?" the girls were screaming.

She opened the envelope, took out the valentine, looked inside it, and, turning to me, she cried, through tears streaking her
cheeks, "How can I ever, ever thank you?"

That's what good ol' Henry did.

The Hurried Easter Bunny

A smart aleck asked the other day when I was going to put on my bunny suit. Some people are like that. Never let a fellow forget. Even after years, that question made me start and look fearfully over my shoulder.

On Easter morning 1959, my wife persuaded me to put on a rabbit costume that, ears and all, seemed 9 feet tall. She borrowed the suit through a friend who knew a radio announcer who had been parading around town in it two weeks interviewing people.

"Next to conversing on the street in broad daylight with a 9-foot-tall Easter rabbit," I told my wife, "the silliest thing I can think of is playing the part of the rabbit."

"Oh, go ahead," she said. "Be a good sport and give the children something to remember."

Early Easter morning, while she was herding the three of them to the front window in the living room, I put on the suit in the kitchen. It was difficult, wearing mittens, to zip the headpiece into place and harder to slip my feet into the furry white bunny slippers.

Every time I bent to put on the shoes, the darned ears clashed with the pots on the stove or tangled with the curtains until I said, "To heck WITH it, this old bunny is going barefoot. (You may say, superior-like, why didn't the fool put on the bunny shoes first and the mittens last, and I say to you that one does not think logically under such circumstances. To become an Easter Bunny is disorienting in the first place.)

I picked up the basket packed with candy eggs in fake green grass, stumbled out the back door, and started, wavering, around the house when Teddy, the collie next door (later deported to the country because of his ferocity) came stalking, head lowered, teeth bared, toward me.

"It's me, Teddy," I screamed. "Or rather," I said, "it is I."

He paid no attention whatever to the shift in grammar. Growling, he picked up speed, bent on investigating the biggest rabbit he had ever seen.

And the fastest.

Gin had the three boys waiting at the front window, an adorable spectacle, no doubt, and was saying to them, "Now if you look closely you just may catch sight of the Easter Bunny bringing you all manner of pretties," when WHOOM-M-M-M-M! — so fast, she said later, she almost missed the hot pursuit — came a gigantic white bunny scattering eggs in all directions as he ran yelling "HOLD OPEN THE BACK DOOR! HOLD OPEN THE BACK DOOR!" while a frenzied collie, snapping at his heels, inspired him to ever greater bounds across the grass.

When it comes to powers of observation, I will hand it to our youngest, then 3, for whom, after all, the whole thing had been staged.

"Dat rabbit," he said, "got feet like Guybo."

Take Off Your Shoes, Chilluns

An arrant conservative, I believe that things, once done, ought to stay put. My creed is "If it don't work, don't fix it."

Word that Memorial Day had been switched to May 26 from its time-honored anchor of May 30 shook me to the roots. Of all the holidays, Memorial Day has been since boyhood my favorite. It meant more than Christmas, the Fourth of July and Valentine rolled into one.

For one thing, Memorial Day made so little demand on those bent on observing it. You didn't have to ask your father for half a dollar to buy your mother a gift at the corner drug store. You didn't need to shovel walks clean of snow and sprinkle them with ashes to earn a half dollar for a valentine to give a girl sitting six desks away to whom you'd never had the nerve to speak. Or ever would. You didn't have to make a covert purchase of fireworks that had been banned both by law and parental command. All you had to do was take off your shoes. For May 30 was the first day in spring on which one could go barefoot. It was the day on which all God's chilluns didn't have to wear shoes.

You can't imagine, or perhaps you don't remember, the discomfort of having your feet encased eight long months in unyielding leather while your sole yearned to go free. Nor the joy on a hot day of walking across a mud flat and feeling the red clay ooze between your toes. Nor the blessed cooling when you thrust your feet into a brawling mountain creek. Nor walking early in the morning across a dew-wet pasture and nudging a cow to get up so you could warm your feet in the space where she had been lying. Nor running across a sun-seared beach to thrust your feet into the white-tumbling, chilling salt-surf. Nor padding through the thick cushion of brown leaves under an old forest's cathedral-lofty trees.

The one thing on which Flower Children and I couldn't agree was their concession to conformity in wearing sandals or wood clogs , thereby missing the earth's kiss on their feet.

May 30 was, no doubt, the furtherest date to which Mothers of the World could postpone shoelessness. The change to May 26 assures a three-day week-end in which families may get together and also get out and spend money to boost the economy. Could a creaky conservative decry that reasoning? Let me take off my shoes. To think it through.

Nature's White Wand

It snowed throughout Virginia as if nature had suddenly had enough of civilization's uncivil ways and flung out a white-gloved hand and said, Stop! — and a white stillness fell across the land.

There had been talk from weather forecasters, who later had scientific explanations of why they had been wrong, about the snow not hitting here and not showing there, but it began in Roanoke and continued until it mantled the city in ermine and even smoothed a white layer over the tracks in Norfolk & Western Railway's vast switching yard.

Sweeping east, defying predictions, the snow on Saturday morning reached Richmond, where as much as an inch customarily throws that city into a tizzy; but this time the snow kept right on falling thickly as if someone above were just pouring it down, curtains and curtains of the finest Irish lace.

The predictions kept escalating, too — four, six, eight and finally more than 12 inches — and Richmonders looked out on still, snow-masked hills and parked autos transformed by the snow's thick coating into numb, dumb, rough-cut wooden block toys of simplest outlines. For a long while, movement ceased as if the Riviera on the James had been shifted to the snowscape of Antarctica.

The snow, still laughing at forecasts, swept down the Peninsula, and into Williamsburg, laying a white sheeting to Duke of Gloucester Street, as if preparing it as a satiny aisle for a bride, then moving on to Newport News, brushing gray ships in a priming coat of white, and even crossing Hampton Roads, dusting Norfolk thoroughly, and persisting eastward until the white flakes, swirling in sea breezes, were dancing and sifting into the white caps of the dark, cold, green-blue, heaving Atlantic Ocean. Nothing escaped nature's weaving white wand.

In our house, the blond labrador retriever discovered the snow first, and barking, brought everybody to the windows and then nipping at ankles until she had her way, raced out the open door and bounded deerlike through the fleecy white world.

She disappeared behind a clump of trees and then reappeared racing, joined by the neighbor's black Labrador retriever running at her side, stride for stride, a black shadow to the blond lab. The two, scarcely more than pups, kept grabbing, as they ran, mouthfuls of this odd arrangement of water that didn't melt until they tried to chew it.

Into the field came two junior-high girls, blond Lisa and brunette Katherine, stocking caps pulled nearly to their noses, turning their heads skyward, looking up through a dizzying tunnel of flakes, swirling down and touching lightly their lips and lashes. It was, said Lisa, like a fine white ash. Or, said Katherine, soft down, white down pulled from snow geese, their laughing eyes outshining the softly falling, spinning, wheeling, white flakes.

The snow was working its magic everywhere. A pyracantha's branches, dripped blood-red berries, crimson against the white snow tufting the prickly green leaves. The great magnolias had turned from glossy green to flat white, each spray of broad pointed leaves looking like white poinsettias. In the magnolia's dark interiors was a constant clatter of falling water, a steady rainstorm, as the snow on the canopy's surface melted and dropped, pelting to the leafy floor, a continuing uproar, a hundred drummers crashing away in the trees' dark caves.

The snow found a row of crape myrtles, bare and beige in the winter, and caught and coated every limb, branch, and tiniest twig with a fringe of white and gave their fine-set crowns luminous frizzy hairdos.

Five boys, aged 9 and 10, wearing brightly stripped ski jackets, were throwing snowballs at one another, running, skidding, falling, antic as the snowflakes. I walked carefully, casual, betraying no awareness of them, remindful that dogs — and boys — can sense dread. Then almost out of their range, I heard them fall silent in the rear, and, at a slight stiffening of my backbone, an acknowledgment of their presence, the snowballs began to thud around me. One found the mark at the nape of the neck and trickled in a cold stream down the spine. Nobody escaped the snow's cold fingers.

Dressing Up

Truth is, spring arrives by inches.
Nature's strip tease.
No, that doesn't quite fit, does it?
Spring is putting on, not taking off, clothes.
There is allure in watching a careful minute-by-minute, article-by-article dressing, right up to the putting on of the perky

hat, a simple shallow little basket of a hat on the back of her head. And then a quick appraising glance in the mirror, and a brief sigh that the ritual is over, the job is done again — a strip tease in reverse.

And so she turns, smiling, ready to go.

If the old Gaiety Theater were still on East Main Street that would make an interesting, even startling apparition for the shocked audience, if a gal walked on stage and began putting clothes on.

Cause a riot, it would. Celebrated ever after in vaudeville lore:

"So there we were sitting down front and Rosa La Rose comes out and begins putting ON her clothes. The damndest thing. Then, at the end, she does a tap dance, fully dressed — and LEAVES!

That's what spring is doing for us.

I found a band of 2-feet-high King Alfred daffodils raising yellow trumpets to the sky, marching down the drive-way border. The sight made me catch my breath at the flash of recollection of she who had planted them, a daffodil planting daffodils.

And, being annuals, they will persist catching us by surprise.

Monday morning presented two calling cards. First it was light enough to see the very twigs as the birds were tuning up and note that the slender branches were showing tiny green buds. One day and soon spring, fully apparelled, would turn and face us, resplendent, smiling, a belt of white daisies girdling her waist, apple blossoms caught in her hair, a golden sun of dandelion at her shoulder, with the elusive scent of wild violets.

And then we will know. Spring, wholly attired, will at long last be here, ready for our full appreciation.

Fencing The Waves

Waking at 4 in the morning in Corolla, giving up after a few minutes trying to reclaim sleep, I switched on the bedside lamp to read. At the bed's foot slept the root-beer brown Lab, tuckered from swimming after a ball hurled by eight grandchildren on the beach. The tanned youngsters platooned the dog, one after another flinging the ball from the beach into the face of oncoming, rolling, rearing, roaring white-crested combers crashing in thunder on the sands. He seemed as tireless as the continuing chain of children or the waves.

Generated by a storm beyond the horizon, waves shouldered their way shoreward, gathering, swelling. The ball fell between the one attacking the shore and its fast-rushing successor rising in a looming wall beneath which Boomer danced and scurried after the ball that had landed in the slight lap between the two waves.

Usually, fencing the wave coming toward him, he managed to stay just out of its charging reach while he searched the white tumult for the ball in its maw.

Now and then the wave swept over him and his taut, slight length could be seen riding it, gleaming bronze and limber, his outthrust dark head protruding arrow-like from the white comb. The wave crashed on the sand in a churning, spreading white wake that the foam-flecked Lab quartered here and there to spot the ball as if he were scouring a field. Retrieving it as much as 100 feet down the shore, he ran to the children and dropped it at the feet of one who threw it back into the heaving sea.

And now he slept on his side, not a muscle moving, his legs, front and rear, extended to their utmost as if he were still running, as if he were caught and mounted forever in that pose. Outside the open window through which blew an ever-cooling breeze, his ocean adversary called, rising, falling, rocking, an eternal susurrus of surf encircling the shore. The dog lifted his head, listening. He began to groom himself, licking one forepaw then the other, concluding by nosing and licking a riffle in the sheet.

He turned, shook his ears, stretched again, sneezing, and, heaving a sigh, lay still, chin extended on my ankles, eyes on my face. I dared not stir a toe nor meet his gaze else he seize any move as a release to spring into action. At a slight change in my expression, his tail beat a drum roll. At a tiny noise, he raised his head, ears cocked, big nose twitching as if to single out a seaweed in the surf, all senses conjoined, sampling, savoring every air current.

The door opened. A barefoot 6-year-old climbed on the bed and laid his blond head beside the brown dog, who kissed him. "Kin Boomer go out?" the boy whispered.